Enlisted Soldier's Guide

Enlisted Soldier's Guide

7th Edition

Revised by
CSM Robert S. Rush, USA (Ret.)

STACKPOLE
BOOKS

Published by
STACKPOLE BOOKS
5067 Ritter Road
Mechanicsburg, PA 17055
www.stackpolebooks.com

Printed in the United States of America

10 9 8 7 6 5 4 3 2 1

Seventh edition

Cover design by Wendy A. Reynolds

Library of Congress Cataloging-in-Publication Data

Rush, Robert S.
  Enlisted soldier's guide / rev. by Robert S. Rush. — 7th ed.
    p. cm.
  Includes index.
  ISBN-13: 978-0-8117-3312-0
  ISBN-10: 0-8117-3312-2
  1. United States. Army—Handbooks, manuals, etc. I. Title.

  U113.R87 2006
  355.00973—dc22
                                        2006017617

STACKPOLE BOOKS

Military Professional Reference Library

Armed Forces Guide to Personal Financial Planning
Army Officer's Guide
Army Dictionary and Desk Reference
Career Progression Guide
Combat Service Support Guide
Combat Leader's Field Guide
Enlisted Soldier's Guide
Guide to Effective Military Writing
Job Search: Marketing Your Military Experience
Military Operations Other Than War
Military Money Guide
NCO Guide
Reservist's Money Guide
Servicemember's Legal Guide
Soldier's Guide to a College Degree
Today's Military Wife
Veteran's Guide to Benefits
Virtual Combat: A Guide to Distributed Interactive Simulation

Professional Reading Library

Fighting for the Future: Will America Triumph?
by Ralph Peters

Guardians of the Republic: A History of the NCO
by Ernest F. Fisher

Roots of Strategy Books 1, 2, 3, and 4

Street Without Joy
by Bernard Fall

The 1865 Customs of Service
for Non-commissioned Officers and Soldiers
by August V. Kautz

Stackpole Books are available at your Exchange Bookstore or
Military Clothing Sales Store, or from Stackpole at
www.stackpolebooks.com *or* **1-800-732-3669**

Contents

Preface

Once upon a time, a bit more than thirty years ago, I stood in the same position as you, the first termer. I had no idea what the Army was about, and outside of a few wise old sergeants who thought to give me the time of day, the only way I could learn about the Army was to experience it. One of the drill sergeant's familiar refrains was "if you don't learn this, you'll die in Vietnam!" Reading the *Enlisted Soldier's Guide* will not guarantee your survival or even ensure your success or failure; however, it will assist you in learning about your Army.

Over a career spanning thirty years there were ups and downs, with the ups far outweighing the downs. I will admit that at every reenlistment or extension I thought of voting with my feet, but something changed over time and I stayed on. The camaraderie, the different duty assignments and countries. After a while it was not The Army, it was *my* Army. This book is dedicated to the first termer from one of those wise, it is to be hoped, old sergeants.

I edited the *Enlisted Soldier's Guide* to provide information that I wanted to know when I was a first termer and what I wanted *my* soldiers to know when I was a sergeant major. As a reference tool, the guide can help soldiers better understand the Army and their roles in it. It includes information about promotion to noncommissioned officer (NCO) rank, uniformed service standards and systems, programs and services, policies and opportunities, soldiers' rights and military law, and other topics soldiers must understand, relate to, and effectively deal with each duty day.

This edition of *Enlisted Soldier's Guide* is directly aligned with an associated Stackpole Books' publication, *NCO Guide*, 8th edition. All chapters of this guide relate to chapters in *NCO Guide*. I mention the relationship between *Enlisted Soldier's Guide* and *NCO Guide* because of the natural relationship between junior soldiers and NCOs. A noncommissioned officer's primary duty is to train junior soldiers to take his or her place, and a junior soldier's duty is to learn what it takes to measure up to earn sergeant's stripes.

Soldiers must handle progressively more authority and responsibility as they work toward becoming leaders and supervisors in the NCO corps. This edition of *Enlisted Soldier's Guide* is an educational resource and ready reference to key Army subjects that will assist soldiers in their initial years. It draws from education, experience, training, and hundreds of sources. The guide begins with discussion of how and why the Army continues to change and ends with a series of ready reference guides. The *Enlisted Soldier's Guide* serves the reader when fellow soldiers have questions about pay, benefits, entitlements, personal appearance, uniforms, and insignia. It also contains aids that quickly lead soldiers to official or other publica-

tions that may contain updates. This edition of *Enlisted Soldier's Guide* has reformed content and improved relevancy. All new material was tightly composed and edited to contain less mundane detail, flow more logically, and be more readable and practical.

The seventh edition contains new or updated information about how to be a better soldier by improving marksmanship and PT (physical training) scores, as well as obtaining promotion points for military and civilian education. It also addresses sensitive contemporary Army issues, such as professional ethics, fraternization, AIDS, discrimination, sexual harassment, and homosexuality, and includes a professional reading and multimedia list. Readers will also find sections on promotions, assignments, uniforms, and the military justice system, as well as how to make the most of a transition from service to civilian life.

As our Army continues to change to counter evolving international threats, as our federal government makes service attractive by offering education and other incentives, as soldiers aim for professional goals, as uniformed traditions remain intact, and as hard career decisions continue to be made, *Enlisted Soldier's Guide* will continue to do its duty. Much of the information in this guide is timeless; that which is not was current at the time of publication. Policies, procedures, regulations, systems, and other aspects of service life change regularly. Remember that nothing is sacred, including this book; when in doubt check the regulation.

This book is what I needed thirty years ago when I was a young soldier. I sincerely hope it serves you in good stead.

Deeds, Not Words

Robert S. Rush, Ph.D.
CSM, USA (Ret.)

Acknowledgments

Hallelujah for the Internet! By using the many sites available to all soldiers, I was able to ensure that the latest information is included in this edition. Many sites contributed to this revision, including the following: Department of the Army; Department of Veterans Affairs; Defense Activity for Nontraditional Education Support; Army Family Advocacy Program; Army Community Services; Civilian Health and Medical Program of the Uniformed Services; American Forces Information Service; Human Resources Command; Enlisted Records and Evaluation Center; Army Career and Alumni Program; Training and Doctrine Command; Army and Air Force Exchange Service; Army Training Support Center; Association of the U.S. Army; Office of the Chief of Public Affairs; Defense Finance and Accounting Service; and Department of Education.

The following organizations also contributed: Army News Service; *SOLDIERS* magazine; *NCO Journal*; Army Continuing Education Services; Army Safety Center; Army Family Liaison Office; Judge Advocate General's Corps; DOD Still Media Records Center; the Center of Military History; and the Army Community and Family Support Center.

I am indebted to my Stackpole editors for their professional support and guidance during production of the *Enlisted Soldier's Guide*, 7th edition. I also want to thank all those old sergeants and officers who had faith in and showed much forbearance with a soldier who spoke his mind perhaps a bit too often. Lastly, I thank my wife, Edith, not only for everything she has done and the support she has shown toward this project, but for the many years she put up with a ragged old ranger who was seldom home. Without her, I would have failed before I had even started.

Code of Conduct

For Members of the Armed Forces of the United States

Serving our country as a member of the armed forces is the noblest public service a citizen of the United States can perform. Since 1955, American soldiers have memorized this Code, which defines the essence of military service and the high standards required of men and women in the military service.

I.

I am an American, fighting in the forces which guard my country and our way of life. I am prepared to give my life in their defense.

II.

I will never surrender of my own free will. If in command, I will never surrender my men while they still have the means to resist.

III.

If I am captured, I will continue to resist by all means available. I will make every effort to escape and aid others to escape. I will accept neither parole nor special favors from the enemy.

IV.

If I become a prisoner of war, I will keep faith with my fellow prisoners. I will give no information or take part in any action which might be harmful to my comrades. If I am senior, I will take command. If not, I will obey the lawful orders of those appointed over me and will back them up in every way.

V.

When questioned, should I become a prisoner of war, I am required to give name, rank, service number, and date of birth. I will evade answering further questions to the utmost of my ability. I will make no oral or written statements disloyal to my country and its allies or harmful to their cause.

VI.

I will never forget that I am an American, fighting for freedom, responsible for my actions, and dedicated to the principles which made my country free. I will trust in my God and in the United States of America.

PART I

The Army

1

The Army of
the Twenty-first Century

Just as the post-9/11 operational environment has fundamentally changed, so too should the expectations of the Americans entering Army service. We will seek individuals ready and willing for warrior service. Bound to each other by integrity and trust, the young Americans we welcome to our ranks will learn that in the Army, every Soldier is a leader, responsible for what happens in his or her presence regardless of rank.

—2005 Army Campaign Plan

Serving in today's Army is one of the finest forms of public service an American citizen can perform. Today's Army has 494,000 Regular Army soldiers on active duty, another 343,000 in the National Guard, and still another 204,000 in the Army Reserve. In all, about a million soldiers wear the Army uniform either full-time or part-time.

Since the Spanish-American War at the end of the nineteenth century, over 41 million Americans have served in the armed forces at home and abroad. There are nearly 26 million veterans alive today. Throughout our history, twenty-four of our forty-two presidents have had military service, and of that number, seventeen served in the Army, ten of whom were generals. Within the last fifty years, only one president did not serve in the military.

To be a soldier is to be a member of a highly respected profession. Public opinion polls have repeatedly shown that the armed forces have the highest trust and confidence of the American people. The country knows military service is tough duty, with high risk and many hardships, and that our soldiers are dedicated to getting the job done—a job that amounts to nothing less than being the defenders of our nation's highest and most important interests.

ARMY HISTORY

The Army's high reputation is due to the professionalism of the soldiers who served in it from the days of its creation over 230 years ago. The American Army was created on June 14, 1775, when the Continental Congress first authorized the muster of

The Army on Parade—Yesterday and Today

troops to serve under its authority. Those soldiers came from the provincial forces of the colonies, which were at that time laying siege to Boston. From its birth, the American Army has relied on the citizen-soldier, exemplified by the militia and the Minutemen who fought the British at Lexington and Concord. Commanded by Gen. George Washington and supported by our French allies, the Continental Army defeated the British at Yorktown and secured the freedoms so eloquently stated in the Declaration of Independence. Thus, the birth of the Army preceded and guaranteed the birth of the nation.

The Army's fundamental purpose is to fight and win the nation's wars by establishing conditions for lasting peace through land force dominance. This dominance is established through integration of the complementary capabilities of all the services. With this fundamental purpose in mind, the framers of the Constitution intended that armies be raised to "provide for the common defense!" and, together with the Navy, to "repel invasion." The Army raised for the nation's defense incorporates two uniquely American ideas: civilian control of the armed forces and reliance on the citizen-soldier. Over the years, the organization and structure of the Army have adapted to each challenge the nation has faced, but these basic ideas have remained unchanged. Throughout the formative years of the nation, the Army responded—on the frontiers, in the War of 1812, in the war with Mexico—in fulfillment of this role. During the Civil War, the Army was called upon to support another clause of the Constitution, to "suppress insurrection." As the nation became a colonial power following the Spanish-American War, the Army was called upon to secure and administer the new territories.

When the United States became a world power in the twentieth century, the Army was called upon to defend our national interests and rights on a wider scale,

which drew us into alliances in regions far removed from our shores. In the combat operations of the World Wars, in Korea, Vietnam, Panama, the Persian Gulf, and today in Iraq and Afghanistan, the Army has responded to the call to duty and performed that duty well. In the sixty years of Cold War, in many locations around the world, the Army performed a deterrent role as part of the containment strategy. In other places, at other times, the Army fulfilled the nation's expectations in operations too small to be called "wars," although no less dangerous. The Army's deployment is the surest sign of America's commitment to accomplishing any mission that occurs on land. To the soldiers on the ground, operations in Grenada (1983), Panama (1989), Kuwait and Iraq (1991), Afghanistan (2002), and Iraq (2003) are indistinguishable from the combat operations of their forefathers. Operations in Somalia, Haiti, Bosnia, and Kosovo, although peace operations, also have been or may prove to be dangerous. Like those who went before them, however, American soldiers responded readily in fulfilling the unlimited-liability aspect of their contract. Knowing that simply joining the Army demands a willingness to place one's life at risk, many have joined and made the ultimate sacrifice.

Today, we are a nation at war, with soldiers serving in far-flung corners of the globe. The global Al Qaeda terrorist network remains the most immediate and serious threat to the United States. Since 1998, Osama bin Ladin has declared all U.S. citizens legitimate targets of attack. Terrorists are capable of planning multiple attacks with little or no warning, as shown by the bombing of our embassies in Africa in 1998, the Millennium plots in 1999, and the World Trade Center and Pentagon attacks in 2001.

Although terrorism is our most important challenge today, there continue to be states that are threats to the United States. The 2003 war in Iraq showed clearly that America's Army—all its armed forces—were well trained and well led. This highly skilled, agile, and flexible force, in relatively small numbers, was able to defeat a well-armed enemy in a country the size of France in a mere thirty days of combat.

There also remains uncertainty about the future of Russia and China—two major powers undergoing great change—plus other issues, such as the potential new threat on the Korean peninsula; the prospects for lasting peace or continuing conflict in the Middle East; genocidal, ethnic, religious, and tribal conflict in Africa; the global impact of the proliferation of military technology; and an array of upcoming leadership changes in many already unstable countries.

THE ARMY MISSION

Protecting the nation's highest and most important interests is the Army's and the other services' mission. The Army's national mission is well stated in Title 10 of the Code of Laws of the United States. When it passed this law, Congress intended to provide an Army that, in conjunction with the other armed forces, would:

- Preserve the peace and security, and provide for the defense of the United States, its territories, its commonwealths and possessions, and any areas occupied by the United States.

- Support U.S. national policies.
- Implement U.S. national objectives.
- Overcome (i.e., *win a war against*) any nations responsible for aggressive acts that endanger the peace and security of the United States.

Today, the Army mission boils down to three major tasks:

- *Deterrence:* to be so competent and powerful that no enemy will risk attacking us, and if he does, to fight and win any resulting engagement, conflict, or war.
- *Power projection:* to be able to move combat forces anywhere in the world and support them on a sustained basis until victory is achieved or peace restored.
- *Military operations other than war (MOOTW):* to support those national and international peacekeeping, humanitarian assistance, disaster assistance, counterinsurgency, counterdrug, counterterrorist, and other related operations that the government determines are in the U.S. national interest.

This is serious business. National security, national defense, and the willingness and ability to fight for those vital interests are what the Army is all about. For the Army to accomplish these tasks, however, it needs the right strategies, tactics, techniques, and procedures; the right organizations; the right equipment; and, above all, trained soldiers. The Army's command structure and its organization exist to see that we have an efficient and effective Army and that it is well led and well trained.

COMMAND OF THE ARMY

Because the Army operates in response to America's most important interests, the U.S. Constitution designates the president as commander in chief. He is assisted by the secretary of defense and the chairman of the Joint Chiefs of Staff, who are in the chain of command for all military operations.

The Army chief of staff is a member of the Joint Chiefs of Staff. He and the secretary of the Army direct the Army to ensure that it is capable of performing the mission and tasks described above. They are the Army's principal advocates in the annual competition for national resources when the Army budget is negotiated within the government. They ensure that the Army is properly organized and equipped, and they make the regulations that govern all aspects of the Army from soldier recruitment through retirement.

ARMY ORGANIZATION

Active Army

For combat, the active Army includes five army-level headquarters as part of all-service unified commands; three three-star corps level headquarters, and ten two-star active-duty division level headquarters.

A variety of other commands, brigades, and groups provide engineer, chemical, civil affairs, intelligence, communications, medical, transportation, supply, mainte-

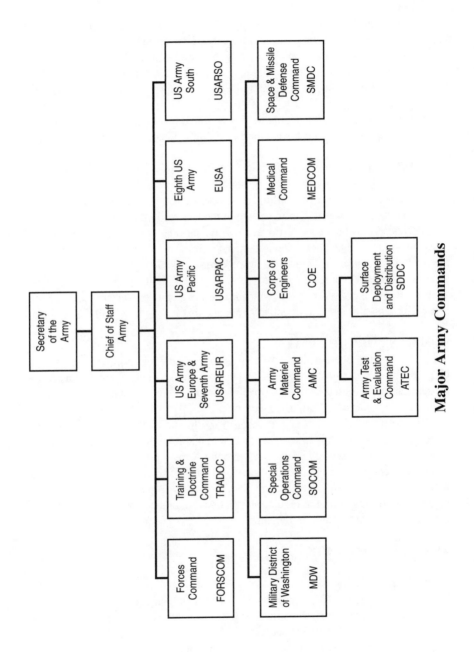

Major Army Commands

nance, military police, and other support services essential to the conduct of combat operations.

Major Army Commands
In addition to the tactical organizations, there is a supporting structure of units that perform a wide range of Army activities, such as command and control, logistics, training, military education, recruiting, research and development, procurement, and engineering and base support activities.

Army National Guard
The Army National Guard has some of the oldest units in the country, whose lineage extends to the years before the United States became independent. The Guard today provides a great amount of potent combat and combat support power to the Army. It contains eight divisions and fifteen "enhanced readiness" combat brigades. Eighty percent of the Army's field artillery is in the National Guard. The National Guard can be called to duty by the governor of a state for a state mission. It can also be called to active federal duty by the President to support a military operation that is beyond the capability of the active Army.

Army Reserve
The Army Reserve was first formed in 1908. It includes both units and individuals who join units when mobilized. The Army Reserve forces are essential to the accomplishment of the Army's mission. These forces provide the bulk of the Army's backup combat support and combat service support, without which many operations could not be carried out. For instance, the Army Reserve contains 100 percent of the Army's railway units, military police enemy prisoner of war brigades, and chemical brigades; 97 percent of all civil affairs units; 85 percent of the psychological operations units; 80 percent of the transportation groups; and 69 percent of the petroleum supply battalions.

Most soldiers will not complete an enlistment without working with units or individuals in the Army Reserve.

The Army in Transition
Transformation is a process that shapes the changing nature of military competition and cooperation through new combinations of concepts, capabilities, people, and organizations. It employs the nation's advantages and protects against asymmetric vulnerabilities. It sustains the U.S. strategic position, thus helping peace and stability in the world.

Tactical Organization of the Army
The Army is currently undergoing transformation from a division-based to a brigade-based force. These brigades are designed as modules, or self-sufficient and standardized brigade combat teams (BCTs), that can be more readily deployed and combined with other Army and joint forces to meet the precise needs of the com-

batant commanders. The total number of brigades will increase from thirty-three to forty-three. The goal for this larger pool of available forces is to enable the Army to generate forces in a rotational manner. At the current operational tempo, this modular force structure will allow active component soldiers to spend at least two years at home following each deployed year, at least four years at home following each deployed year for the Army Reserve soldiers, and five years at home following each deployed year for National Guardsmen.

Armies. Field Armies, most of which will be numbered, will become the Army component of a Joint Major Command and will be referred to geographically. Army headquarters will be capable of assuming the duties of a Joint Task Force (JTF) or a Joint Force Land Component Command (JFLCC)—with augmentation from other services—and controlling operations. Soldiers assigned to one of these commands will wear the patch of a traditional numbered army and perpetuate its lineage and honors. Third U.S. Army/U.S. Army Central, provides the Army component of Central Command; the Fifth U.S. Army, U.S. Army North, represents the Army in Northern Command; and the Sixth U.S. Army is the Army component of Southern Command. The Army component within the U.S. European Command is the Seventh Army, and the U.S. Army Pacific (no designation as of this writing) is the Army component of Pacific Command.

Corps and Divisions. These units will consist of a headquarters of about 800 and 1,000 Soldiers respectively who are capable of functioning as a Joint Task Force and a Joint Force Land Component Command. The three-star corps will perpetuate the lineages and honors of a historical corps. The two-star divisions will perpetuate the lineages and honors of a historical division. When the Army's restationing plan is complete, the ten active division headquarters will all be in the United States.

Brigades

The modular brigade combat team (BCT) is a stand-alone, self-sufficient, and standardized tactical force of between 3,500 and 4,000 soldiers. These units are more capable of independent action than current division-based organization, with strategic responsiveness greatly improved.

There are three common organizational designs for ground BCTs and five designs for support brigades. The three designs include a heavy brigade with two armor-mechanized infantry battalions and an armed reconnaissance battalion; an infantry brigade with two infantry battalions and an armed reconnaissance and surveillance battalion; and a Stryker (eight-wheel drive armored combat vehicle) brigade with three Stryker battalions and a reconnaissance and surveillance battalion. Four of the five types of support brigades perform a single function each: aviation; fires; sustain; and battlefield surveillance. The fifth, maneuver enhancement brigade, is organized around a versatile core of supporting units that provide engineer, military police, air defense, chemical, and signal capabilities. Modularity increases each unit's capability by building in the communications, liaison, and logistics capabilities needed to permit greater operational autonomy and support the

ability to conduct joint, multinational operations—capabilities that previously were at much higher organizational echelons.

Below are the active division headquarters and brigade combat teams perpetuating the honors and lineages associated with that division and their anticipated locations:

ANTICIPATED ACTIVE DIVISION AND BRIGADE COMBAT TEAM LOCATIONS

Fort Benning, Ga.	1 Brigade Combat Team affiliated with the lineage of the 3rd Infantry Division.
Fort Bliss, Tex.	1st Armored Division headquarters: 4 Brigade Combat Teams.
Fort Bragg, N.C.	82nd Airborne Division headquarters: 4 Brigade Combat Teams.
Fort Campbell, Ky.	101st Airborne Division headquarters: 4 Brigade Combat Teams.
Fort Carson, Colo.	4th Infantry Division headquarters: 4 Brigade Combat Teams.
Fort Drum, N.Y.	10th Mountain Division headquarters: 3 Brigade Combat Teams.
Fort Hood, Tex.	1st Cavalry Division headquarters: 4 Brigade Combat Teams.
Fort Hood, Tex.	3rd Armored Cavalry Regiment: 1 Brigade Combat Team.
Fort Knox, Ky.	1 Brigade Combat Team affiliated with the lineage of the 1st Infantry Division.
Fort Lewis, Wash.	2nd Infantry Division headquarters: 3 Stryker Brigade Combat Teams.
Fort Polk, La.	1 Brigade Combat Team affiliated with the lineage of the 10th Mountain Division.
Fort Richardson, Alaska	1 Brigade Combat Team affiliated with the lineage of the 25th Infantry Division.
Fort Riley, Kans.	1st Infantry Division headquarters: 3 Brigade Combat Teams.
Fort Wainwright, Alaska	1 Stryker Brigade Combat Team affiliated with the lineage of the 25th Infantry Division.
Fort Stewart, Ga.	3rd Infantry Division headquarters: 3 Brigade Combat Teams.
Schofield Barracks, Hawaii	25th Infantry Division headquarters: 1 Brigade Combat Team / 1 Stryker Brigade Combat Team.

ANTICIPATED ACTIVE DIVISION AND BRIGADE
COMBAT TEAM LOCATIONS *continued*

Fort Irwin, Calif.	11th Armored Cavalry Regiment: 1 Brigade Combat Team (minus).
Korea	1 Brigade Combat Team affiliated with the lineage of the 2nd Infantry Division.
Germany	2nd Armored Cavalry Regiment: 1 Stryker Brigade Combat Team.
Italy	173rd Airborne Brigade: 1 Brigade Combat Team.

Army National Guard Divisions

Until they are federalized by order of the president, Army National Guard divisions are under the authority of their respective state governors and are available for missions within their states. State missions usually include disaster assistance, protection of key assets or facilities during periods of civil unrest, and similar tasks. In recent years, more and more units from the reserve components have been deployed overseas to support national missions. In all cases, however, National Guard divisions have the same combat function as active Army divisions when called to federal duty in time of crisis or war. These divisions are:

28th Infantry Division, Harrisburg, Pennsylvania
29th Infantry Division, Fort Belvoir, Virginia
34th Infantry Division, St. Paul, Minnesota
35th Infantry Division, Fort Leavenworth, Kansas
38th Infantry Division, Indianapolis, Indiana
40th Infantry Division, Los Alamitos, California
42nd Infantry Division, Troy, New York
49th Armored Division, Austin, Texas

Nondivisional Organizations

Soldiers assigned to combat service support and combat support organizations can serve in divisional or "nondivisional" units. Nondivisional units are also tactical formations, but their organization varies, depending on type. The most common types of nondivisional units are commands, brigades, and groups; these formations usually command battalions, which are in turn composed of companies. Nearly all soldiers are assigned to a company of one type or another. For instance, there are engineer, air defense artillery, and signal brigades; transportation commands and groups; signal commands and signal brigades; and military intelligence and special forces groups.

BRANCHES OF THE ARMY

The Army has twenty-four active-duty branches organized into four major categories: combat, combat support (CS), combat service support (CSS), and special branches (SB).

Combat Arms

Infantry. Infantry is the oldest of the combat arms. Its mission is "to close with the enemy by fire and maneuver to destroy or capture him, and to repel his assault by fire, close combat, and counterattack." Today's infantryman can move by land, sea, or air. The modern infantryman may fight on foot or go into action by parachute, helicopter, assault boat, or Bradley fighting vehicle. The infantry can operate at night, under any climatic conditions, and it can overcome natural and man-made obstacles that would stop other forces.

Light infantry units are rapidly deployable and are especially useful in missions conducted in complex and urban terrain due to their streamlined nature and lack of dependence on masses of heavy equipment for transportation. Air assault infantry units are more heavily equipped and although fully capable of dismounted operations, typically incorporate the large numbers of helicopters available in the air assault division's aviation groups. Airborne infantry units are uniquely qualified and equipped for arrival in combat by parachute but are fully capable of dismounted or air assault operations as well. Mechanized infantry are the most heavily armed and protected infantry, riding into battle in Bradley infantry fighting vehicles (IFVs), which are armed with 25mm automatic cannons, antitank missiles, and machine guns. The new interim brigade is equipped with the wheeled Stryker series vehicle, which provides mobility and protection to the infantrymen riding within.

Ranger infantry are trained to go into battle by parachute, special operations helicopter, small boat, or dismounted. Although trained as infantry, ranger infantry units are increasingly being used as special operations forces.

Armor. Armor branch includes both armor and armored cavalry and is the modern successor to the horse cavalry. Armor operates in a combined arms team with infantry, artillery, and the other combat and combat support branches. Armor tactics emphasize mobility, firepower, and shock action to overcome and destroy enemy forces in rapid actions. Armored cavalry units exist in Army division and at corps level to conduct the reconnaissance and other security missions. The M1 series tank is armor's principal weapon system; it is a world-class tank. Like the Bradley IFV, the Bradley cavalry fighting vehicle in the armored cavalry units furnishes great speed and mobility, as well as maximum firepower and armored protection for use on the forward edge of the battle area.

Field Artillery. A historic branch of the Army, the field artillery mission is more challenging than ever before—to destroy, neutralize, or suppress the enemy by cannons, rockets, and missile fire and to integrate all supporting fires into the combined arms operation. Howitzers, rockets, and missiles are the muscle of the field artillery. Currently, towed field artillery systems include the M102 and M119A1

105mm howitzers and the M198 155mm howitzer. Self-propelled artillery systems include the M109-series 155mm howitzer and the Multiple Launched Rocket System (MLRS). The artillery's current ground-to-ground missile system is the Army Tactical Missile System (ATACMS), which is fired from the MLRS launcher and provides long-range fires against personnel and material targets. Artillery units provide fire support teams (FISTs) that plan and coordinate artillery fire in support of infantry and armor combat teams and call for and adjust artillery fires on enemy targets. The FIST uses many tools, including the ground/vehicular laser locator designator to determine ranges to targets and the designation of targets for laser-guided munitions, such as the tank-killing Copperhead round or the Hellfire missile. When the tactical situation warrants, the FIST may employ naval gunfire and joint close air support, as well.

Air Defense Artillery. The mission of the air defense artillery (ADA) is to protect the force and selected geographical assets from attack by enemy aircraft and missiles and to conduct antiaircraft surveillance. With its multicapable, phased-array radar and long-range, high-altitude missiles, the Patriot battery is the most formidable air defense system in the world today. It has the capability to intercept incoming tactical ballistic missiles, a role it performed with success in the Gulf War. While the Patriot provides long-range protection, the Avenger missile system, mounted on a high-mobility multipurpose wheeled vehicle (HMMWV) and found in divisions and corps, is a formidable weapon against low-flying aircraft and unmanned aerial vehicles.

Combat Engineers. Today's combat engineers provide the battlefield commander with mobility, countermobility, and survivability support. Combat engineer units are located primarily in divisions and corps. They provide bridging, mine laying, mine clearing, obstacle construction and removal, electric power, topographic support (terrain analysis), and a variety of combat construction and land-clearing tasks for combat units before, during, and after an attack, defense, or retrograde operation. As a secondary mission, combat engineers are trained to fight as infantry.

Aviation. Aviation branch provides combat and combat service support aviation to the combined arms Army maneuver unit from aviation brigades located at division, corps, and higher echelons. Combat missions include attack, air assault, reconnaissance, show of force, intelligence, and logistical (air delivery) support. Its principal equipment is the UH-1 and UH-60 (Black Hawk) utility and troop transport helicopter, the AH-64 (Apache) and AH-1 (Cobra) attack helicopters, the CH-47D (Chinook) cargo and transport helicopter, and the OH-58D small observation helicopter.

Special Forces. Special Forces (SF) is the Army's newest separate branch. As the name indicates, SF provides the Army with special tactics and techniques to accomplish very special missions, which range from special reconnaissance, direct action, foreign internal defense, unconventional warfare, and counterterrorism. SF mobile training teams travel all over the world to assist allied armies with modern training. Soldiers destined to SF units require considerable extra training and are

specially selected. In addition to their traditional roles, SF branch includes units dedicated to civil affairs and military government and psychological operations.

Combat Support Branches

Chemical Corps. The Chemical Corps provides expertise in the area of nuclear, biological, and chemical (NBC) operations and defense. This includes use of nuclear and chemical weapons during war, training units on NBC defense, reconnaissance of the NBC battlefield, and decontamination of units and equipment contaminated by NBC hazards. The Chemical Corps is also responsible for providing large-area smoke and obscurants on the battlefield and for the use of field flame weapons and techniques against enemy forces.

Military Intelligence. Military Intelligence (MI) branch is responsible for providing a large number of critical intelligence support services to the battlefield commander. These include intelligence and information collection, counterintelligence support, cryptologic and signals intelligence, electronic warfare, operations security, enemy order of battle analysis, interrogation of enemy prisoners of war (EPWs), aerial surveillance, imagery (aerial and other photography) analysis, and related work.

Military Police. Military Police (MP) provide combat operations against opposing forces in U.S. rear areas of a battlefield. They provide traffic control to expedite movement of critical combat resources to the front. They process EPWs and evacuate them from the battle area. MPs provide security for critical facilities such as command posts and special ammunition sites, and they conduct law-enforcement operations much along the lines of the order given by General Washington in 1776 to the Army's first provost martial to "apprehend deserters, marauders, drunkards, rioters, and stragglers."

Signal Corps. As one of the Army's high-technology branches, the Signal Corps performs a broad range of communications-related tasks in support of the Army mission. These range from procuring, installing, operating, maintaining, and reconfiguring communications networks from the battlefield level to the Pentagon. It leads the Army's digitization effort for information management on the battlefield.

Combat Service Support Branches

Adjutant General Corps. One of the oldest branches in the Army, the Adjutant General (AG) Corps operates the military personnel system from a soldier's accession at a military processing station to his or her retirement or departure from the service. AG units are found at all levels from division on up. AG soldiers are also responsible for band operations and for operation of the military postal system.

Finance Corps. One of the Army's smallest branches, the Finance Corps is responsible not only for soldier pay matters, but also for the payment and auditing of accounts of the various vendors and contractors who sell items to the Army. One of the Finance Corps's most time-sensitive functions is the funding of contingency contracts usually needed in overseas areas to purchase supplies and services for deploying forces.

Ordnance Corps. Ordnance soldiers perform one of the Army's most important missions: repair and maintenance of equipment and materiel, supply and maintenance of ammunition, and explosive ordnance disposal (EOD). Given the extensive array of high-technology weapon systems, other sophisticated equipment, missiles, and munitions in the Army, and the need to maintain these items in the highest state of readiness, the Ordnance Corps is staffed with a variety of units at all echelons of service.

Quartermaster Corps. Along with the Ordnance and Transportation Corps, the Quartermaster (QM) Corps forms the basis of Army logistics. QM soldiers supply the Army. This includes all aspects of supply—procurement, cataloging, inventory, storage, distribution, salvage, and disposal of material. It also includes the vital commodities of food, fuel, and water and the battlefield distribution networks that get these commodities to the fighting forces. The QM Corps pioneered the technology of aerial delivery, including air-drop and parachute delivery of personnel and supplies. It provides the Army's parachute riggers. The QM Corps also provides the Army with essential field services such as laundry, bath and shower facilities, clothing exchange, and mortuary support.

Transportation Corps. As the name implies, the Transportation Corps (TC) provides motor, air, rail, and water transport in support of Army operations worldwide. It operates the Army's line-haul truck fleets, ocean ports, railroads, and watercraft and coordinates logistic air operations. It operates motor transport depots and trailer transfer points. It also provides movement control units that schedule transportation assets in and through the battle area. Transportation companies and battalions are found at all echelons in the Army.

Special Branches

Chaplain Corps. Chaplains provide religious support to soldiers and their families. Chaplains of most major faiths and chaplain's assistants are found on most Army posts in the United States and overseas to provide regular religious services, military community services, and personal counseling.

Judge Advocate General (JAG) Corps. The JAG Corps is primarily a branch of trained officer-attorneys and enlisted paralegal specialists who serve in the Army as judges, trial attorneys, defense attorneys, and legal counsel to commanders, soldiers, and families.

Medical Corps. Part of the Army Medical Department (AMD), and working under the Army Surgeon General, the Medical Corps is the part of the department that provides the medical doctors who staff Army hospitals and clinics throughout the world and provides the surgeons for the Army's field and battlefield hospitals in combat areas.

Dental Corps. Also part of the AMD, the Dental Corps provides the Army with dentists and dental technicians.

Veterinary Corps. The Army uses veterinary medicine doctors for care of Army animals, for meat inspection, and for preventive veterinary medicine support to Army communities.

Medical Service Corps (MSC). The MSC provides allied medical scientist support to the Army. This includes medical supply, ambulance support, pharmacists, optometrists, biochemists, physiologists, podiatrists, audiologists, entomologists, epidemiologists, and sanitary engineering and environmental health support.

Army Nurse Corps (ANC). The ANC was the first of the branches of the Army to admit women. As its name indicates, it provides commissioned and non-commissioned nursing services of all types to the Army mission at home stations and on battlegrounds around the world.

Army Medical Specialist Corps. Therapists, dieticians, and physician assistants constitute the members of this professional medical branch that supports soldiers as part of the Army Medical Specialist Corps (AMD).

TYPES OF UNITS

Enlisted soldiers are trained for and serve in each of the above branches. All enlisted soldiers progress through basic combat training (BCT) and advanced individual training (AIT) for their military specialty. Officers are commissioned through the U.S. Military Academy at West Point, the Reserve Officers' Training Corps (ROTC), or the Officer Candidate School (OCS) and attend a basic course for their branch. Once initial training is completed, all soldiers—enlisted and officer—are assigned to units within the Army, and all work together to accomplish the Army's missions.

Even though there are many different types of units, the size and designation of units is fairly standard.

Designation	Symbol	Size	Usually Led By
Fire team	•(-)	About 5	Sergeant
Squad	•	10–15	Staff sergeant
Section	••	10–15	Staff sergeant
Platoon	•••	About 40	Lieutenant
Battery, company, troop	|	100–200	Captain
Battalion, squadron	||	400–800	Lieutenant colonel
Group, regiment	|||	3–5 battalions	Colonel
Brigade	X	3–5 battalions	Colonel
Division	XX	4–6 brigades	Major general
Corps	XXX	Several divisions	Lieutenant general
Army	XXXX	Several corps	General

For every officer leading an organization, there is a noncommissioned officer to assist him or her.

- A sergeant first class (SFC) platoon sergeant assists the platoon leader.
- A first sergeant (1SG) assists the commander of a company.
- A command sergeant major (CSM) assists commanders at all levels at battalion and above.

Today, the Army sits at the crossroads at the beginning of the new millennium. Computerization, modernization, and digitization on the battlefield—from target acquisition to logistical support—are leading to an increased reliance on small-unit leaders and soldiers and on a smaller yet more capable force. Operations are devolving to smaller, more capable, self-sustaining units digitally linked to artificial intelligence, analysis, combat support, and combat service support nodes that provide real-time information on the battlefield, whether it be a battlefield in a traditional sense or a peacekeeping operation.

To operate all the digitized high-technology equipment, as well as fight in the mud, the Army—as in the past—will continue to require trained, disciplined, and cohesive soldier teams. To attain this goal, the Army's enlisted training system operates for the purpose of producing the kind of soldiers needed on the modern battlefield.

2

The Enlisted Training System

While you are on active duty, your opportunity for military training is extensive. The enlisted training system (ETS) is a subsystem of the Enlisted Personnel Management System (EPMS). It is characterized by progressively higher levels of performance capability, experience, and rank. Five "skill levels" of training have been established to support the ETS. They are administered in two distinct but closely related phases: Initial Entry Training (IET) and the Noncommissioned Officer Education System (NCOES).

IET provides a foundation of professional and technical knowledge needed to perform at the first duty station; combined with subsequent individual training in the unit, the soldier qualifies at skill level one (SL-1) in one of the Army's military occupational specialties (MOSs). The next four skill levels are taught through the NCOES.

CAREER MANAGEMENT FIELDS

The military occupational specialties (MOSs) of all enlisted soldiers from private to sergeant major are grouped into career management fields (CMFs). A CMF is a grouping of related MOSs. MOSs are grouped so that soldiers in one specialty have abilities and aptitudes appropriate for training and assignments in other specialties within that CMF. This flexibility means that a soldier can move laterally within a CMF as well. Training leads to progression and promotions. Each soldier has a career path mapped out for him or her, identifying appropriate schooling, assignments, and opportunities.

As soldiers climb the promotion ladder within a CMF, new recruits fill in the lower rungs of the ladder, preparing themselves for upward mobility as well. The Army has established career paths for each CMF so soldiers can be counseled on the training and education they will need.

Within each CMF, the EPMS has identified the skills necessary for successfully functioning at each rank. Soldiers seeking promotions need to constantly prepare themselves for the next higher skill level. SL-1 includes skills, proficiencies, and abilities typically needed to perform efficiently up through the rank of specialist. SL-2 relates to sergeant; SL-3 to staff sergeant; SL-4 to sergeant first class; and SL-5 to master sergeant through command sergeant major. Because MOSs are grouped

into CMFs, the skills necessary for SL-2 in one CMF will not necessarily be the same skills required at that level in a different CMF.

Included among the CMFs for enlisted soldiers are the following:

11 Infantry	42 Adjutant General
13 Field Artillery	44 Financial Management
14 Air Defense Artillery	46 Public Affairs
15 Aviation	56 Religious Support
18 Special Forces	63 Mechanical Maintenance
19 Armor	74 Chemical
21 Engineer	79 Recruiting and Retention
25 Communications and Information Systems Operations	88 Transportation
	89 Ammunition
	91 Medical
27 Paralegal	92 Supply and Services
31 Military Police	94 Electronic Maintenance and Calibration
33 Electronic Warfare/Intercept Systems Maintenance	96 Military Intelligence
37 Psychological Operations	98 Signals Intelligence/Electronic Warfare Operations
38 Civil Affairs	

The CMFs are organized into three branches: combat arms, combat support, and combat service support. The ETS recognizes the distinction necessary among branches, but leadership training is required to some degree in all three branches.

INITIAL ENTRY TRAINING

Every soldier in the Army has gone through initial entry training (IET). The two phases of IET are basic training (BT) and advanced individual training (AIT), which is MOS training.

Generally, soldiers entering the combat arms branch or the military police receive one-station unit training (OSUT); they remain in the same unit for their BT and AIT. Soldiers entering combat support or combat service support branches generally change duty assignments for their AIT, primarily because of the technical nature of many MOSs in these branches. The primary functions of IET are to prepare recruits for military life and to provide soldiers with basic combat skills and SL-1 technical training.

Drill sergeants are key figures in preparing recruits for the rigors of Army life. It is the responsibility of a drill sergeant to teach a new soldier about the Army and to help him or her appreciate how individuals contribute to the military structure. The drill sergeant instills self confidence, self-respect, and self-discipline in young soldiers so they can perform their duties as soldiers. Equally important, the drill sergeant must ensure that soldiers are physically fit.

It is essential that each soldier be proficient in the combat basics regardless of the branch in which he or she will serve. Marksmanship, field fortifications, first aid, hand-to-hand combat, nuclear, biological, and chemical (NBC) defense, and small-unit teamwork are emphasized.

All soldiers are given additional training in basic combat skills during the advanced individual training (AIT) phase of initial entry training (IET). Field training exercises are used to combine specialized MOS training the soldier must receive with basic soldier skills that need to be reinforced. AIT highlights the specific skills soldiers will need to perform in their MOS at SL-1.

Upon completion of IET, soldiers go to their units with skills sufficient to effectively contribute to the team. Training, however, is by no means complete. Field units provide continuing on-the-job training to round out the soldier's initial training and to enhance the first-termer's potential.

UNIT AND INDIVIDUAL TRAINING

Upon assignment to a unit, the new soldier practices and refines the individual soldier skills learned in BT and AIT. The Individual Training and Evaluation Program (ITEP) provides a formal structure for the soldier's ongoing training. The ITEP focuses on Common Task Training and the Commander's Evaluation.

Common task training (CTT) emphasizes combat skills that *all* soldiers must perform. Tasks such as map reading, communications, and NBC defense are reinforced through performance-oriented, hands-on training. Each year, soldiers must pass a battery of common skills tests that evaluate their ability to perform basic skills.

The Commander's Evaluation (CE) is a hands-on test designed to help unit leaders determine the proficiency level each soldier has achieved in relationship to standards outlined in the soldier's job book and appropriate soldier's manual.

Although the focus of each soldier's training is on developing individual soldier skills, unit leaders are responsible for ensuring that the unit can per-

All Soldiers Learn Common Task Training

form collective tasks. At the unit level, the Army Training and Evaluation Program (ARTEP) is to assist commanders in identifying appropriate training standards for the accomplishment of collective unit tasks. Each commander evaluates his or her unit's wartime mission and assesses which tasks require emphasis in the unit's training plans. The commander uses ARTEP manuals to develop a unit training strategy and then develops, executes, and evaluates unit training.

NONCOMMISSIONED OFFICER EDUCATION SYSTEM

The second phase of the enlisted training system (ETS) is the Noncommissioned Officer Education System (NCOES), which has a single goal: to train noncommissioned officers (NCOs) to be trainers and leaders of soldiers who work under their supervision. The NCOES prepares soldiers to perform at the next higher skill level and combines leadership study with technical training. It provides an extensive network of courses at all levels of the NCO corps. It is conducted in service schools and NCO academies (NCOAs).

Listed below are the Army's NCO academies (listed by location) with their courses and Web sites, which contain welcome letters and provide packing lists, directions, phone numbers, and mailing addresses:

Aberdeen Proving Ground, MD; Basic Noncommissioned Officer Course (BNCOC)/Advanced Noncommissioned Officer Course (ANCOC)
www.goordnance.apg.army.mil/

Camp Jackson, Korea; Primary Leadership Development Course (PLDC)
ncoa.korea.army.mil/

Fort Benning, GA; PLDC/BNCOC/ANCOC
www.infantry.army.mil/ncoa/

Fort Bliss, TX; PLDC/BNCOC/ANCOC/U.S. Army Sergeants Major Course (USASMC)
airdefense.bliss.army.mil/secure/ncoa/

Fort Bragg, NC; PLDC
www.bragg.army.mil/ncoa/default.htm

Fort Campbell, KY; PLDC
www.campbell.army.mil/ncoa/ncoa.htm

Fort Drum, NY; PLDC
www.drum.army.mil/garrison/ncoacad/index.htm

Fort Eustis, VA; BNCOC/ANCOC
www.eustis.army.mil/ncoa/

Fort Gordon, GA; BNCOC/ANCOC
www.gordon.army.mil/rncoa/

Fort Hood, TX; PLDC
www.hood.army.mil/NCOA/

Fort Huachuca, AZ; BNCOC/ANCOC
huachuca-usaic.army.mil/SCHOOL/NCOA/index.htm

Fort Jackson, SC; BNCOC/ANCOC
www.army.mil/ncoa/index.htm

Enlisted Training System

Rank		Skill Level
CSM, SGM 1SG, MSG	SMC	SL5
SFC	N C O E S ANCOC	SL4
SSG	BNCOC	SL3
SGT	PLDC	SL2
PVT-SPC	Initial Entry Training (IET) · OSUT · BCT AIT	SL1

Fort Knox, KY; PLDC/BNCOC/ANCOC
www.knox.army.mil/school/ncoa/ncoa.htm
Fort Lee, VA; BNCOC/ANCOC
www.quartermaster.army.mil/NCO/
Fort Leonard Wood, MO; BNCOC/ANCOC
www.wood.army.mil/mncoa/default.htm
Fort Lewis, WA; PLDC
www.lewis.army.mil/ncoa/index.htm
Fort Polk, LA; PLDC
www.jrtc-polk.army.mil/ncoa/
Fort Richardson, AK; PLDC
www.usarak.army.mil/ncoa/index.htm
Fort Rucker, AL; BNCOC/ANCOC
www-rucker.army.mil/NCOA/test%20web%20page.htm
Fort Sam Houston, TX; BNCOC/ANCOC
ncoa.amedd.army.mil/
Fort Sill, OK; PLDC/BNCOC/ANCOC
sill-www.army.mil/usancoa/
Fort Stewart, GA; PLDC
www.stewart.army.mil/Display.asp'Page=55A55D2D-9BC5-48C6-9FFD-8E45D30C5A04
Grafenwoehr, Germany; PLDC
www.grafenwoehr.army.mil/7ATC/default.htm
NCOA Hawaii; PLDC
(not available)
Updates can be found at
www.hrc.army.mil/site/active/epncoes/ncoalink.htm

The four levels of the NCOES are the Primary Leadership Development Course (PLDC), the Basic NCO Course (BNCOC), the Advanced NCO Course (ANCOC), and the U.S. Army Sergeants Major Academy (USASMA).

Many first-term soldiers will have the opportunity to attend the Primary Leadership Development Course (PLDC). This four-week, non-MOS-specific leadership course is conducted at sixteen noncommissioned officer academies (NCOAs) worldwide. The course provides basic leadership training for soldiers selected for promotion to sergeant and provides soldiers with the skills, knowledge, and behaviors needed to lead a team-size unit and serves as the foundation for further training and development. PLDC is conducted in an NCO academy live-in environment using the small-group instruction method with practical application, followed by hands-on, performance-orientated training conducted in a field environment, culminating with an extensive field training exercise (FTX). Training focuses on self-discipline; professional skills; leading, disciplining, and developing soldiers; and caring for soldiers and their families. Other areas include the planning, executing, and evaluating of individual or team training and the planning and executing of missions/tasks assigned to a team-size unit. Successful completion of PLDC establishes the foundation for further training and leader development. Small-group leaders assess the students' leadership potential and evaluate their ability to apply lessons learned and effectively lead their classmates in a tactical environment.

Attendance at PLDC is mandatory for promotion to sergeant. Priority of attendance goes to the sergeants who have not previously attended, E-4 (P), or, E-4, who have been serving in leadership positions. Soldiers may appear before promotion boards; however, they cannot be promoted until they complete PLDC. Conditional promotions may occur when a soldier meets the cutoff score while operationally deployed.

Noncommissioned Officer Education System Equivalency for PLDC

Personnel support battalion (PSB) commanders may grant active component (AC) Primary Leadership Development Course (PLDC) equivalency to soldiers that successfully complete any of the following training:

Reserve Component Primary Leadership Course (RC-PLC).

Reserve Component Primary Noncommissioned Officer Course (RC-PNCOC).

Reserve Component Primary Leadership Development Course (RC-PLDC), BNCOC (must have completed phases I and II) or ANCOC (phase I).

Any of the several U.S. Marine Corps (USMC) NCO Courses above the Corporal's Course.

Any branch of service Officer Candidate School (OCS).

Reserve Officers' Training Corps (ROTC) (from any service) advanced camp.

U.S. Army or USMC Warrant Officer Candidate School.

The following courses, among many others, are not equivalent to AC PLDC: any nonresident corresponding study programs, courses taught at the USMC institute in Washington, D.C., or any U.S. Air Force or U.S. Navy NCO training.

The BNCOC, conducted at NCOAs, is designed to produce hard-hitting squad and section leaders who can lead and train soldiers in combat. The length of the course varies according to the MOS. Graduation from BNCOC is required for consideration of promotion to staff sergeant.

The ANCOC stresses MOS-related tasks, with emphasis on technical and common leader combat skills required to train and lead other soldiers at the platoon or comparable level. Courses are presented at NCOAs and vary in length according to MOS requirements. ANCOC is required for consideration of promotion to sergeant first class.

The USASMA prepares master sergeants and first sergeants for troop and staff assignments throughout the Army and the Department of Defense. Graduation from the U.S. Army Sergeants Major Course at the USASMA must precede promotion to sergeant major.

Other Military Training Opportunities
Soldiers may apply for a number of additional qualification training courses. The following courses are open to all MOSs:

Air Assault Course
Obstacle courses, physical training, aircraft safety, Pathfinder operations, combat assaults, sling-loading operations, rappelling from UH-60 Blackhawk helicopters, twelve-mile road marches with rucksack and rifle—this ten-day course is packed with challenge. To attend, soldiers must receive permission from their commander and pass the Army Physical Fitness Test (APFT) (in the seventeen- to twenty-one-year-old age group).

Airborne Course
Airborne training is available on a voluntary basis for enlisted personnel without regard to current assignment who will be assigned to an airborne unit after training. This functional training conducted by the U.S. Army Infantry School is designed to qualify volunteers in the use of the parachute as a means of deployment and through mental and physical training, to develop leadership, self-confidence, and aggressive spirit. Graduates receive an additional skill identifier (ASI) designated by a (P). Eligible personnel volunteering for airborne training should submit applications according to the instructions contained in AR 614-200 and should be physically qualified for parachute duty in accordance with AR 40-501.

Ranger Training
This voluntary training conducted by the U.S. Army Infantry School, Fort Benning, Georgia, is designed to develop leadership skills and provide a knowledge of Ranger operations involving direct combat with the enemy. Nonairborne enlisted graduates receive a special qualification identifier (G) for their MOS code, while those who are airborne qualified receive a V. Ranger training is available on a voluntary basis prin-

cipally for enlisted soldiers who are in the following MOSs: any Infantry or Special Forces MOS, 12B—Combat Engineer, 13F—Fire Support Sergeant, 14S—Avenger Crewman, 19D—Cavalry Scout, and 19K—Armor Crewman. Ranger School is now also available to combat support (CS) and combat service support (CSS) soldiers within the combat arms exclusion policy. Because many of the tasks evaluated at Ranger School are outside the CS/CSS arena, successful completion of a pre-Ranger program is essential for CS/CSS success. Submit applications according to the instructions contained in AR 614-200. In my opinion, this is the best small-unit leadership training in the Army, if not the world, bar none!

Special Forces Training

Special Forces training is available for all male soldiers with any MOS; however, combat arms is preferred. Applicants must be in the rank of specialist (SPC) (P) through staff sergeant (SSG) and meet the course criteria as outlined in AR 614-200, Chapter 5, Section I, *Special Forces Assignments* (policy and selection criteria). Soldiers who meet the prerequisites and who volunteer for Special Forces training must be airborne qualified and must attend and successfully complete the three-week Special Forces Selection and Assessment Course, which assesses tactical skills, leadership, physical fitness, motivation, and a student's ability to cope with stress. Students are in a temporary duty (TDY) and return status during the course. Those who pass are scheduled to attend the Special Forces Qualification Course. Soldiers who attend the qualification course must complete a common phase, an MOS-specific phase, and a final phase that combines and tests what was learned in the first two phases. Depending on the MOS (weapons, engineering, communications, medical, intelligence), the qualification course can vary from twenty-six to fifty-seven weeks, depending on the MOS. Language training may also be required. The primary training site for Special Forces training is Fort Bragg, North Carolina.

DISTANCE LEARNING

The Army has entered the digital age with soldiers attending classes at their post; where through digital and video teleconferencing (VTC) links they attend courses presented by schools and instructors located at far-off institutions. Soldiers attending courses, whether through a resident school, a Total Army Schools System (TASS) Training Battalion, or a digital learning facility, receive the same credit for successfully completing training, with documentation in the soldier's Military Personnel Records Jacket (MPRJ) reflecting identical codes for any of the training types. All diplomas, certificates, or DA Form 1059 will be the same and not reflect nonresident, distant learning, reserve component, or other similar remarks. Promotion and evaluation boards will not discriminate against soldiers who completed their professional military training through distant learning.

First priority for all components is mission immediate training required for mobilization, activation, deployment, or other critical, time-sensitive requirements. Second priority is to quota-managed training, as directed by Headquarters, Depart-

ment of the Army (HQDA), such as MOS reclassification and NCOES courses with the reserve components, and NCOES, additional skill identifier (ASI), and special qualification identifier (SQI) courses, and MOS reclassification for active duty. Third priority is to reserve component ASI/SQI courses and civilian training. The remaining priorities are to functional training courses, self-development courses, and training courses provided to the civilian community.

Soldiers may split their training phases, with some at the resident school or at a TASS Battalion and the remainder conducted through distant learning while at their home station. One of the considerations for determining training location is whether the costs of TASS or distant learning exceed the costs of sending a soldier to the proponent school for the full resident course.

SKILL RECOGNITION PROGRAM

The Skill Recognition Program provides ways to get recognition within the civilian sector for skills learned in service. This recognition can come in the following forms:

Army Apprenticeship. This program provides participants with documentation of apprentice skills acquired while in the Army that is understood by civilian industry. It improves the performance and motivation of soldiers, provides a recruiting incentive for MOSs that are related to skills with apprenticeships, and improves the supervisor-soldier relationship.

Occupations with apprenticeships are those that are learned through experience and on-the-job training and are supplemented by related technical instruction. They involve manual, mechanical, or technological skills and knowledge requiring a minimum of 2,000 hours of work experience plus related instruction. They do not fall into the categories of selling, management, clerical, or professional skills requiring advanced knowledge and academic degrees. These apprenticeship occupations are identified in Department of Labor pamphlets and appendix I, AR 621-5.

Enrollment is open to soldiers who perform satisfactorily on the job and possess an MOS (primary or secondary) that relates to the program and that has been registered with the Bureau of Apprenticeship Training. Also eligible are soldiers who possess a qualifying MOS in which they were initially registered but are no longer serving because of priorities and mission requirements.

Certification. Some Army MOSs correspond to civilian occupations that require licensing or certification as a prerequisite for employment in certain states or businesses. Certification requirements and agencies are listed in Army apprenticeship or industry recognition pamphlets in the AR 621 series.

Involvement in these programs is voluntary. Army training programs are not altered to meet civilian standards for skill recognition programs. As a prerequisite to registration, certification, or formal recognition, however, some civilian agencies might require additional nonmission-related training or experience before recognizing a soldier as fully qualified. When this is necessary, the soldier must acquire the additional training and experience through local trade or vocational schools, or by other means.

Programs stress individual initiative. An individual cannot be enrolled in more than one occupational skill area within an apprenticeship program at any one time. The soldier may, however, change to another occupational area or program as many times as desired, provided prerequisites are met.

FUNCTIONAL ACADEMIC SKILLS TRAINING

Functional Academic Skills Training (FAST), formerly called Basic Skills Education Program (BSEP), provides instruction in academic competencies necessary for job proficiency and preparation for advanced training. FAST, available at Army Learning Centers (ALCs), helps improve soldiers' job performance and helps them meet reenlistment eligibility and MOS classification requirements. Because this program is self-paced using instructional material (software at those ALCs that are computer-equipped), FAST is available during duty and off-duty hours. FAST covers reading, writing, arithmetic, and other subjects that soldiers must comprehend to excel in service.

NCO EVALUATION SYSTEM

Some first-term soldiers will reach the rank of sergeant during their first enlistment and will begin receiving written NCO Evaluation Reports (NCOERs) from their immediate supervisors. The NCOER provides formal recognition of duty performance, a measurement of professional values and personal traits, and is the basis for performance counseling by rating officials. Subsequent school selection, promotion, assignment, MOS classification, and qualitative management are based largely on information found in the NCOER. The NCOER is designed to strengthen the NCO Corps's ability to meet the professional challenges of the future.

3

Service in Today's Army

Peter J. Schoomaker and Anthony W. Vassalo provide a compelling guide to the Army's future in "The Way Ahead" (*Military Review*, March–April 2004):

> Flexible, adaptive, and competent Soldiers infused with the Army's Warrior Culture fight wars and win the peace. Soldiers remain the centerpiece of our combat systems and formations. American Soldiers, possessed of a fierce warrior ethos and spirit, fight in close combat, dominate key assets and terrain, decisively end conflicts, control the movement of people, protect resource flows, and maintain post-conflict stability. We must never forget that it is the Soldier—fierce, disciplined, well trained, and well equipped—who ultimately represents and enables the capabilities we as an Army provide the Joint Force and the Nation.

CHARACTERISTICS OF ARMY SERVICE

For over 225 years, the Army has employed its military doctrine, organization, procedures, and ideals of service to meet whatever challenge the nation has asked of it in the realm of national defense, military deterrence, and warfighting. Today, and for the foreseeable future, Army service will be characterized by a number of key attributes all soldiers need to understand.

Continuous Training

Training is the cornerstone of military life. The Army has an extensive program of *individual* and *unit* training that is virtually continuous. Individual training is the responsibility of the Army's enlisted NCOs. Unit training is the responsibility of the unit's leaders and commanders. Unit training is accomplished during recurring field training exercises (FTXs) and other collective training events. Every FTX, whether it lasts one day or several weeks, measures how ready individual soldiers, their units, and larger collective organizations are to perform their respective missions in war. Soldiers find out how fit, tough, trained, and ready they are during an FTX, especially when they get cold, hot, tired, wet, hungry, or thirsty and encounter other

unpleasant conditions or forces, such as the simulated "enemy" opposing force found at major training centers. Training also occurs in combat theaters so that soldiers remain familiar with tasks not accomplished daily as well as to absorb "lessons learned."

Professional Competence

The Army of the new millennium incorporates intellectual ingenuity, technological innovation, and a set of corporate values that have shaped America's Army throughout its more than 200-year history. Our Army will continue to need skilled, versatile, and highly motivated soldiers capable of accomplishing their mission in ever-changing environments. Today's soldiers will become the leaders of tomorrow's soldiers. They are the young men and women who will provide to America a corps of leaders who have an unmatched work ethic, who have a strong sense of values, who treat others with dignity and respect, who are accustomed to hard work, who are courageous, who thrive on responsibility, who know how to work as a team, and who are positive role models for all around them. Today's Army is manned with professionally competent soldiers and leaders. They know their jobs, and they do them well.

World-Class Missions

America's Army is the best land combat force in the world, serving the nation every day at home and abroad. It is often the commitment of our Army into trouble spots

Semper Paratis, **"Always Ready"**

that makes the difference between success and failure of America's national security policy. When ground troops deploy, the world knows the United States means business. Land forces remain decisive and provide the most visible and sustained form of U.S. commitment. Since 1989, the Army has had forty-three major deployments, including ongoing operations in Iraq, Afghanistan, the Sinai, the Philippines, Kosovo, and Bosnia. In the forty years prior to 1989, there were only ten.

Hundreds of thousands of soldiers are involved in vital roles, missions, and functions on a daily basis. In 2005, approximately 640,000 soldiers were serving on active duty, with 315,000 from all components—Active Army (155,000), Army National Guard (113,000), and Army Reserve (47,000)—deployed or forward stationed in more than 120 countries to support operations in Iraq, Afghanistan, and other theaters of war and deter aggression, while securing the homeland. Soldiers from the Army National Guard and the Army Reserve are making a vital contribution, with 150,000 soldiers mobilized and performing a diverse range of missions worldwide. In addition to their duties overseas, soldiers from all components of the Guard and the Reserve are supporting civil authorities during disaster relief operations, such as those which occurred in Louisiana and Mississippi.

An Army of Values
Soldiers learn and draw strength from those soldiers and leaders who nurture and encourage the development of values as inalienable professional attributes. Soldiers are expected to live by and exemplify those values. Internalizing these values—living by them—is what builds professionalism in America's Army and character in our nation. Values and traditions are the soul of the Army.

The Army lives by seven bedrock values to which all soldiers must adhere. Army values follow the acronym LDRSHIP:

ARMY VALUES

Loyalty	Being faithful to the country, the Army, your unit, and other soldiers in good times and bad.
Duty	Performing your military responsibilities and fulfilling your legal obligations faithfully and reliably under all conditions.
Respect	Treating all people with dignity and courtesy and as you would wish to be treated.
Selfless service	Putting the welfare of the nation, the Army, and your colleagues before your own welfare.

ARMY VALUES *continued*

Honor   Having the personal integrity, courage, and honesty
                         to know and support what is right without being
                         forced to do so.

Integrity   Doing what's right, legally and morally, and not
                         allowing yourself to be corrupted by that which is
                         not. This includes taking responsibility for your
                         actions.

Personal courage   Being brave and doing your duty in the face of fear,
                         danger, or adversity.

Additionally, two personal characteristics go hand in hand with values. They are:

Teamwork   Working or performing duties in cooperation with
                         others.

Discipline   Controlling your personal behavior to avoid doing
                         wrong, and focusing your talents and skills on
                         doing well what is required.

These values have served the Army well in peacetime and in war. Values, along
with professional job competence, contribute directly to mission success. Soldiers
who develop within themselves a sense of mental and moral strength—courage—
will accomplish the mission when in combat. Understand also that commitment to
the unit's mission takes priority over personal wishes, wants, pleasures, and, perhaps, needs. It means sincere involvement—doing something—to find solutions to
problems and just not paying lip service to them.

Although soldierly values and character attributes are not new, there is a
renewed interest in them. The Soldier's Code best encapsulates the compact among
the soldier, the leader, and the Army.

An Army of Standards
Today's Army is also an army of standards. There are two types of standards: standards of *personal behavior* and standards of *duty performance*. The standards of
personal behavior apply to all ranks. The standards of duty performance apply to all
soldiers according to their military occupational specialties and the levels of responsibility and authority they hold.

   Standards are those principles or rules by which behaviors and tasks are measured as successfully accomplished. When members of a squad, section, or platoon share and adhere to the Army values and to the standards that flow from them, they are a more cohesive organization. Soldiers will measure other soldiers by the standard as it gradually becomes a criterion for acceptance by the whole team.

   Army Field Manual (FM) 1 [FM 100-1], titled simply *The Army*, capstones the Army's guiding beliefs, standards, and ideals succinctly in one word—duty. Duty means to fulfill your obligations. It is behavior required by moral obligation, demanded by custom, or enjoined by feelings of rightness. It requires the impartial administration of standards without regard to friendship, personality, rank, or other bias. It is one of the key Army values.

SOLDIER'S CREED

I am an American Soldier.

I am a Warrior and a member of a team.

I serve the people of the United States and live the Army Values.

I will always place the mission first.

I will never accept defeat.

I will never quit.

I will never leave a fallen comrade.

I am disciplined, physically and mentally tough,

trained and proficient in my warrior tasks and drills.

I always maintain my arms, my equipment and myself.

I am an expert and I am a professional.

I stand ready to deploy, engage, and destroy the enemies

of the United States of America in close combat.

I am a guardian of freedom and the American way of life.

I am an American Soldier.

The Soldier's Code expands the Soldier's Creed:

SOLDIER'S CODE

I.

I am an American soldier, a protector of the greatest nation on earth—sworn to uphold the Constitution of the United States. I will always perform my duties to the utmost of my abilities and will strive to exhibit the moral and physical courage expected of a soldier. Throughout my years as a soldier and after, I will put my obligations before self. My word is my bond.

II.

I will treat others with dignity and respect, and expect others to do the same. I will not tolerate soldiers being treated differently because of race, color, sex, religion, or national origin. I will notify my chain of command if I observe instances which affect the good order and discipline of the organization.

III.

I will honor my Country, the Army, my unit, and my fellow soldiers by living the Army values. I will obey the lawful orders of my superiors and will uphold the standards established by the leadership.

IV.

No matter what situation I am in, I will never do anything for pleasure, profit, or personal safety which will disgrace my uniform, my unit, or my country.

V.

I expect my leadership to discipline me when I do wrong and commend me when I exceed expectations. I rely on my leadership to establish an organizational climate where I can learn and grow as an individual. Lastly, I am proud of my country and its flag. I want to look back on my time in the Army and say that I am proud to have served my country as a soldier.

CURRENT TRENDS IN THE ARMY

Army Transformation: New Doctrines for New Missions

Assigned Army missions affect how the military is structured, trained, and employed. The Army's new regional focus, combined with major troop reductions overseas, puts enormous emphasis on strategic mobility. Airlift and sealift mobility improvements being made today will enable deployment of an Army light division and a heavy brigade to any crisis area in about two weeks, and two heavy divisions in about a month. The new brigade combat teams will be able to deploy in ninety-six hours.

New Structures

The Army is currently undergoing transformation from a division-based to a brigade-based force. These brigades are designed as modules, or self-sufficient and standardized Brigade Combat Teams, that can be more readily deployed and combined with other Army and joint forces to meet the precise needs of the combatant commanders. These were described in Chapter 1.

AN ERA OF CONFLICT

The end of the Cold War had three key strategic events: the collapse of international communism, the demise of the Soviet Union, and an end to bipolar competition. These events, in turn, are affecting power and security relationships throughout the world. One result is the relative dispersal of power away from the states of the former Soviet Union toward other regional power centers. Another is the potential struggle within regions as the dominant states vie for position within the emerging power hierarchy. A third is that in many regions the "lid has come off" long-simmering ethnic, religious, territorial, and economic disputes.

Terrorism

The United States continues to face a variety of threats from terrorist organizations such as al Qaeda and Sunni extremist groups. The primary threat for the foreseeable future is a network of Islamic extremists hostile to the United States. The network is transnational and has a broad range of capabilities, to include mass-casualty attacks. The most dangerous and immediate threat is Sunni Islamic terrorists that form the "al Qaeda associated movement."

Osama bin Ladin and his senior leadership no longer exercise centralized control and direction. We now face an "al Qaeda associated movement" of like-minded groups who interact, share resources, and work to achieve shared goals. Some of the groups in the movement provide safe haven and logistical support to al Qaeda members, others operate directly with al Qaeda, and still others fight with al Qaeda in the Afghanistan/Pakistan region.

Remnants of the senior leadership still present a threat. As is clear in their public statements, bin Ladin and Ayman al-Zawahiri remain focused on their strategic objectives, including another major casualty-producing attack against the homeland.

The Global Jihadist Movement

The global jihadist movement predates al Qaeda's founding and was reinforced and developed by successive conflicts in Afghanistan, Bosnia, Chechnya, and elsewhere during the 1990s. As a result, it spawned several groups and operating nodes and developed a resiliency that ensured that destruction of any one group or node did not destroy the larger movement. Since 2001, extremists, including members of al Qaeda and affiliated groups, have sought to exploit perceptions of the U.S.-led global war on terrorism and, in particular, the war in Iraq to attract converts to their movement. Many of these recruits come from a large and growing pool of disaf-

fected youth who are sympathetic to radical, anti-Western militant ideology. At the same time, these extremists have branched out to establish jihadist cells in other parts of the Middle East, South Asia, and Europe, from which they seek to prepare operations and facilitate funding and communications. Foreign fighters appear to be working to make the insurgency in Iraq what Afghanistan was to the earlier generation of jihadists: a melting pot for jihadists from around the world, a training ground, and an indoctrination center. In the months and years ahead, a significant number of fighters who have traveled to Iraq could return to their home countries, where they might strengthen existing extremist networks with their new skills and experience in the communities to which they return.

Afghanistan

Afghanistan, once the safe haven for Osama bin Ladin, has started on the road to recovery after decades of instability and civil war. Hamid Karzai's election to the presidency was a major milestone. The September 2005 elections for a new National Assembly and local district councils scheduled for spring 2006 will complete the process of electing representatives. President Karzai still faces a low-level insurgency aimed at destabilizing the country, raising the cost of reconstruction, and ultimately forcing Coalition forces to leave. The development of the Afghan National Army and a national police force is going well, although neither can yet stand on its own.

Iraq

Self-determination for the Iraqi people will largely depend on the ability of Iraqi forces to provide security. Iraq's most capable security units have become more effective in recent months, contributing to several major operations and helping to put an Iraqi face on security operations. Insurgents are determined to discourage new recruits and undermine the effectiveness of existing Iraqi security forces.

The lack of security is hurting Iraq's reconstruction efforts and economic development, causing overall economic growth to proceed at a much slower pace than many analysts expected a year ago. Alternatively, the larger uncommitted moderate Sunni population and the Sunni political elite may seize the postelectoral moment to take part in creating Iraq's new political institutions if victorious Shia and Kurdish parties include Sunnis in the new government.

The Army is trained and ready "to be persuasive in peace and invincible in war." Military operations conducted during this war provided evidence to soldiers that the Army's goals of having an army that is responsive, rapidly deployable, agile, versatile, lethal, survivable, and sustainable (as discussed earlier) may already be at hand. The future role of the Army in Iraq will certainly be to assist in the transition to peace until other international arrangements can be put in place and become effective.

Iran

Iran is important to the United States because of its size, location, energy resources, military strength, and hostility to U.S. interests. It actively supports terrorist groups in the region, such as Hezbollah, and could encourage increased attacks in Israel and

the Palestinian Territories to derail progress toward peace. Iran also aids insurgents in Iraq to drive the United States out of that country and ultimately the Middle East. In the near term, Iran's goal is a weakened, decentralized, and Shia-dominated Iraq that is incapable of posing a threat to Iran. The country's mullah-dominated government will also continue its weapons of mass destruction and ballistic missile programs. Its drive to acquire nuclear weapons is a key test of international resolve and the nuclear nonproliferation treaty.

The government in Tehran has the only military in the region that can threaten its neighbors and Gulf stability. Its expanding ballistic missile inventory presents a potential threat to states in the region. As it fields new longer range medium-range ballistic missiles (MRBMs), Iran will have missiles with ranges to reach many of our European allies. Although the country maintains a sizable conventional force, it has made limited progress in modernizing its conventional capabilities. Air and air defense forces rely on out-of-date U.S., Russian, and Chinese equipment. Ground forces suffer from personnel and equipment shortages. In addition, the equipment is also poorly maintained. Intelligence services estimate that Iran can briefly close the Strait of Hormuz, relying on a layered strategy using predominately naval, air, and some ground forces. Last year it purchased North Korean torpedo and missile-armed fast attack craft and midget submarines, making marginal improvements to this capability.

Iran is and will remain a threat to the national security interests on the United States for the foreseeable future.

Syria

The Syrian government likely weighs opportunities and risks with an unstable Iraq. It sees the problems we face in Iraq as beneficial because our commitments in Iraq reduce the prospects for action against Syria. It is probably concerned, however, about potential spillover of Iraqi problems, especially Sunni extremism, into Syria. We have little evidence of active regime support for the insurgency, but Syria offers safe haven to Iraqi Baathists, some of whom have ties to insurgents. Syria continues to support Lebanese Hezbollah and several rejectionist Palestinian groups, which its government argues are legitimate resistance groups. While the country is making minor improvements to its conventional forces through purchases of modern anti-tank guided missiles and overhauling of some aircraft, it cannot afford major weapon systems acquisitions.

North Korea

After more than a decade of declining or stagnant economic growth, Kim Jong Il's military capability has significantly degraded. The North's declining capabilities are even more pronounced when viewed in light of the significant improvements over the same period of the Republic of Korea (ROK) military and the U.S.-ROK Combined Forces Command. Nevertheless, the North maintains a large conventional force of over one million soldiers, the majority of which may be deployed south of Pyongyang.

North Korea continues to prioritize the military at the expense of its economy. The "military first policy" has several purposes. It serves to deter U.S.-ROK aggression.

Nationwide conscription is a critical tool for the regime to socialize its citizens to maintain the Kim family in power. The large military allows the dictator to use threats and bravado in order to limit U.S.-ROK policy options. Suggestions of sanctions, or military pressure by the United States or the Republic of Korea are countered by the North with threats that such actions are "an act of war" or that it could "turn Seoul into a sea of fire." Inertia, leadership perceptions that military power equals national power, and the inability for the regime to change without threatening its leadership also explain the continuing large military commitment.

The North Korean People's Army remains capable of attacking South Korea with artillery and missile forces with limited warning. Such a provocative act, absent an immediate threat, is highly unlikely, counter to Pyongyang's political and economic objectives, and would prompt a South Korean–U.S. Combined Forces Command (CFC) response it could not effectively oppose.

China

Beijing's military modernization and military buildup is tilting the balance of power in the Taiwan Strait. Improved Chinese capabilities threaten U.S. forces in the region.

China remains keenly interested in coalition military operations in Afghanistan and Iraq and is using lessons from those operations to guide its People's Liberation Army's (PLA) modernization and strategy; however, it will take several years before these lessons are incorporated into the armed forces. The government in Beijing remains concerned over the U.S. presence in Iraq, Afghanistan, and Central Asia. It may also think it has an opportunity to improve diplomatic and economic relations—including access to energy resources—with other countries distrustful or resentful of U.S. policy. China continues to develop or import modern weapons. Priorities include submarines, surface combatants, air defense, ballistic and antiship cruise missiles, and modern fighters. The PLA must overcome significant integration challenges to turn these new, advanced, and disparate weapon systems into improved capabilities. The government also faces technical and operational difficulties in numerous areas. The PLA continues with its plan to cut approximately 200,000 soldiers from its army to free resources for further modernization, an initiative that began in 2004.

China is increasingly confident and active on the international stage—trying to ensure it has a voice on major international issues: securing access to natural resources—and countering what it sees as U.S. efforts to contain or encircle China.

Russia

Despite an improving economy, Russia continues to face endemic challenges related to its post-Soviet military decline. Seeking to restore itself as a great power, the Russian government has made some improvements to its armed forces, but has

not addressed difficult domestic problems that will limit the scale and scope of military recovery.

Russian conventional forces have improved from their mid-1990s low point. Moscow nonetheless faces challenges if it is to move beyond these limited improvements. Significant procurement has been postponed until after 2010 and the Kremlin is not spending enough to modernize Russia's defense industrial base. Russia also faces increasingly negative demographic trends and military quality of life issues that will create military manning problems.

Moscow has been able to boost its defense spending in line with its recovering economy. Russia's gross national product averaged 6.7 percent growth over the past five years, predominately from increased energy prices and consumer demand. Defense should continue to receive modest real increases in funding, unless Russia suffers an economic setback. Budget increases will help Russia create a professional military by replacing conscripts with volunteer servicemen and focusing on maintaining, modernizing, and extending the operational life of its strategic weapons systems—including its nuclear missile force.

The Balkans
International peacekeeping forces in Bosnia and Kosovo continue to operate in a complex environment that poses significant challenges to the establishment of a stable and enduring peace. The Bosnian factions should continue to generally comply with the military aspects of the Dayton Accords and Stabilization Force (SFOR) directives. Montenegro's potential drive for independence presents the next potential crisis. Ethnic Albanians from across the political spectrum in Kosovo continue to insist on independence. While the threat to U.S. and allied forces in the Balkans from organized military forces remains low, they will continue to face a threat from land mines and various forms of low-level, sporadic, and random violence, which could include high-profile attacks by rogue elements or terrorists.

On the other hand, the entrance of Romania and Bulgaria into the NATO Alliance is a positive development for regional security. The U.S. may also establish training bases in Bulgaria in the near future.

South Asia
The tense rivalry between India and Pakistan over Kashmir is our most important security concern on the subcontinent. While neither side wants war, both see their security relationship in zero-sum terms. India's larger economy and more robust military is balanced by Pakistan's threat to retaliate with nuclear weapons if the two nations go to war. With frequent low-level clashes, the potential for miscalculation and rapid escalation is constant.

Latin America
The scourge of narcotrafficking, related money laundering, weapons and contraband smuggling, insurgency, and the recent disruption in the Venezuelan oil industry all combine to provide threatening conditions for some countries and governments of

the region and for U.S. interests. The potential for more serious insurgency and more widespread terrorism and crime in several areas of Central and South America and the Caribbean continues to demand our vigilance.

In summary, although the United States will not likely see a global "peer competitor" within twenty years, the threats facing the United States in the next decade will be of an uncertain order of magnitude. The world remains a very dangerous and complex place, and there is every reason to expect U.S. military requirements to be at about the same level of the past several years, and that use of U.S. military forces will be required along the full spectrum of operations.

THE BEST TIME TO SERVE

As ironic as it may seem, morale in heavily engaged and deployed Army units is higher than in units doing peacetime training and garrison duties. This is probably because soldiers like doing constructive and visible Army missions. Although training is one of the Army's most important missions, actually performing the functions for which we are trained seems to be more rewarding.

The Army also seems to have stabilized in terms of its size and in the opportunities for professional advancement. Soldiers who work hard at their duties, perform to standard in training and conduct, and participate professionally in any operation are rewarded not only with decorations but also with promotion to higher ranks. The skills learned in the Army—both the technical skills and the skill of working on a team toward a cooperative goal—are treasures of a lifetime.

The Army also received significant pay raises during the first years of this millennium. Army salaries, when considering all the benefits and allowances and taking into account what they would cost if they had to be purchased out of a civilian salary, are now quite competitive. And pay increases with length of service and advancement in rank and responsibility.

Above all, Army duty is exciting, interesting, and personally rewarding. How many civilians get to be part of a world event? Very few. Soldiers do all the time. As U.S. interests in the world expand, the deployment of American forces to trouble spots around the world to deter enemies, protect international friends, and keep the peace between warring factions will continue to be missions worth training for and successfully executing.

The issues that soldiers are concerned about on a daily basis would fill thick volumes, with pay and entitlements; housing, including barracks and Army family housing; medical care for soldiers and their families; and a stable retirement system leading the list. Daily discussions about chow, guard duty, uniform costs, women in combat (or male attitudes toward them), homosexuals, the quality of training, leadership, supervision, field training exercises, the weather, separation hardships, marital discord, blisters and other ailments, orders, directives, and verbal instructions all point to the old adage that soldiers are happy when they have the opportunity to complain.

Some aspects of Army life are as follows:

- Soldiers of every race, gender, and creed are successful if treated equally and held to the same standards.
- Soldiers will get from combat training what they put into it.
- Most leaders and supervisors are competent; those who aren't fall by the wayside.
- Field training is critical to combat readiness.
- Separation from loved ones occurs in many occupational sectors of American society and must be understood and dealt with by the chain of command.

In recent years, members of the Army have had to deal with increasing deployments, assaults on their benefits, and, worse yet, fellow soldiers undermining the traditional key values by bad behavior. Nevertheless, in the Army family, plenty of good people do care and go about their business because it must be done. Selfless service calls for personal sacrifice and dedication to duty, regardless of the circumstances. No one gets rich on Army pay. If elements of the nation seem less than caring, well, that's just how it is, so don't sweat it.

Sergeant Major of the Army Kenneth O. Preston had these final words of wisdom to soldiers serving in today's Army: "You are the next 'Greatest Generation.' Be proud of your service to your nation."

4

Real-World Issues

Soldiers excel in their duty performance and have successful careers when they obey the requirements of law and Army policy and use a little common sense in other matters that can cause needless problems. Many of the issues confronting civilians also confront soldiers, but the Army has policies and rules to guide the conduct of soldiers.

THE LAW OF WAR

The Army has been tarred by a few soldiers operating outside the bounds of military discipline and law. Although their misdeeds have been exposed by fellow soldiers and investigated by the chain of command, their actions have brought great discredit to not only themselves, but the Army and our nation.

The United States and its military abides by the laws of war. Its soldiers are expected to comply with both the spirit and intent of these laws in all of their actions. It is only this respect for, and obedience to, the reign of law that differentiates our Army from wanton hordes of looters, destroyers of life and property, and other immoral persons. Nevertheless, the very nature of war can lead some of the fighting forces to fall prey to violence and disorder and to participate in unlawful actions. These actions, at whatever level and for whatever reason, cannot be permitted to exist or continue. Only when all members understand that every member of the Army must be absolutely opposed to any unlawful conduct and that any such conduct will be met with immediate action will the United States be living up to its national goals. If something looks wrong, question it. If you walk by, you may be acquiescing to establishing a standard for patterns of abuse.

The attack of noncombatants and protected property is illegal. You must be able to distinguish "noncombatants" from "combatants" and distinguish "protected property" from "military objectives." Combatants are defined as follows: Anyone engaging in hostilities in an armed conflict on behalf of a party to the conflict. Combatants are lawful targets unless "out of combat." Military objectives are lawful targets (Army Field Manual (FM) 27-10: *The Law of Land Warfare*, para. 40, and GP I, art. 52(2)).

RULES OF ENGAGEMENT

The *DOD* (Department of Defense) *Dictionary* defines Rules of Engagement (ROE) as "directives issued by competent military authority that delineate the circumstances and limitations under which [U.S.] forces will initiate and/or continue combat engagement with other forces encountered."

Army training about ROE envisions two general circumstances for using weapons: in self-defense and to accomplish the mission. Whether ROE are "permissive" (allowing more use of force) or "restrictive" (limited use of force) depends on the anticipated conditions extant in the mission—e.g., presence or absence of quantities of small arms and light weapons; existing, organized opposition groups, armed and unarmed; competency of local security forces, etc.

Remember that in all cases and regardless of ROE, a soldier always has the inherent right of self-defense.

FRATERNIZATION

The Army has always had policies concerning senior-subordinate relationships. This is nothing new, and it is not just a problem relating to gender.

Army policy states that relationships between soldiers of different rank that involve or give the appearance of partiality, preferential treatment, or the improper use of rank or position for personal gain, and that are prejudicial to good order, discipline, and high unit morale, will be avoided.

Prohibited Relationships

Relationships between soldiers of different rank—regardless of military service—are prohibited if they:

- Compromise, or appear to compromise, supervisory integrity or the chain of command.
- Cause actual or perceived partiality or unfairness.
- Involve the improper use of rank or position for personal gain.
- Are exploitative or coercive in nature.
- Create an actual or predictable impact on discipline, authority, morale, or mission accomplishment.

Prohibited relationships between officers and enlisted people, trainers and trainees, and recruiters and recruits include:

- Any business relationships, except landlord-tenant relationships or one-time transactions.
- Borrowing or lending money, commercial solicitation, and any other type of ongoing financial or business relationship.
- Shared living accommodations other than those directed by operational requirements.
- Dating and other intimate or sexual relationships.
- Gambling.

The reason for this policy is clear. Officers have both punitive and reward power over the personnel in their units. Fraternization or inappropriate association by an enlisted soldier and his or her officers will surely be interpreted as an attempt to obtain favorable treatment. Since officers are legally bound not to fraternize with enlisted soldiers, it is best for enlisted soldiers not to seek these improper associations. Normal team-building associations such as community organizations, religious activities, family gatherings, unit-based social functions, and athletic teams or events are permitted and encouraged.

These prohibitions do not negate a leader's responsibility for the professional development of soldiers. Leaders cannot stop mentoring, coaching, and teaching soldiers because they fear being accused of fraternization or worse. They must continue to encourage individual study and professional development and to mentor the continued growth of their subordinates' military careers.

EQUAL OPPORTUNITY

Equal opportunity (EO) means exactly what the words indicate: Every soldier in the Army shall have an equal opportunity to serve his or her country and obtain the benefits of military service, including training, schooling, promotion, and assignments, without regard to race, religion, ethnic background, national origin, or gender.

Army policy is to base all personnel decisions on merit and excellence of duty performance. Equal opportunity does not mean creating quotas for promotions, assignments, or apportionment of duties based on a soldier's race or other defined category, for this, too, is against the law. Rather, the purpose of EO is for all soldiers to compete on an equal basis for schooling, promotions, and assignments. Soldiers who do their jobs best, who maintain the standards and values mentioned in the previous chapter, will win in these professional competitions regardless of their race or gender. In the Army, these rules are well understood and enforced. Equal opportunity for minorities in the military service has been a success story. It is seen as proof that the Army's EO policies are working, notwithstanding the existence of some individual acts of prejudice that unfortunately still occur.

Gender discrimination is defined as discrimination based solely on an individual's gender in a subgroup "female" or "male." Discrimination based on gender is often linked to a set of assumptions based on sex-role stereotypes concerning the abilities, competence, status, and roles of the particular subgroup, resulting in a disparate treatment of or impact on those groups. We've all seen it in one form or another—male soldiers serving as aides and drivers to male generals because of concerns about having women as their assistants, or an attractive female soldier in the operations shop rather than down in the motor pool working in her MOS.

To prevent the occurrence of discrimination, the Department of the Army has placed the responsibility for EO in the hands of unit commanders and has articulated the connection between EO and unit readiness by enforcing the policy through the traditional chain of command. AR 600-20, *Army Command Policy*, states:

The chain of command, whether military or civilian, has the primary responsibility for developing and sustaining a healthy climate. This responsibility entails, but is not limited to, promoting positive programs that enhance unit cohesion, esprit, and morale; communicating matters with EO significance to unit personnel and higher headquarters; correcting discriminatory practices by conducting rapid, objective, and impartial inquiries to resolve complaints of discrimination; encouraging the surfacing of problems and preventing reprisal for those who complain; and taking appropriate action against those who violate Army policy.

Under current regulations, commanders have the legal authority to deal with cases of unlawful discrimination or sexual harassment (see the next section). AR 600-20, paragraph 4-4, "Soldier Conduct," provides that ensuring proper conduct of soldiers is a function of command. Commanders rely on all leaders in the Army to "take action against military personnel in any case where the soldier's conduct violates good order and discipline." Although this charge is not punitive, the commander's inherent authority to impose administrative sanctions and to prosecute specific offenses under the Uniform Code of Military Justice (UCMJ) provides commanders with sufficient authority to enforce Army policy against discrimination and harassment.

SEXUAL HARASSMENT

The Department of Defense defines sexual harassment as a form of sex discrimination that involves unwelcome sexual advances, requests for sexual favors, and other verbal or physical conduct of a sexual nature when:

- Submission to such conduct is made either explicitly or implicitly a term or condition of a person's job, pay, or career; or
- Submission to or rejection of such conduct by a person is used as a basis for career or employment decisions affecting that person; or
- Such conduct has the purpose or effect of unreasonably interfering with an individual's work performance or creates an intimidating, hostile, or offensive working environment.

This definition emphasizes workplace conduct. To be actionable as an "abusive work environment," harassment need not result in concrete psychological harm to the victim but need only be so severe or pervasive that a reasonable person would perceive—and the victim does perceive—the work environment as hostile or offensive. Any person in a supervisory or command position who uses or condones any form of sexual behavior to control, influence, or affect the career, pay, or job of a military member or civilian employee is engaging in sexual harassment. Similarly, any military member or civilian employee who makes deliberate or repeated unwelcome verbal comments, gestures, or physical contact of a sexual nature in the workplace is also engaging in sexual harassment and is subject to punishment under the provisions of the UCMJ.

Sexual harassment can include verbal abuse, profanity, off-color jokes, sexual comments, threats, barking, growling, oinking, or whistling at passers-by to indicate a perception of their physical appearance. It also includes nonverbal abuse such as leering, ogling (giving a person the "once over"), blowing kisses, licking lips, winking, leaving sexually suggestive notes, and displaying sexist cartoons and pictures. Unwanted physical contact such as touching, patting, hugging, pinching, grabbing, cornering, kissing, blocking a passageway, and back and neck rubs may also constitute sexual harassment.

EXTREMISM
Although the Constitution guarantees freedom of speech and association, soldiers do not have the right to use these freedoms to infringe upon the rights of others.

Policy
Chapter 4-12 of AR 600-20, *Army Command Policy*, makes it clear that participation in extremist organizations or activities is inconsistent with the responsibilities of military service. It defines extremist organizations and activities as those "that advocate racial, gender, or ethnic hatred or intolerance; advocate, create, or engage in illegal discrimination based on race, color, sex, religion, or national origin; advocate the use of or use force or violence or unlawful means to deprive individuals of their rights under the [U.S.] Constitution or the laws of the United States, or any state, by unlawful means."

By regulation, soldiers are prohibited from the following actions in support of extremist organizations or activities:

1. Participating in a public demonstration or rally.
2. Attending a meeting or activity with knowledge that the meeting or activity involves an extremist cause when on duty, when in uniform, when in a foreign country (whether on or off duty or in uniform), when it constitutes a breach of law and order, when violence is likely to result, or when in violation of off-limits sanctions or a commander's order.
3. Fundraising.
4. Recruiting or training members (including encouraging others to join).
5. Creating, organizing, or taking a visible leadership role in such an organization or activity.
6. Distributing literature on or off a military installation the primary purpose and content of which concerns advocacy or support of extremist causes, organizations, or activities, and it appears that the literature presents a clear danger to the loyalty, discipline, or morale of military personnel or if the distribution would materially interfere with the accomplishment of a military mission.

Penalties for violations of these prohibitions include the full range of statutory and regulatory sanctions, both criminal (Uniform Code of Military Justice [UCMJ]) and administrative.

Command Authority

Commanders have the authority to prohibit military personnel from engaging or participating in any other activities that the commander determines will adversely affect good order and discipline or morale within the command. This includes, but is not limited to, the authority to order the removal of symbols, flags, posters, or other displays from barracks, to place areas or activities off-limits (see AR 190-24), or to order soldiers not to participate in those activities that are contrary to good order and discipline or morale of the unit or pose a threat to health, safety, and security of military personnel or a military installation.

HOMOSEXUALITY

The armed forces exclude persons whose presence would create an unacceptable risk to the armed forces' high standards of morale, good order, discipline, and unit cohesion, which are the essence of military capability. That exclusion applies to persons who demonstrate a propensity or intent to engage in homosexual acts. The Department of Defense has stated that the suitability of persons to serve in the Army is based on their *conduct* and their ability to meet required standards of duty performance and discipline.

Homosexuality is incompatible with military service.

A "homosexual act" means any bodily contact, actively undertaken or passively permitted, between members of the same sex for the purpose of satisfying sexual desires, and any bodily contact (for example, hand-holding, slow dancing, or kissing) that a reasonable person would understand to demonstrate a propensity or intent to engage in such an act.

A "statement by a person that he or she is a homosexual or bisexual or words to that effect" means language or behavior that a reasonable person would believe was intended to convey the statement that a person engages in, attempts to engage in, has a propensity to engage in, or intends to engage in homosexual acts. This may include statements such as "I am a homosexual," "I am gay," "I am a lesbian," "I have a homosexual orientation," and the like.

A "homosexual marriage or attempted marriage" means that a person has married or attempted to marry a person known to be of the same biological sex (as evidenced by the external anatomy of the person involved).

Separation Policy

Homosexual conduct is grounds for separation from the Army. Only a soldier's commander is authorized to initiate fact-finding inquiries involving homosexual conduct. A commander may initiate a fact-finding inquiry only when he or she has received credible information that there is a basis for discharge. Commanders are responsible for ensuring that inquiries are conducted properly and that no abuse of authority occurs.

A fact-finding inquiry may be conducted by the commander personally or by a person he or she appoints. It may consist of an examination of the information

reported or a more extensive investigation as necessary. The inquiry should gather all credible information that directly relates to the grounds for possible separation. Inquiries shall be limited to the actual circumstances directly relevant to the specific allegations.

If a commander has credible evidence of possible criminal conduct, he or she shall follow the procedures in the *Manual for Courts-Martial*, ARs 27-10 and 195-2. A commander will initiate an inquiry only if he or she has credible information that there is a basis for discharge. Credible information exists when the information, considering its source and the surrounding circumstances, supports a reasonable belief that a soldier engaged in homosexual conduct. It requires a determination based on known facts, not just a belief or suspicion.

A basis for discharge exists if the soldier has engaged in a homosexual act, the soldier has said that he or she is a homosexual or bisexual, the soldier has made some other statement that indicates a propensity or intent to engage in homosexual acts, or the soldier has married or attempted to marry a person of the same sex. Credible information exists, for example, when a reliable person states that he or she observed or heard a soldier engaging in homosexual acts or saying that he or she is a homosexual or bisexual or is married to a member of the same sex. Credible information also exists when a reliable person states that he or she heard, observed, or discovered a soldier making a spoken or written statement that a reasonable person would believe was intended to convey the fact that the soldier engages in, attempts to engage in, or has the propensity or intent to engage in homosexual acts.

Additionally, credible information exists when a reliable person states that he or she observed behavior that amounts to a nonverbal statement by a soldier that he or she is homosexual or bisexual—that is, behavior that a reasonable person would believe intended to convey the statement that the soldier engages in, attempts to engage in, or has the propensity or intent to engage in homosexual acts. Commanders or appointed inquiry officers shall not ask, and soldiers shall not be required to reveal, whether a soldier is heterosexual, homosexual, or bisexual. Upon receipt of credible information of homosexual conduct, however, commanders or appointed inquiry officials may ask soldiers if they engaged in such conduct. The soldier should first be advised of the DOD policy on homosexual conduct and rights under the UCMJ. The prohibition against homosexual conduct is a long-standing element of military law that continues to be necessary in the unique circumstances of military service.

AIDS
Military readiness, medical, and personnel policies associated with human immunodeficiency virus (HIV) and acquired immunodeficiency syndrome (AIDS) protect the Army's ability both to fulfill its constitutional role and to confidentially identify, evaluate, and provide an appropriate level of care for infected members.

Policy
Active soldiers are tested biennially for the AIDS virus, reserve component soldiers every five years. Soldiers who are HIV-positive will not be deployed outside the

continental United States (CONUS). (Alaska, Hawaii, and Puerto Rico are considered CONUS in this definition.) The fact that HIV-positive soldiers are nondeployable does not preclude their assignment to table of organization and equipment (TOE) or modified table of organization and equipment (MTOE) units, except for Ranger and Special Forces units, which are totally closed. Soldiers who are HIV-positive are eligible for all military professional development schools and may also attend formal military training to qualify them for reclassification, provided the schooling does not exceed twenty weeks.

Mandatory testing and HIV prevention awareness are being emphasized Army-wide. Soldiers and their families must learn to understand how to avoid and prevent the spread of the disease. For more information, request from the Association of the U.S. Army a copy of its Institute of Land Warfare Paper No. 6, titled "AIDS and Its Impact on Medical Readiness."

MARRIAGE OF JUNIOR ENLISTED SOLDIERS

The old saying "If the Army wanted you to have a wife, it would have issued you one" has gone by the boards. So has the quaint custom whereby a soldier had to get his company commander's permission to get married. Although much of this was done as a courtesy to inform the commander, it did give the company commander—the "old man"—a chance to talk to the young soldier and to discuss the pros and cons of getting married at this particular stage of life.

Marriage is a commitment to fidelity, love, mutual support, and mutual sacrifice. Junior-grade soldiers should make a serious self-assessment to determine whether they are ready to assume these responsibilities. There are several areas to consider:

Money. Can you afford to be married? The wise soldier, like the wise civilian, makes a careful evaluation of whether his or her salary can support a marriage at this time.

Maturity. Sociologists tell us that the kinds of things you believe are important in a spouse when you are very young are likely to be different after about the age of twenty-five. The wise soldier thinks twice about the real meaning of marriage and whether he or she is on solid emotional ground before making the commitment to being a husband or a wife. If you are a member of a church or religious faith, you should check with your chaplain, since many denominations now require multiweek prenuptial counseling before the clergyman will perform the marriage service. If your denomination requires this, take advantage of it, for it is in your and your fiancé's interest to do so.

Duty and Deployment. In recent years, America has experienced a large increase in the number of deployments to far-flung locations. In nearly all cases, deployments for married soldiers mean family separation. Although the Army has programs and family support groups for the spouses and families of deployed soldiers, all soldiers should consider the impact of their absence on their marital situation and the burdens this places on the spouse. For some, this will be no problem. For those who might have married too young or with too little income, it can spell unhappiness for both the soldier and the spouse.

Dual-Service Marriages. Some soldiers believe that if they marry a fellow soldier, they will not have to face the problems of separation during deployment or field exercises. This might be the situation at the moment of a marriage proposal, but it is not a guarantee that two soldiers will always share the same duty or even be in the same unit. The Army tries to assign married service couples to the same post or as close as possible within the same geographic location, depending on MOS vacancies, but you might not always end up in the same unit. Hundreds of dual-service couples have faced this situation without problems, but you should be aware of it before tying the knot. See chapter 12, "Assignments," for more details.

DIVORCE

Divorce is hard on everyone involved, and the military seems to have a larger number of divorces than the general American population. The Army has available a number of family counseling services. The Family Services Center (discussed later), the post or unit chaplain, or even your sergeants and officers can help if you want to save your marriage. If your differences seem irreconcilable, then check with your local legal office to determine the legal requirements for divorce in your state.

SPOUSE AND FAMILY ABUSE

Do not ever, under any circumstances, abuse your spouse or children in any manner, physically or mentally. It is both a criminal and a moral offense. If you even suspect that you have tendencies to abuse family members less strong than you are, seek counseling immediately. The Army is a rough-and-tumble profession, and the Army requires tough soldiers. Keep the rough-and-tumble out of your family.

SOLDIER PREGNANCY AND SINGLE PARENTHOOD

For several years now, the Army has afforded pregnant soldiers options other than immediate discharge. Today, a pregnant soldier is faced with a number of choices based on Army policy, and she needs to understand these policies up front. These choices are spelled out in chapter 10, "Career Decisions."

Staying in the military as a mother of a newborn child does not afford the military mother special privileges. Although the Army is concerned for the welfare of the child, it does not adjust the assignment process to accommodate the new mother. Instead, the Army requires each soldier with dependents unable to care for themselves to file an approved family care plan. Because the soldier must be ready to deploy anywhere in the world on a moment's notice, the family care plan is necessary so that the Army knows that the child will be cared for in the event the mother is deployed overseas with her unit or assigned to an area where dependents are not authorized.

Married mothers usually face fewer problems, since the spouse will automatically have custody of the children and is assumed to be capable of caring for them if the mother is deployed or assigned to a no-dependents area. Unmarried military mothers have to make other guaranteed arrangements for children and document them in their family care plans, which are registered with the first sergeant.

INDEBTEDNESS

Nothing will make your first sergeant or company commander more upset than receiving letters from your creditors because you have bought more than your salary can pay for. This is not just a soldier problem, it's a DOD-wide problem affecting airmen, sailors, and marines as well, predominantly those in the junior enlisted grades.

The major culprits leading to indebtedness are:
- The "gotta-have-it-now" attitude.
- Undisciplined use of credit cards.
- Buying big-ticket items that are not really needed.
- Excessive entertainment.

The reason first sergeants and company commanders are upset with soldier indebtedness is because it takes so much of their time to deal with it. One military service, for instance, had the incredible record of receiving 123,000 letters of indebtedness; furthermore, 99,000 bad checks passed through the post exchange and another 75,000 passed through the commissary—in one year!

To reduce the size of this problem, the DOD has issued a compact disk training program called "Financial Tips" that is available at the education center.

A good source of information for soldier financial planning is Stackpole's *Armed Forces Guide to Personal Financial Planning*, 5th edition, which was written specifically to help servicemembers manage money and is chock full of sound advice. Likewise, Stackpole's *Servicemembers Legal Guide* is an excellent source of information on marriage, divorce, or the legal aspects of indebtedness.

ALCOHOL AND DRUG ABUSE

A drug is defined as "any substance that by its chemical nature alters structure or function in the living organism (AR 600-85)." This definition includes alcohol, glue, and aerosols, among many others. The harm and misery these substances have caused to soldiers are incalculable.

Soldiers who use drugs and those who sell drugs do not belong in the U.S. Army. A soldier who relies on alcohol to make it through the day or one who feels that he or she must turn to some drug to get by or get high should have the personal courage to quit or to seek help from the local Army Substance Abuse Program (ASAP).

Alcohol Abuse

AR 600-85 states that the use of alcohol is legal, provided the consumer is of legal age. Alcohol is socially acceptable, if used in moderation. Excessive use of alcohol is not condoned or accepted as part of any military event.

Drug Abuse

An NCO who is caught buying, selling, or using illegal drugs will be punished and separated from the Army. Junior enlisted personnel who abuse drugs may face the same consequences but more often receive nonjudicial punishment under Article 15

of the Uniform Code of Military Justice (UCMJ), including loss of pay, reduction in grade, and the stigma of conviction attached to their official files.

Soldiers caught using drugs are referred to a mandatory ASAP for rehabilitation. The Army, however, has a very strict "no-tolerance" attitude toward drug abuse, and ASAP treatment does not necessarily mean that the Army will not initiate separation action against the soldier. Don't do drugs.

PART II

The Soldier

5

Self Development

Everyone has room to improve. Every soldier in your pay grade is competing for that same promotion you desire. The farther you go up the ladder, the more you must compete for the next higher position. You must realize that you have control over how competitive you are. . . . Study one area, one task, once a week. It may take an hour or two away from your free time, but you will find the rewards will be worth it.
—CSM Walter J. Jackson in *Soldier's Study Guide*

The Army's system for promotion is discussed in detail in chapter 13. This chapter offers thoughts and proven methods for developing yourself in your current profession—soldier. Individual development is one of the keys to promotion, and the first step in that process is to set a goal for yourself.

SETTING PROFESSIONAL GOALS
Everyone wants to be promoted at some point in his or her career. No one can stay forever at the same rank. The Army's retention control points force you to move up or out. Look at where you want to be five years down the road and begin working to that end today. Waiting until you are a specialist or corporal to start working toward sergeant means that it will take you longer to acquire the necessary promotion points than soldiers who started when they were privates first class.

In all military occupational specialties (MOSs), some common elements are necessary for promotion. The three items common to all soldiers in the grades private to specialist are:
1. Develop MOS skills.
2. Qualify with your assigned weapon.
3. Maintain physical fitness.

With the new changes in the promotion system, much of your fate rests in your own hands. Work hard to identify yourself to the chain of command (and later the promotion board) as the best soldier.

Soldiers seeking promotion can directly influence their qualifications by making improvements in all three key elements. First, you should be performing duties

in your primary MOS at the authorized or next higher grade. Take advantage of any opportunity to serve in a leadership position at the next higher grade. Second, attend any locally available military schools that you can at this stage in your career. The schools found at your installation can vary from air assault, combat lifesaver, nuclear, biological, and chemical (NBC) defense, or field sanitation. Finally, you should take advantage of every opportunity to attend military and civilian schools that improve your skills. Begin taking Army correspondence courses early in your career. Take college courses if you are in a position to do so. The additional military and civilian education you obtain on your own shows the chain of command that you are a self-starter seeking to improve yourself. Additionally, military and civilian schooling will improve your chances for promotion by converting educational credit into promotion points.

To keep things in perspective, however, remember that leaders look to your duty performance when recommending you for initial promotions. In an interview conducted in 1998, Sgt. Maj. of the Army Robert E. Hall commented that he "would like every soldier to get a master's degree—a master's degree in soldiering."

Seek Advice

You should actively seek information and guidance from your chain of command, mentors, and career adviser. You must play an integral part in the decision and assignment process to help attain the goals you have set. Your career branch at the Human Resources Command (HRC) is also there to assist you in determining what is right for you, both professionally and personally. You should maintain communication with your branch to inquire about your next assignment or school. For information or assistance, call (800) 394-3763 in the United States or Defense Switched Network (DSN) 221-3763, or check the HRC enlisted management Web site at *www.hrc.army.mil/site/Active/enlist/ENLIST.htm.*

As mentioned in chapter 2, the Primary Leadership Development Course (PLDC) is the first level of the Noncommissioned Officer Education System (NCOES) and is a requirement for promotion to the rank of sergeant. This course prepares specialists and corporals (E-4) for leadership and increased levels of responsibility. Promotions (chapter 13) are governed by AR 600-8-19, *Enlisted Promotions and Reductions.* Department of the Army (DA) controls the time in service (TIS) and time in grade (TIG) requirements for promotion. Commanders have the latitude to waive both TIS and TIG to promote outstanding soldiers ahead of their peers. DA controls the rate of promotion to sergeant (E-5) and staff sergeant (E-6), but the local battalion selects the soldiers for promotion at locally conducted promotion boards.

MOS KNOWLEDGE

The Army rewards selfless, dedicated, confident, competent service. If you are among the best in your MOS at your skill level, NCOs and officers will view your professional potential favorably. It will help promotion, school, and training selection boards identify and select you to be among the soldiers who will lead the Army in the twenty-first century. Ignoring your professional self-development can result

Job Training Is Continuous

in substandard job performance or, worse, mission failure at a critical time and place. Your knowledge in your occupational specialty, whatever it is, is important. Like all the MOSs in your unit, your technical expertise is essential to the accomplishment of your unit's mission. Be an expert in your MOS.

MILITARY EDUCATION
If you wait for the Army to send you to school to acquire military education promotion points, you have to go through PLDC (4 points per week) plus an additional forty-two weeks of military school to reach the 200-point maximum in this promotion category (unless you opt for Ranger and Special Forces training). The quickest way to achieve your 200-point goal is through the Army correspondence course program. Start earning points when you are a private or private first class, and have your military education maxed out when you are first eligible for promotion to sergeant. These same points carry over for promotion to staff sergeant.

Army Correspondence Course Program
A variety of exportable training courses specific to your career management field (CMF) and MOS are available through the Army Correspondence Course Program (ACCP). Courses and subcourses on specific topics developed by respective proponent schools are designed for your professional development. You may enroll in this program as an individual student or via the group enrollment program. Students enrolling in individual study decide which courses to take and when to study the lessons and take the examination. Students register and enroll

through the Army Institute for Professional Development (AIPD) Web site: *www.atsc.army.mil/accp/aipd.htm.* Group enrollment allows a soldier to use these courses to supplement individual training. The program provides professionally designed training that a supervisor can readily administer, and it awards promotion points to those who successfully complete each subcourse. The group leader takes care of all administrative requirements.

A course consists of one or more subcourses designed to support a specific professional field, skill qualification development, or MOS-related tasks. Subcourses are issued in the sequence listed in each course. A subcourse is a basic unit of training covering one subject area, containing one or more lessons and a final examination.

The credit hour is the basic work unit for a correspondence course. The number of credit hours assigned to a subcourse is based on the estimated time required for an average student to read the material and complete all the exercises and the examination. Five hours of subcourse work equates to one military education promotion point.

AR 351-20, *Army Correspondence Course Program Catalog,* lists all courses and subcourses available to soldiers. Of special interest are the Green Book courses, which combine two series of correspondence courses (*www.atsc.army.mil/accp/grn-book.asp*). The Primary Leadership Subjects (ACCP Course Number: 553BD21) cover math skills, reading comprehension, study methods, management, and writing mechanics/composition. Soldiers in the rank of private through specialist or corporal are eligible to take this course. The course covers subjects such as math skills, reading comprehension, study methods, management, and writing mechanics and composition. Soldiers in the grade of private first class, specialist, or corporal interested in progressing would also do well to take the Primary Leadership Development Preparatory Course. This course has two phases and consists of twenty-two subcourses.

Army Training Extension Courses
Army training extension courses (TECs) are oriented toward common skills and critical MOS tasks. Proponent schools develop TECs, and soldiers in the MOS validate them. This self-paced training medium is for individuals and groups. Generally, soldiers use TECs in groups as part of unit training or for individual study. The courses are usually distributed to unit learning centers, but you can requisition individual lessons. TECs are designed in various formats—printed, audiovisual, audio, and job performance aids. Printed lessons are, however, the most predominant form.

Other Sources for Individual Development
Two books written especially for soldier development and promotion are Walter J. Jackson's *Soldier's Study Guide,* 4th edition (Mechanicsburg, PA: Stackpole Books, 2000) and Audie G. Lewis's *Career Progression Guide for Soldiers* (Mechanicsburg, PA: Stackpole Books, 2003). Both books should be available in post exchange bookstores or military clothing sales stores, or from the publisher.

IMPROVING BASIC LANGUAGE SKILLS

Reading and writing are critical skills for all soldiers. The Army depends on and must have in its ranks soldiers who read, comprehend, and communicate effectively in writing. Your ability to read, comprehend, and respond in writing to orders and directives from superiors is very important for all leaders. Your reading ability will be assessed when you attend the mandatory NCOES's PLDC, the first rung in the NCOES ladder. You must read at the tenth-grade level or face a likely consequence of nonenrollment.

If you have trouble reading and writing, get help at your local Army Education Center. An education counselor will assist you in identifying any literacy shortcomings. Once you know your reading and writing weaknesses, the counselor can help you enroll in courses designed to turn the weaknesses into strengths. It is better to discover and fix reading deficiencies and writing defects before some critical point in your career.

Much of Army writing is hard to understand and therefore wastes the time of the readers. When you write a military document, be sure to follow this important rule: Put the meaning of your communication in the first paragraph, in the first sentence, if possible. When you write clearly and simply, the material is easy to comprehend.

Common writing problems involve misuse of sentence structure, grammar, punctuation, mechanics, usage, tense, agreement, and "gobbledygook"—avoidable "padding" that hides meaning. Avoid gobbledygook; keep explanations of points you must make to a minimum. Use military jargon only if it is necessary. Avoid the overuse of acronyms. If you have to use acronyms, explain them before using them. One of the best sources to refine your writing skills is William A. McIntosh's *Guide to Effective Military Writing*, third edition (Mechanicsburg, PA: Stackpole Books, 2003).

The best way to improve your writing skills and your reading ability is to read a variety of books, magazines, and newspapers. Reading stimulates the intellect and increases your understanding of people and events. Read more than one book on a subject; challenge yourself to comprehend complex ideas and issues. Stay tuned to topics that pertain to national events, such as human rights, free enterprise, democracy, liberty, and prosperity. Read stories in daily newspapers about business, politics, and environmental issues, about how these matters relate in the global marketplace, and how they affect other nations.

Stay informed. Read to understand America's role in the world, the Army's role in America, and your role in America's Army.

PERSONAL REFERENCE LIBRARY AND RECOMMENDED READING

What follows are the books and poetry that most affected my attitudes toward my service as an enlisted man and that I recommend to others. Most lend a historical perspective and deal with issues we are all faced with: duty, morale, ethics, training, and leadership, especially that of the small unit in extreme circumstances. Many look at leaders who are looking at themselves.

Books that are on the Army reading list are marked with an asterisk (*).

Nonfiction
*Stephen Ambrose, *Band of Brothers*
Center of Military History, U.S. Army, *American Military History*
*T. R. Fehrenbach, *This Kind of War*
Ernest F. Fisher, *Guardians of the Republic: A History of the Noncommissioned Officer Corps of the U.S. Army*
*Charles Heller and William Stoft, *America's First Battles: 1776–1965*
*David Hogan, *A Concise History of the U.S. Army: Two Hundred and Twenty-five Years of Service*
Elbert Hubbard, *A Message to Garcia*
*John Keegan, *The Face of Battle*
*Paul Kennedy, *Rise and Fall of the Great Powers*
Gerald Linderman, *The World within War*
Dandridge "Mike" Malone, *Small Unit Leadership*
*Harold Moore and Joe Galloway, *We Were Soldiers Once . . . and Young*
Robert S. Rush, *GI: The US Infantryman in World War II*
Sam Watkins, *Co. Aytch*

Fiction
R. A. Heinlein, *Starship Troopers*
Jean Larteguy, *The Centurions*
*Anton Myrer, *Once an Eagle*
Guy Sager, *Forgotten Soldier*

Poetry
Rudyard Kipling, "The 'Eathen" and "If"
Robert W. Service, "The Quitter"

Other Works
Other recommended history and historical figure books include *The Civil War* by renowned author Shelby Foote and *Ernie's War: The Best of Ernie Pyle's World War II Dispatches* edited by David Nichols.

Though they were not intended as literary works, the U.S. Constitution and the Bill of Rights are worth your time as well, as are other historic government documents. Read about civic matters to learn more about the U.S. government and the Army's role in it.

Stackpole Books, publisher of *Enlisted Soldier's Guide*, offers more than 100 other titles of interest to the military reader.

Soldiers, the official monthly magazine of the Army, is also a recommended source of feature information about unit activities and Army people. It is now published online at *www.dtic.mil/soldiers*. Although not an official publication of the army, *Army Times* weekly newspaper and *Army* magazine, the monthly journal of

the Association of the U.S. Army, are important publications containing professional information.

Official Doctrine and Guidance
You should also read material about specific subjects that become increasingly important to professional soldiers. Study the following: Field Manual 6-22 [FM 22-100], *Military Leadership*; FM 3-22.9 [FM 23-9], *M16A1 Rifle Marksmanship*; FM 3-22.20, [FM 21-20], *Physical Fitness Training*; FM 7-10 [FM 25-101], *Battle Focused Training*; AR 27-10, *Military Justice*; STP 21-1, *Soldier's Manual of Common Tasks Skill Level 1*; and STP 21-24SMCT 1, *Soldier's Manual of Common Tasks Skill Level 2*. All these publications should be available in your company or at your local MOS library and are available online at the Training and Doctrine Digital Library at *www.atsc.army.mil*.

EXPLORING THE INFORMATION SUPERHIGHWAY: THE ARMY ONLINE AND THE WORLD WIDE WEB
The Army has entered the information superhighway, with dozens of sites currently online and more established daily. Computer literacy is becoming important for soldiers of all ranks, because it enables them to receive and transmit text and supporting communications across vast electronic networks. No longer do you have to thumb through old copies of the *Army Times* or look for the latest Human Resources Command (HRC) message to find information vital to your career. Just go to the HRC home page and view the most up-to-date information concerning your MOS. Entire books are online at the Center of Military History's home page. Need to prepare a class on the most current techniques to breach a minefield? Try the Center for Army Lessons Learned. It's all there—you just have to look.

The Internet
The Internet is the worldwide free-enterprise network of computers that links distant sites. It is a combination of tens of thousands of computer servers linked to computer users via telephone lines or direct circuits, all connected through the world's telephone companies. Each server is a separate "site" with a unique numeric name. Another name for part of the Internet is the World Wide Web, shortened to *www* or the Web.

Web Pages
A Web page is the graphical presentation of a document on the Web. Usually each page contains one type or grouping of information with "links" to other subpages or to other Web pages at different sites. Web pages can be as simple as text pages or can be as complex as pages with pictures, animated images, video clips, and attached sound files.

U.S. Army Online

Listed below are some of the more popular Web sites that deal with military issues. No longer do you have to wait in the dark for the word to be passed down on Army issues. You can now go to the source.

ACES GI to Jobs Web site
www.armyeducation.army.mil/COOL
Adjutant General Directorate
www.hrc.army.mil/site/active/tagd/index.htm
APFT Score Converter
www.everettsoftware.com/APFT16.htm
Army and Air Force Exchange Service
www.aafes.com/
Army Career and Alumni Program (ACAP)
www.acap.army.mil/
Army Continuing Education System
www.armyeducation.army.mil/
Army Correspondence Course Program
www.atsc.army.mil/accp/aipdnew.asp
Army Distance Learning
www.tadlp.monroe.army.mil/
Army Electronic Product Support (AEPS)
aeps.ria.army.mil/
Army Enterprise Architecture
www.army.mil/ciog6/offices/SAISIO/SAISIOE/ent_arch_home.html
Army home page
www.army.mil/
Army Housing
www.housing.army.mil/
Army Knowledge Online access page
www.us.army.mil
Army National Guard
www.arng.army.mil/
Army Public Affairs
www4.army.mil/ocpa/
Army Publishing Agency (USAPA)
www.usapa.army.mil/
Army Reserve
www.goarmy.com/reserve/nps/
Army Retirement Services
www.armyg1.army.mil/rso/mission.asp
Army Sergeants Major Academy
www.bliss.army.mil/usasma/default.htm

Army Training Information Management Program (ATIMP)
www.atsc.army.mil/atimp/
Army Training Requirements and Resources System (ATRRS)
www.atrrs.army.mil/
Army Vision 2010
www.army.mil/2010/
Assignment Satisfaction Key (ASK) (active duty enlisted only)
isdrad06.hoffman.army.mil/ask/index.html
Association of the U.S. Army
www.ausa.org/
Available electronic forms
www.army.mil/usapa/eforms/
CALL (Center for Army Lessons Learned)
call.army.mil/
Career Branch Newsletters
www.hrc.army.mil/site/active/enlist/cb-let.htm
Center of Military History (CMH)
www.army.mil/cmh-pg/default.htm
Combat Developments Directorate for Combat Service Support
www.cascom.army.mil/DCD_CSS/Multi/index.htm
Command and General Staff College
www-cgsc.army.mil/
Common Task Testing
www.atsc.army.mil/itsd/ctt.asp
Corps and Division Doctrine
www-cgsc.army.mil/cdd
Defense Finance and Accounting Service
www.dod.mil/dfas/
DefenseLink
www.defenselink.mil/
Defense News
www.defensenews.com/
Department of Veterans' Affairs
www.va.gov/
DOD Dictionary
www.dtic.mil/doctrine/jel/doddict/acronym_index.html
Enlisted National Guard Association
www.ngaus.org/
GulfLink
www.gulflink.osd.mil/
Headquarters, Department of the Army
www.hqda.army.mil/hqda/
Human Resources Command
www.hrc.army.mil/indexflash.asp

Human Resources Command Army Reserve
www.hrc.army.mil/site/reserve/
Human Resources Command, Enlisted Promotions
www.hrc.army.mil/site/active/select/enlisted.htm
Installations and Facilities
www.army.mil/organization/
Instant Map "Mapquest"
www.mapquest.com/
Leadership Resources
www.wyattresources.net/leadership.html
Medals and Ribbons
www.hrc.army.mil/site/active/tagd/awards/index.htm
Military Family Research Institute
www.mfri.purdue.edu/
Military Network
www.military-network.com/
Military Review Magazine
www.leavenworth.army.mil/milrev/index.htm
My Pay Military and Civilian
www.dod.mil/dfas/
"NCO Education System Newsletter"
www.hrc.army.mil/site/active/EPncoes/newsletter.htm
NCOES Information Papers
www.hrc.army.mil/site/active/enlist/guide/ncoes.htm
Office of the Chief, Army Reserve (OCAR)
www.armyreserve.army.mil/usar/home/
OPM (Office of Personnel Management) Retirement Programs
www.opm.gov/retire
Pentagon Library
www.hqda.army.mil/library/
Per Diem
secureapp2.hqda.pentagon.mil/perdiem/
PS Magazine
www.logsa.army.mil/psmag/psonline.cfmv
Retention and Reenlistment
www.armyreenlistment.com/
Soldiers Magazine online
www4.army.mil/soldiers/
Thrift Savings Plan
www.tsp.gov/
Training and Doctrine Digital Library
www.train.army.mil/
Training Support Center, Army (ATSC)
www.atsc.army.mil/

TRICARE home page
www.tricare.osd.mil/
TRICARE OCHAMPUS
www.defenselink.mil/dodgc/doha/tricare.html
USAJOBS (OPM)
www.usajobs.opm.gov
U.S. Army Reserve
www.armyreserve.army.mil/usar/home/U.S.
Veterans' Affairs OEF/IF Operation Enduring Freedom/Iraqi Freedom Web site
www.seamlesstransition.va.gov/

PROFESSIONAL ASSOCIATIONS

Association of the U.S. Army

The Association of the U.S. Army (AUSA) is a private, nonprofit organization established in 1950. It supports active and reserve component members, Army civilians, retirees, and Army families. Its goals are as follows:

- People support for those in the Army.
- Industry support of the Army.
- Public education about the Army.
- Professionalism within the Army.

AUSA's legislative affairs office stays on top of issues that affect soldiers during and after service. The association pushes for pay equity, adequate military housing, cost-of-living allowances, and standard subsistence allowances for all personnel, as well as full reimbursement of expenses for official travel and changes of station, quality medical and dental care, and an upgraded retirement system.

Regular membership costs are stepped according to grade: $20 per year for grades E-1 through E-4, $25 for E-5 through E-7, and $30 for E-8 and E-9. Among its membership benefits are opportunities to participate in chapter activities and discount product and service programs.

For more information, check the AUSA Web site at *www.ausa.org* or call (800) 336-4570. You can also write to Association of the U.S. Army, 2425 Wilson Blvd., Arlington, VA 22201, or e-mail them at *ausa.info@ausa.org*.

Noncommissioned Officers Association

The Noncommissioned Officers Association (NCOA) is a federally chartered, nonprofit, fraternal association founded in 1960. The NCOA seeks to promote health, prosperity, and scholarship among its members and their families through legislative and benevolent programs to improve benefits for soldiers, veterans, and their families and survivors. Through its office near the Pentagon, NCOA actively lobbies Congress, the White House, the Department of Veterans Affairs, the military services, and other federal agencies to fulfill its goals. It monitors state and local administrative and legislative activities affecting NCOA members, conducts a

nationwide outreach program for hospitalized veterans, and operates fellowship and intern programs for undergraduate college students.

Annual membership for NCOs costs $30. The association offers many member benefits, including a certified merchants program and a buying network. Members also receive the *NCOA Journal* and may qualify for the NCOA Visa card.

For more information, write to Noncommissioned Officers Association, ATTN: Membership Processing, P.O. Box 105636, Atlanta, GA 30348-5636; call (800) 662-2620; or check the Web site at *www.ncoausa.org*.

National Guard Enlisted Association

The National Guard Enlisted Association (EANGUS) exists to promote the status, welfare, and professionalism of the enlisted members of the National Guard of the United States and promote adequate national security.

EANGUS has a home page on the Internet at *www.eangus.org*. Users can access the congressional database system, the Senate, the House, EANGUS's *New Patriot* magazine and newsletter, *Congressional Quarterly*, *Legislative Updates*, and more. E-mail capability puts you in touch with the various departments at the national office that can answer your questions regarding membership, events, and legislative issues.

For more information, call toll-free (800) 234-EANG or write to Enlisted Association of the National Guard of the United States, 3133 Mount Vernon Ave., Alexandria, VA 22305; e-mail address: *eangus@eangus.org*.

6

Marksmanship

Every soldier must be a proficient marksman with his or her assigned weapon. Proper shooting is a physical skill that, like riding a bicycle, can be learned. When practiced often for short periods, it becomes a skill that will be retained. Marksmanship is learned on the zero range and the qualification range; in combat, it is the individual soldier's ultimate defense. Marksmanship fundamentals include assuming a steady position, aiming, breathing in a controlled manner, and squeezing the trigger. Knowing these fundamentals develops fixed and correct firing habits for instinctive application.

The mechanics for zeroing the M16 series weapons, found in FM 3-22.9, *Rifle Marksmanship M16A1, M16A2/3, M16A4, and M4 Carbine*, are not described here. The basic techniques presented below apply to all positions.

FUNDAMENTALS

Position

To assume the prone position, face the target, spread your feet a comfortable distance apart, and drop to your knees. Using the butt of the rifle as a pivot, roll onto your nonfiring side. Place the rifle butt in the pocket formed by the firing shoulder, grasp the pistol grip in your firing hand, and lower the firing elbow to the ground. Adjust your left and right elbows until your shoulders and feet are about level to provide the steadiest possible position. Your elbows provide additional support, and your feet, shoulder width apart, add stability. Rest the handguard in the V formed by the thumb and forefinger and across the heel of your nonfiring hand with the hand on the sandbag, ensuring that all the weapon's weight is on the sandbag and not on your elbows. Place the butt of the stock firmly into the pocket formed by the firing shoulder. Wrap your hand around the hand grip. The three lower fingers come around the pistol grip and meet the thumb to form the grip. The grip should be like a good, firm handshake. If you put on a "death grip," the muscle tension will cause you to shake.

Your body must lie in a relaxed, flat position. Point your toes out so your feet lie sideways, flat against the ground. Start with your feet and think about the posi-

tion of all body parts, working up to your fingers. If you are using muscles to hold your position, you will shake. Keep your forearm vertical under the rifle, straight up and down. When you angle your arms, you are using muscles to hold them still. Gravity will do this for you if you keep your forearm vertical.

Place your cheek firmly against the stock of the rifle, putting your eye close to and directly behind the rear peep sight. You can tell that you have a good position when there is absolutely no movement of the weapon as you sight on the target, exhale, hold your breath, and squeeze the trigger. This way, your head rides with the rifle as it recoils, and it will not kick you. It just pushes your shoulder, and you ride with it.

Aim

You begin the aiming process by aligning the rifle with the target when assuming a firing position. Point the rifle naturally at the desired point of aim. If you use muscles to adjust the weapon onto the point of aim, you will find that they automatically relax as the rifle fires; and the rifle will move toward its natural point of aim, which is the point at which the rifle naturally rests in relation to the aiming point. Because this movement begins just before the weapon discharges, the rifle is moving as the bullet leaves the muzzle. This causes inaccurate shots with no apparent cause (recoil disguises the movement). Since the rifle becomes an extension of your body, it is necessary to adjust your position until the rifle points naturally at the preferred aiming point on the target.

Once you are in position and aimed toward your target, the method for checking for the natural point of aim is to close your eyes, take a couple of breaths, and relax as much as possible. Upon opening your eyes, your sights should be positioned at the aiming point (target). You can change the deviation of the natural point of aim by shifting your body left or right. Elevation can be changed by leaving your elbows in place and sliding your body forward or rearward. This raises or lowers the muzzle of the weapon, respectively. By adjusting the weapon and body as a single unit, rechecking, and readjusting as needed, you can achieve a true natural point of aim.

Once your natural point of aim is established, aim your weapon at the exact point on the target.

Four aspects contribute to aiming: your shooting eye, the rear sight, the front sight, and the target. The distance between the sights does not change. The distance from your eye to the rear sight can change when you have different stock welds. The relationship between your eye and the rear sight is important. Once you find the right position for your eye, note the relationship between your nose and the stock or action of the rifle. Each time you aim, put your nose in the same place. This will help you keep your sight picture consistent. This is called a stock weld. When zeroing, it is critical to use the same aim point, regardless of the strike of the shot group, so that you do not chase the shot groups trying to hit center using "holdoff."

Aiming involves four elements: sight picture, sight alignment, aiming point, and focus.

Sight Picture

In aiming, you are concerned with correctly pointing your rifle so the bullet will hit the target when you fire. To do this, you must have the rear sight, the front sight post, and the target or aiming point in their proper relationship. This is known as sight picture. A correct sight picture is obtained when the sights are aligned and the aiming point (target) is in the correct relationship to the front sight post. The sight picture includes two basic elements: sight alignment and placement of the aiming point.

Sight Alignment

Alignment is critical. Any movement you make during firing that changes the relationship of the front and rear sights by one-tenth of an inch will cause a miss on a 300-meter target by five feet. When you look through the rear aperture, your mind must form an imaginary pair of crosshairs, one vertical and one horizontal. Align these crosshairs with the front sight post. Bring the top of the front sight post up even with the horizontal line and center it, ensuring that there is an equal amount of the front sight post on each side of the vertical line.

Although a small misalignment can cause problems, don't get wrapped around the axle with the thousandths of an inch—just do it correctly. Remember, it must be done the same way each and every time.

CORRECT
SIGHT PICTURE

CORRECT
SIGHT ALIGNMENT

CORRECT PLACEMENT
OF AIMING POINT

Aiming Point

When zeroing, the aiming point is the center mass of the black 250-meter scaled silhouette of the 25-meter target. If the aiming point is correctly positioned, an imaginary vertical line drawn through the center of the front sight post will appear to split the aiming point.

1. Position the front sight just to the right or left of the target, just far enough so the whole target next to the front sight post can be seen.

2. Raise or lower the front sight post so the top of the sight is halfway between the top and bottom of the target.

3. Smoothly move the front sight straight over to the target, without raising or lowering the post, and stop when the post is centered on the target.

If the sight picture gets too blurry, relax, blink your eyes, take a breath, and start over at step 1.

Focus

Remember that the human eye cannot focus on two objects at the same time. A correct sight picture has the rear sight and target blurry and the front sight in focus. The line of sight goes from the eye through the rear sight aperture (the mind forms the imaginary crosshairs). The front sight post is then brought into the line of sight and correctly aligned with the imaginary crosshairs. This is critical to good shooting and scores. Whether shooting at 25, 100, or 600 meters, you must always focus on the front sight post.

Dominant Eye

Some shooters have problems aligning the target with the sights because of their eyesight. To determine which eye is dominant, extend one arm to the front and point the index finger skyward to select an aiming point. With both eyes open, align the index finger with the aiming point; then close one eye at a time while looking at the aiming point. With one eye, the finger will appear to move off the aiming point; with the other eye, the finger will stay on the aiming point. The dominant eye is the eye that does not move the finger from the aiming point. Some individuals may have difficulty aiming because of interference from the dominant eye, if this is not the eye used in the aiming process. Such individuals must close the dominant eye while shooting.

Breathe

If you don't breathe during weapon firing, you will shake. There is a correct way to breathe when shooting. Try this exercise: Take a breath. Let it out. While exhaling, notice that there is a point at which you don't feel it necessary to continue exhaling or to start breathing in again. Now try it again. This time, when you get to that point, stop breathing for a second or two. It's easy!

This is the place in your breathing cycle where you want to take your shot. Since you can hold it for only a second or two at most, you must time the rise and fall of the rifle, the sight alignment and picture, and the trigger squeeze to coincide with that point. Notice that when you inhale, the muzzle of the rifle drops. It rises again when you exhale. When your chest expands, your shoulder rises; your forearm that supports the rifle does not move, so the muzzle drops. You must time this rise and fall so that the target is sighted at that point.

SEQUENCE FOR BREATHING AND FIRING

1. Breathe. Inhale and exhale to the natural respiratory pause. Check for consistent head placement and stock weld. Ensure that eye relief is correct. At the same time, begin aligning the front blade with the target at the desired point of aim.

2. Relax. As you exhale, relax as many muscles as possible while maintaining control of the weapon and position.

3. Aim. If you have a good, natural point of aim, the rifle points at the desired target during the respiratory pause. If the aim is off, make a slight adjustment to acquire the desired point of aim. Avoid "muscling" the weapon toward the aiming point.

4. Squeeze. As long as the sight picture is satisfactory, squeeze the trigger. The pressure applied to the trigger must be straight to the rear without disturbing the lay of the rifle or the desired point of aim.

Squeeze

Squeeze is nothing more than squeezing the trigger straight to the rear without disturbing the sight picture. You begin the trigger squeeze and continue until the rifle fires, while maintaining sight alignment. The part of the finger that should touch the trigger is the pad of flesh directly opposite the quick of the fingernail—not the fingertip, and no further back than the first joint.

When you pull the trigger, you must apply steadily increasing pressure until the gun fires. The shot should come as a surprise every time. If you anticipate and flinch, you will never be able to shoot well. The normal reflex action of the body is such that you will miss if the trigger is not squeezed. Your concentration should be so centered on sight alignment, focus, and trigger control that you can ignore the recoil and just let it happen.

Follow-Through

You will have less tendency to jerk, flinch, and buck if you follow through after your shot. Follow-through is the act of continuing to apply all the marksmanship fundamentals as the weapon fires as well as immediately after it fires. Follow-through involves:

- Keeping the head in firm contact with the stock—stock weld.
- Keeping the finger on the trigger all the way to the rear.
- Continuing to look through the rear aperture or scope tube.
- Keeping muscles relaxed.
- Avoiding reaction to recoil and noise.
- Releasing the trigger only after the recoil has stopped.

Hearing Protection

The biggest mistake you can make is not wearing hearing protection. Not only can you damage your hearing, but the noise will be loud, and you will begin to associate the noise with the recoil. In your mind, the noise and the recoil will be one and the same.

Acting As a Coach

If you are acting as a coach, watch for the following:

- Ensure that the firer assumes a good steady position.
- Make sure that the firer applies correct pressure during trigger squeeze.
- Determine whether the firer flinches, jerks, or bucks by watching the firer's head, shoulder, trigger finger, and nonfiring hand and arm.
- Make sure that the firer breathes correctly by watching his or her back occasionally.
- Make sure that the firer releases pressure on the trigger and lowers his or her rifle when the trigger is not squeezed within three to five seconds.
- Check shoulder placement of the rifle butt and pressure in the shoulder pocket. It should be snug; the top of the butt should be level with the top of the shooter's shoulder and not falling off the side of the shoulder.
- Check that the back of the nonfiring hand is fully supported by the sandbag.

References

FC 23-11, *Unit Marksmanship Trainer's Guide*
FM 3-22.9, *Rifle Marksmanship*

7

Physical Fitness
and Weight Control

The real value of being physically fit is as clear today as it was on distant battle-fields long—and not so long—ago. Soldiers not physically fit put themselves and their comrades at risk during wartime. It is difficult to survive in 130-degree heat or at altitudes above 5,000 feet in body armor when you are not in shape.

Mental toughness goes hand in hand with physical fitness. Soldiers who fought and won more recent battles can attest to the value of physical strength and mental endurance. Soldiers today—active and reserve—must be fit to fight.

Infantrymen, medics, cooks, mechanics, tankers, engineers, artillerymen, and air defenders all serve on the same team.

According to Army policy, soldiers must train to accomplish their wartime Mission Essential Task List (METL). A unit METL includes all its critical wartime tasks. So, soldiers should have in their physical training programs events that fully prepare them to accomplish METL, or wartime, tasks.

In an artillery unit, one physically demanding METL task might be to load a 202-pound, eight-inch explosive projectile into a howitzer. In an armored unit, a METL task could be to remove, repair, and replace a track pad on a disabled M1 tank. An airborne infantry METL might read: "On order, parachute at night with full combat load from a C-141 jet aircraft, then move on foot to find, close with, and kill the enemy." By now, you should fully grasp the importance of physical fitness to the accomplishment of a unit's METL.

THE FIVE COMPONENTS OF FITNESS
The five components of fitness give soldiers the ability to handle military emergencies.
1. Cardiorespiratory endurance enables the body to deliver nutrients and remove waste at the cellular level.
2. Muscular strength is applying the greatest amount of force possible in a single movement.
3. Muscular endurance is the ability to perform repeated movements with moderate resistance for given periods of time.

70

4. Flexibility is the ability to move joints of the body through their entire range of motion.
5. Body composition deals with the proportion of lean body mass (muscle, bone, and essential organ tissue) to body fat.

THE SEVEN PRINCIPLES OF EXERCISE

PROVRBS (pronounced "proverbs")—progression, regularity, overload, variety, recovery, balance, and specificity—are the principles behind a proper physical training program. These principles lead to a positive training effect and physical excellence each time you exercise. Violate any principle, and your program will be less rewarding.

Progression

The intensity of each successive exercise period must gradually be increased so that physical strength improves gradually (progress). A safe improvement rate is about a 10 percent increase in cardiorespiratory and muscular ability every ten days. That is, you should strive to reduce your elapsed time on a run by about 10 percent every ten days to two weeks until you achieve the desired goal. You should try to increase the number of endurance-related exercises such as push-ups and sit-ups by about 10 percent during the same period, and you should push and pull toward the same level of improvement in muscular strength during the period.

Regularity

Exercise must be performed at regular intervals, at least three to five times a week. Soldiers must also rest, sleep, and eat properly on a regular basis.

Overload

Overloading means going for the "max" during each exercise session and doing so safely to achieve a positive training effect. Overloading means working your heart at a relatively high percentage of its maximum capacity, based on your current physical condition, sex, and age. This is called the training heart rate. Your unit master fitness trainer (MFT) can help you determine your rate so that you train at the proper intensity when running or doing other aerobic exercises. Overloading also means working to muscle failure when doing muscular strength or endurance routines. With push-ups and sit-ups, this means using several timed sets (such as a sixty-second set, followed by a twenty-second rest, followed by a forty-five-second set, followed by a twenty-second rest, followed by a thirty-second set, and doing as many repetitions per set as possible). Over time, as you become more fit, your training heart rate intensity is increased and the timed sets are lengthened.

Variety

Variety means breaking up the weekly training routine with various exercises to reduce boredom and increase motivation. A program can include different kinds of

Unit Physical Training Can Be Done Anywhere

runs, such as ability group runs, circuit training, slow distance runs, fast continuous runs, relays, and so forth. Strength and endurance workouts can be outdoors or at the gym and include free weights, Nautilus machines, Kaiser or pneumatic machines, universals, mat routines, partner-resisted exercises, timed sets, sandbag circuits, and so forth. Of course, units should train collectively, so periodic cohesion runs and formation routines should be included.

Recovery
Recovery provides a twenty-four to forty-eight-hour rest between exercising the same muscles. Hard days of training should be alternated with easier days, or the muscles exercised each day should be alternated. Improper recovery leads to muscle fatigue, which can cause injury. During rest periods, muscle damage is repaired and waste is metabolized.

Balance
Balance entails balancing the principles of exercise so that they lead to the five components of fitness. It means that as you progress through your exercise program, you should balance upper-body and lower-body routines, back muscle and abdomen routines, and rest and recovery periods. For example, balance endurance runs with sprints so that you can run fast and far for as long as possible.

Specificity
The last principle, specificity, involves what the balance principle seems to tell you to avoid: working on a specific ability. Specificity, however, deals with specific

muscles and muscle groups or with a specific kind of run to address areas that need improvement.

Suppose you were an infantry scout who had real trouble climbing over tall obstacles. You would need to focus on your lack of upper-body climbing strength without violating the other principles of exercise. By adding a rope-climbing routine to your overall exercise program, you would comply with the principles of exercise and overcome a specific METL-related deficiency.

Most soldiers are required to participate in an organized physical training program. The program will undoubtedly emphasize the "big three" of the Army's Physical Fitness Test (APFT)—push-ups, sit-ups, and running—but it should also offer a variety of calisthenics and individual fitness training.

DESIGNING AN INDIVIDUAL FITNESS PROGRAM[1]

Many soldiers do not know how or what to do to increase their physical fitness beyond the present level. This is not because they are uncaring, but because many were never taught how. Many organizations and schools still conduct physical training (PT) en masse, which normally consists of push-ups, sit-ups, and a run. Additionally, many remedial PT programs are not geared to deficiencies, concentrating instead on running rather than the soldier's weakness.

The following individual PT program was developed for soldiers with little time to devote to PT. It is a modification of a successful PT program found in a light infantry battalion and is based on the principles found in FM 21-20. This program may help you increase your physical readiness without a major cost in time.

The program was validated using forty students in a Reserve Officers' Training Corps (ROTC) program. Students exercised three times per week for twenty to twenty-five minutes, not including the run. The following results were achieved: after one month, the average Physical Fitness Test score for students increased by 15 to 20 points, from an average of 192 to 212; at the end of three months, students went from an average of 212 points to 243; the next three months saw average scores climb to 267, with the low score 242 and the high 300. Since this is an individual program, it is designed to fit every soldier's physical ability. The program takes a soldier gradually to a higher level of physical fitness.

Individual Fitness Program Analysis

Take a look at your last APFT. From your scores, you can determine where your starting point for your individual fitness program should be. If you haven't taken an APFT in the last three to four months, you may want to assess your physical abilities before beginning the program.

To conduct a self-assessment, do as many correct push-ups and sit-ups as you can in a one-minute period, and then run as hard as you can for a timed half mile.

---

[1] Published by the author in *NCO Journal* (summer 1993) and republished in *NCO Journal* (summer 1997).

Multiply your push-up and sit-up scores by 1.25 to find an entry point into the charts. Multiply your half-mile time by four.

The Program

The following, if done correctly, will bring you to muscle failure. This exercise regime is designed to be done every other day, as your muscles need twenty-four to forty-eight hours to recover from hard usage.

To get your starting numbers of exercises, look at the charts below. The numbers along the top of the charts are the numbers of push-ups or sit-ups that you performed. Follow the number down the column to give you the number of repetitions of each exercise you should begin with in your individual program.

PUSH-UP IMPROVEMENT
APFT NUMBER PUSH-UPS

#	10	15	20	25	30	35	40	45	50	55	60	65	70	75	80	85
Push-ups	4	6	8	10	12	14	16	18	20	22	24	26	28	30	32	34
Diamonds	2	3	4	5	6	7	8	9	10	11	12	13	14	15	16	17
Wide-arm	2	3	4	5	6	7	8	9	10	11	12	13	14	15	16	17
Turn and bounce	5	6	7	8	9	10	12	14	16	18	20	22	24	26	28	30

SIT-UP IMPROVEMENT
APFT NUMBER SIT-UPS

#	10	15	20	25	30	35	40	45	50	55	60	65	70	75	80	85
Sit-ups	4	6	8	10	12	14	16	18	20	22	24	26	28	30	32	34
Crunches	4	5	6	7	8	8	9	9	10	10	11	12	13	14	15	16
Flutter kick	5	6	7	8	9	10	12	14	16	18	20	22	24	26	28	30
Leg spreader	5	6	7	8	9	10	12	14	16	18	20	22	24	26	28	30

Running

Using the following running chart will help you both increase your aerobic and anaerobic stamina and better your two-mile-run time. Enter the table using your two-mile-run time, or multiply your half-mile assessment by four. For example, if your run time is 26:15, enter the chart at +26. This program is designed to be run every other day, although there is no harm in running more than three times per week.

RUNNING IMPROVEMENT

Minutes	+12	+13	+14	+15	+16	+17	+18	+19	+20	+21	+22	+23	+24	+25	+26
⅛ mile	—	—	—	—	—	:48	:51	:55	:59	1:03	1:07	1:10	1:14	1:18	1:22
¼ mile	1:07	1:15	1:23	1:30	1:37	1:45	1:52	2:00	2:08	2:15	2:23	2:30	2:37	2:45	3:00
½ mile	2:45	3:00	3:15	3:30	3:45	4:00	4:15	4:30	4:45	5:00	5:15	5:30	5:45	6:00	6:15

Fast run															
	—	—	—	—	—	½ mi	½ mi	½ mi	½ mi	½ mi	½ mi	½ mi	½ mi	½ mi	½ mi
	—	—	—	—	—	4:00	4:15	4:30	4:45	5:00	5:15	5:30	5:45	6:00	6:15
	—	—	1 mi	1 mi	1 mi	1 mi	1 mi	1 mi	1 mi	1 mi	1 mi	1 mi	1 mi	1 mi	1 mi
	—	—	6:30	7:00	7:30	8:00	8:30	9:00	9:30	10:00	10:30	11:00	11:30	12:00	12:30
	2 mi	2 mi	2 mi	2 mi	2 mi	2 mi	2 mi	2 mi	2 mi	2 mi	2 mi	2 mi	2 mi		
	11:30	12:30	13:30	14:30	15:30	16:30	17:30	18:30	19:30	20:30	21:30	22:30	23:30		
	2+ mi	2+ mi													
	14:30	15:30													

Long run

Sprint Day

This program will increase your anaerobic ability and decrease your run time. Enter the sprint portion of the chart at your run time row. Do four sprints each of two distances, alternating your sprints between the distances. Begin with the lesser distance for your speed. Attempt to beat the time listed. Rest one minute before you run the longer sprint. Rest two minutes between the longer and shorter sprints. If you feel that you are not being properly stressed, and as you develop your wind, decrease the amount of rest time between sprints. For those with run times of +17 to +26, when the 220 sprint goal is met, move up to the quarter-mile (440) and half-mile (880) runs.

Fast Run Day

Begin with the lesser distance for your speed. When you beat the time for that distance, move to a longer distance within the same column. When you surpass the time for the distance at the bottom of the column, move to the left one column, maintaining the same distance. When you move one column to the left on the fast run, move your sprint goals to the same column.

Long and Slow Run

Run at least thirty minutes for a good cardiovascular workout. Run for time during this session, not necessarily for distance.

Sequence of Exercises: Push-Up and Sit-Up Improvement

1. Regular push-ups × three sets with one minute rest between sets. Form is important; if you can't do the push-ups properly, go to your knees and continue until you have finished the sets. After three workouts, add two push-ups to each set. (Example: Start with six push-ups on Wednesday, and go to eight push-ups the next Wednesday.)

2a. Regular sit-ups × three sets with one minute rest between sets. If you can't do all the sit-ups properly, lower the angle of your legs until they are almost parallel to the ground. After three workouts, add two sit-ups to each set. (Example: Start with eight sit-ups on Wednesday, and the next Wednesday, go to ten sit-ups.)

2b. Alternative to sit-ups: Add one set of all ten crunches every third workout. (Example: Start with six crunches on Wednesday, and the next Wednesday, go to seven crunches). See the next section on proper crunch position.

3. Diamond push-ups: Put your hands together under your chest in a diamond shape. Perform the push-ups. Go to your knees if necessary. Add one diamond after every three workouts.

4. Wide-arm push-ups: Place your hands as far apart as possible. Perform the push-ups. Go to your knees if necessary. Add one wide-arm after every three workouts.

5. Add one set of all ten crunches every third workout. (Example: Start with six crunches on Wednesday, and the next Wednesday, go to seven crunches.) See illustration on crunch positions. Note: If you do exercise 2b instead of sit-ups, do one less repetition of the crunch.

6. Turn and bounce: Start with your arms parallel to the ground, palms facing up. The exercise is an eight-count movement at a slow cadence. Pivot slowly at the waist to the right for 4 counts and then to the left for four counts. Add two turns and bounces after every three workouts.

7. Flutter kicks: Put your hands under your buttocks. Lift your feet six to eight inches off the ground to start. Begin by lifting your legs in sequence six to eighteen inches. Keep legs slightly bent to reduce the strain on your back. One repetition equals four counts. Add two flutter kicks after every three workouts.

8. Leg spreaders: Put your hands under your buttocks. Lift your feet six to eight inches off the ground to start. Begin by spreading your legs eighteen to thirty inches, then back together. Keep legs slightly bent to reduce the strain on your back. One repetition equals four counts. Add two leg spreaders after every three workouts.

Crunches

Start with your arms crossed across your chest, hands grasping your shoulders. Use the stomach muscles to crunch up, not the neck and shoulder. Try not to stop between sets.

1. Legs bent at 90 degrees, legs together

2. Legs bent at 90 degrees, knees apart, soles of feet together

3. Legs bent at 90 degrees, feet in air, knees together

4. Legs bent at 90 degrees, knees apart, soles of feet together

5. One leg bent at 90 degrees, foot on ground, one leg straight and 6 to 12 inches off ground

6. Same as number 5 but legs reversed

7. One leg bent at 90 degrees, foot in air, one leg straight and 6 to 12 inches off ground

8. Same as number 7 but legs reversed

9. Legs bent at 90 degrees, legs spread, feet on ground

10. Legs bent at 90 degrees, legs in air

Crunches Exercise Positions

ARMY PHYSICAL FITNESS TEST

Soldiers taking the APFT are encouraged to make a maximum effort to pass and excel. The test is administered at least every six months for active duty and yearly for reserve component soldiers. Described in detail in chapter 14 of FM 21-20, the APFT includes timed push-ups, sit-ups, and a two-mile run (or alternative aerobic event in certain circumstances).

Push-up Event

The push-up measures the endurance of the chest, shoulder, and triceps muscles. The first event is a two-minute push-up test. The push-ups must be properly completed to be counted as valid repetitions. The starting position is as follows:

- Hands are placed a comfortable distance apart.
- The body must remain in a generally straight line.
- Arms are straight and fully extended.
- Feet may be up to twelve inches apart.

To execute a repetition, bend your elbows, evenly lowering your body until your upper arms are parallel with the ground. Then straighten your arms until they are fully extended. Throughout the repetition, your body should remain generally straight, and your hands and feet must not break contact with the ground. Only your hands and feet may touch the ground during this exercise. If you fail to maintain proper form for the entire repetition, it will not be counted.

Sit-up Event

The second event is a two-minute sit-up test that measures the endurance of the abdominal and hip-flexor muscles. To assume the starting position for this exercise, do the following:

- Lie flat on your back.
- Bend your knees so that your feet are flat on the ground and a ninety-degree angle is formed by the upper and lower portions of your legs.
- Place your feet together or up to twelve inches apart.
- Clasp your hands behind your head with your fingers interlocked.

To execute a correct repetition, raise your body to the vertical position with the base of your neck above the base of the spine. Lower your body so your back touches the ground. The repetition will not be counted if you fail to reach the vertical position, arch your back, raise your buttocks off the ground, fail to keep your fingers interlocked and behind your head, or allow your knees to exceed a ninety-degree angle. Another soldier will assist you during this exercise by holding your feet firmly on the ground.

PUSH-UPS

Age Group	Male Min.	Male Max.	Female Min.	Female Max.
17–21	42	71	19	42
22–26	40	75	17	46
27–31	39	77	17	50
32–36	36	75	15	45
37–41	34	73	13	40
42–46	30	66	12	37
47–51	25	59	10	34
52–56	20	56	9	31
57–61	18	53	8	28
62+	16	50	7	25

SIT-UPS

Age Group	Male/Female Min.	Male/Female Max.
17–21	53	78
22–26	50	80
27–31	45	82
32–36	42	76
37–41	38	76
42–46	32	72
47–51	30	66
52–56	28	66
57–61	27	64
62+	26	63

Two-Mile Run

The two-mile run or alternative aerobic event measures cardiorespiratory and leg muscle endurance. Instructions for each APFT event in FM 21-20 must be read verbatim before each event is administered.

The current APFT standards are shown on the following chart.

TWO-MILE RUN

Age Group	Male Min.	Male Max.	Female Min.	Female Max.
17–21	15:54	13:00	18:54	15:36
22–26	16:36	13:00	19:36	15:36
27–31	17:00	13:18	20:30	15:48
32–36	17:42	13:18	21:42	15:54
37–41	18:18	13:36	22:42	17:00
42–46	18:42	14:06	23:42	17:24
47–51	19:30	14:24	24:00	17:36
52–56	19:48	14:42	24:24	19:00
57–61	19:54	15:18	24:48	19:42
62+	20:00	15:42	25:00	20:00

ARMY FITNESS REGULATIONS

Army Physical Fitness Badge

The Army Physical Fitness Badge is awarded to soldiers attaining a score of 90 points in each event, for a total of 270 points. Under the current standards, soldiers must score 270 points annually to continue to wear the badge. Doing well on the APFT also assists soldiers in obtaining promotion points up to the rank of staff sergeant, ranging from 50 points to 10 points. Fit soldiers also receive verbal commendations and other accolades, are retained in service and selected for advanced military schooling, and can be promoted if they meet other selection criteria, including presenting a sharp military appearance.

Medical Profiles

Soldiers on permanent profile may be unable to take some or all of the APFT events for medical or other authorized or unavoidable reasons. In order to get credit for the APFT, however, the two-mile run or an alternative aerobic event must be taken and

passed. Alternative aerobic events include the 800-yard swim, 6.2-mile bicycle ride (in one gear), and 2.5-mile walk. Like the run, the alternative events must be completed unassisted in a prescribed amount of time relative to age and gender. Unlike the run, the other events are not scored; test takers either pass or fail the event. Soldiers who fail any or all of the events must retake the entire test. In case of test failure, commanders may allow soldiers to retake the test as soon as they are ready. Soldiers without a medical profile will be retested no later than three months following the initial APFT failure.

Failure to Pass

In compliance with Army retention policy, soldiers who have six months or more time in service who fail two consecutive record APFTs must be processed for separation for unsatisfactory performance under chapter 13 of AR 635-200, *Enlisted Personnel*. Receipt of a "chapter 13" for fitness failure indicates that the soldier is unqualified for service because he or she will not develop sufficiently to participate in further training or become a satisfactory soldier. It also means that failures would be likely to recur, and the soldier is unlikely to be able to perform duties effectively in the future, as well as lacking the potential for advancement or leadership. Entry-level soldiers (those with less than six months time in service) who repeatedly fail diagnostic and record APFTs may be separated under chapter 11 of the *Enlisted Personnel* regulation. A "chapter 11" covers inability, lack of reasonable effort, or failure to adapt to the military environment.

WEIGHT CONTROL

AR 600-9, *The Army Weight Control Program*, states that each soldier (commissioned, warrant, or enlisted) is responsible for meeting service weight-control standards. To help soldiers meet their responsibility, height and weight screening tables are published in the weight-control regulation. The regulation's proponent agency, the Office of the Deputy Chief of Staff for Personnel (ODCSPER), recommends that soldiers strive to remain at least 5 percent below their individual screening table weight maximum. Soldiers should individually attain and maintain an acceptable weight and body composition through self-motivation or involvement in an official weight-control program. For some, the weight-control guidance is easy to follow. For others, weight can be a real problem.

Dealing with Body Fat

If a soldier consistently exceeds the personal weight goal, he or she should seek the assistance of master fitness trainers for advice in proper exercise and fitness and health-care personnel for a proper dietary program. Soldiers exceeding the screening table weight or identified by the commander or supervisor for a special evaluation will have their body fat measured using the tape test method. When men are tape tested, they have the abdomen and neck measured; women have the hips, forearm, neck, and wrist measured. All measurements are taken three times and must be within one-quarter of an inch to be considered valid.

Weight-Control Program

To help soldiers fight fat, the Army provides educational and other motivational programs to encourage personnel to attain and maintain proper weight and body fat standards. Programs include nutrition education sessions conducted by qualified health-care personnel, as well as exercise programs. Commanders will enforce body fat standards and monitor, measure, and, if necessary, place individuals into the Army Weight Control Program and continue to monitor them, in compliance with AR 600-9. Soldiers entered into the program are not allowed to reenlist or extend their enlistment, are considered nonpromotable, and are not assigned to command positions (e.g., squad leader, platoon sergeant, first sergeant, or command sergeant major).

Further, overweight soldiers are denied attendance at professional military or civilian schooling. AR 351-1, *Individual Military Education and Training*, states that personnel who do not meet body fat standards are not authorized to attend professional military schooling. All soldiers scheduled for attendance at schooling will be screened prior to departing the home station or losing command. Their height and weight will be recorded on their temporary duty orders, DD Form 1610, or on their permanent-change-of-station (PCS) packet. Soldiers exceeding established screening weights will not be allowed to depart their commands until the commander has determined that they meet the standards.

School commandants will take the following action upon determining that a student has arrived exceeding established body fat composition standards. Soldiers arriving at any Department of the Army (DA) board select school or professional military school as a permanent change of station (PCS) who do not meet body fat standards will be processed for disenrollment and removed from the DA board select list. Personnel arriving at professional military schools (other than DA board select or PCS schools) who do not meet body fat composition standards will be denied enrollment and reassigned in accordance with AR 600-9.

Actions to initiate mandatory bars to reenlistment or initiation of separation proceedings for soldiers who are eliminated for cause from NCOES courses, will be in accordance with AR 601-280, *Army Reenlistment Program*, and AR 635-200, *Enlisted Personnel*. Additionally, soldiers who by the definition in AR 600-9 are considered weight-control failures will be processed for separation from the Army.

Soldiers who are entered into the weight-control program and then successfully meet their body fat reduction goal will be removed from the program and monitored for a year. Failure to meet the standards at any time during the monitoring period will result in initiation of separation action.

Soldiers who consider themselves too fat—or who come close to qualifying for the Army Weight Control Program—should look at modifying their lifestyles and eating habits for life. Soldiers interested in an improved diet may seek guidance in appendix C of AR 600-9, "Nutrition Guide to the Weight Control."

WEIGHT FOR HEIGHT TABLE
(SCREENING TABLE WEIGHT)

Height (in inches)	Male Age				Female Age			
	17–20	21–27	28–39	40+	17–20	21–27	28–39	40+
58	—	—	—	—	109	112	115	119
59	—	—	—	—	113	116	119	123
60	132	136	139	141	116	120	123	127
61	136	140	144	146	120	124	127	131
62	141	144	148	150	125	129	132	137
63	145	149	153	155	129	133	137	141
64	150	154	158	160	133	137	141	145
65	155	159	163	165	137	141	145	149
66	160	163	168	170	141	146	150	154
67	165	169	174	176	145	149	154	159
68	170	174	179	181	150	154	159	164
69	175	179	184	186	154	158	163	168
70	180	185	189	192	159	163	168	173
71	185	189	194	197	163	167	172	177
72	190	195	200	203	167	172	177	183
73	195	200	205	208	172	177	182	188
74	201	206	211	214	178	183	189	194
75	206	212	217	220	183	188	194	200
76	212	217	223	226	189	194	200	206
77	218	223	229	232	193	199	205	211
78	223	229	235	238	198	205	210	216
79	229	235	241	244	203	209	215	222
80	234	240	247	250	208	214	220	227

*Note: For screening purposes, body fat composition is to be determined in accordance with appendix B, AR 600-9.

ALLOWABLE BODY FAT

Age Group:	17–20	Age Group:	21–27
Male (% body fat):	20	Male (% body fat):	22
Female (% body fat):	30	Female (% body fat):	32
Age Group:	28–39	Age Group:	40 & older
Male (% body fat):	24	Male (% body fat):	26
Female (% body fat):	34	Female (% body fat):	36

"Program." According to the guide, proper nutrition and regular exercise are necessary to help you lose weight and improve your state of fitness. It says, "Invest in yourself." Here are some examples of how this can be done:

- Make a decision to lose weight and shape up.
- Get motivated.
- Develop a strategy (diet, exercise routine, lifestyle changes).
- Carry out this strategy and enjoy the payoff—a healthy appearance, an improved self-image, a sense of accomplishment, and a feeling of pride.

Studies show that the average American man eats 2,360 to 2,640 calories per day. The average woman eats between 1,640 and 1,800. Reducing calories taken in leaves fewer calories for the body to burn to lose weight. Army Master Fitness Training Course material states that a healthy man can safely take in as few as 1,500 calories per day, and a healthy woman can consume as few as 1,200.

Vegetables, fruits, and complex carbohydrates, such as whole-grain breads, are "secret weapons" for anyone trying to maintain a healthy diet. They are filling and satisfying because they are high in fiber and generally lower in calories.

8

Continuing Civilian Education

Enlisting in today's Army usually comes with a monetary bonus for civilian education. That education can start while you are on active duty if your duty assignment and location permit. In addition, civilian education counts for a maximum of 100 promotion points. Each college credit hour gained through an accredited source is worth $1^1/_2$ promotion points, and an associate's degree (normally sixty credit hours) garners you an additional 10 points, for a total of 100 points.

ARMY CONTINUING EDUCATION SYSTEM

The Army Continuing Education System (ACES) through its many programs promotes lifelong learning opportunities and sharpens the competitive edge of Army 2010 and beyond. ACES is committed to excellence in service, innovation, and deployability. Today's soldier can take advantage of numerous educational programs. The comprehensive Web site for Army education is at *www.armyeducation.army.mil.*

Your *Army Continuing Education System Record*, DA Form 669, serves a very important purpose during your military career—or it can collect dust. Maintained at your local Army Education Center, it contains information used by education counselors to document your pursuit of higher education. Semester after semester throughout your career, you should (whenever the mission allows) contribute course completion slips to your record. Consider that you are making regular deposits to an intellectual savings account, which will grow with enormous interest—the kind that Army promotion boards and civilian employers will have for you as your educational value increases.

Invest in yourself; the Army does and benefits in the process. The Army Continuing Education System mission is, in part, to improve the combat readiness of the Army by planning, researching, and implementing educational programs and services to support the professional and personal development of quality soldiers and their adult family members, according to AR 621-5. In support of the mission, ACES supports five goals, three of which apply to soldiers, as follows:
- Develop confident, competent leaders.
- Support the enlistment, retention, and transition of soldiers.
- Provide personal development opportunities for soldiers.

The ACES meets its mission goals by providing quality educational programs and services throughout the Army. Education and training mutually support and enhance the combat readiness of the Army and are essential elements in the NCO Development Program. ACES programs and services are designed to expand soldiers' skills, knowledge, and behavior. Programs and services discussed later in this chapter contribute to the three pillars of leader development: institutional training, operational assignments, and self-development.

Individual development, supported by ACES, is a planned, progressive, sequential program that leaders use to enhance and sustain the leadership plan discussed earlier.

Under the guidelines of AR 621-5, soldiers should meet the following educational objectives:

- Master academic skills needed to perform duties of their primary MOS and meet prerequisites for the NCO Education System.
- In cases of exception to the enlistment rule regarding having a high school diploma, earn a high school diploma or equivalent before completing a first enlistment.
- Earn a college degree, license, or professional certificate in an MOS related discipline, as recommended in DA Pamphlet 600-25, *The NCO Professional Development Guide.*

ARMY EDUCATION CENTER COUNSELORS
Counselors help soldiers establish realistic educational goals and provide counseling through the attainment of the goals. They also help soldiers get the maximum benefit from limited tuition assistance and other resources. Soldiers who are new to an installation are required by AR 621-5 to receive education counseling within the first thirty days of their arrival and then receive follow-up counseling as needed.

Soldiers should not need a regulatory push to receive educational counseling; however, they should take advantage of the valuable advice and assistance that counselors provide. Counselors help with school selection, application procedures, prerequisite assessments, and financial aid.

When they cannot help locate financial aid for formal courses of instruction, counselors can recommend free alternative methods of obtaining educational credit. (See Defense Activity for Nontraditional Education Support (DANTES), College Level Examination Program (CLEP), and Graduate Record Exam (GRE) under "Independent Study and Examination Programs for College Credit.")

HIGH SCHOOL COMPLETION PROGRAM
The High School Completion Program (HSCP) is an off-duty program that provides soldiers and adult family members the opportunity to earn a high school diploma or equivalency certificate. It is open to all non–high school graduates. Tuition assistance (TA) is authorized for soldiers up to 100 percent of the tuition costs of courses. ACES will pay TA only to accredited institutions and will not pay fees covering such items as books, matriculation, graduation, and parking.

COLLEGE DEGREE PROGRAMS

Thousands of degree programs are available to soldiers—too many to list here. But you may use dedicated resources to find out more information about obtaining an associate's, bachelor's, or master's degree in arts or science.

If you want to take college courses but are concerned about your ability to comprehend course material, use DA Pamphlet 351-20, *Army Correspondence Course Program Catalog.* It is filled with offerings that will teach you the basics of many subjects. For example, suppose you want to earn an electrical engineering degree. You could contact your local education center to request the basic electricity course listed in the pamphlet. The course is open to "any student who meets the basic qualifications for correspondence study." After successfully completing seventeen sequential electricity subcourses, you should be fully prepared to enroll in a college course that deals with the subject of electricity. Apply this method to other subjects, and you will see the value of "boning up" through correspondence studies.

SERVICEMEMBERS OPPORTUNITY COLLEGES (SOC)

Under the Servicemembers Opportunity Colleges (SOC), there are degree and certification programs in which a soldier can be awarded a degree or certificate for an academic or technical course of study. The programs were developed to provide common curricula in disciplines related to Army MOSs.

The SOC is a network of schools across the country and overseas that have recognized and responded to soldiers' expectations for postsecondary education. The schools must have liberal entrance requirements, allow soldiers to complete courses through nontraditional modes, provide academic advisement, offer maximum credit for experiences obtained in service, have residence requirements that are adaptable to the special needs of soldiers, have a transfer policy that recognizes traditional and nontraditional learning obtained at other schools, promote the SOC, and provide educational support to servicemembers. Under the Servicemembers Opportunity College Army Degree Program (SOCAD), the college must limit the residence requirement and offer a flexible curriculum.

The SOCAD student agreement gives the soldier a one-time evaluation of everything the soldier has done that can be credited toward the college degree and lists what the soldier must take to graduate. The SOCAD colleges require a soldier to take no more than 25 percent of his or her coursework with that college to receive a degree—not necessarily on campus, but from their offerings and elsewhere. Once a soldier completes residency, future courses taken at other colleges will be accepted and applied toward the soldier's original degree plan.

EARMYU

Another new initiative toward assisting soldiers in achieving their educational goals is the Electronic Army University (*eArmyU*). This program is entirely online, offering soldiers a streamlined "portal" approach to a variety of postsecondary degrees and technical certificates. All courses allow soldiers to study on their own schedule.

Highly motivated soldiers can complete degree and certification requirements regardless of work schedules, family responsibilities, and deployments.

eArmyU Benefits
All eligible soldiers receive 100 percent tuition up to $250 per semester hour, whichever is less, with a ceiling of $4,500. Tuition Assistance (TA) covers tuition, fees, books, academic advisement, library resources, and administrative and technical support. Tuition Assistance for eCourse enrollees is on a course-by-course basis, subject to the availability of funds. Effective February 1, 2005, eligible E4, E5, and E6 soldiers, with less than ten years service, who reenlist may participate in the Technology Package (laptop) option, if they meet eligibility requirements. Added to the existing education programs and services available, this online program helps to ensure all soldiers have the opportunity to fulfill their personal and professional educational goals while simultaneously building the technology, critical thinking, and decision-making skills required to fully transform the Army.

Soldier Eligibility
To be eligible for participation in this program, soldiers must be regular active-duty or active guard reserve enlisted soldiers with at least three years remaining on their enlistment. Soldiers may extend or reenlist to meet this requirement. More information on *eArmyU* can be found at *www.earmyu.com/default.asp.*

COLLEGE CREDIT FOR MILITARY EXPERIENCE
Army Education Center counselors can help you complete DD Form 295, *Application for the Evaluation of Learning Experiences during Military Service.* The completed form is used to inform institutions, agencies, and employers about in-service educational achievements. Schools use the form to determine how many and what kinds of college credits to award soldiers based on military education, training, and experience. Your pursuit of a degree should include completing and forwarding DD Form 295 to the college or university of your choice.

The American Council on Education (ACE) evaluates Army service school courses and recommends the number of semester hours of credit that civilian schools may award based on a soldier's military training and experience. Examples include vocational, lower-level baccalaureate and associate's degree, upper-level baccalaureate, and graduate-level credits. These recommendations are published in the *Guide to the Evaluation of Educational Experiences in the Armed Services (ACE Guide).*

INDEPENDENT STUDY AND EXAMINATION PROGRAMS
FOR COLLEGE CREDIT
If you are working on an undergraduate (associate's or bachelor's) degree, you should know about independent ways to earn credit. Credit can be earned through the following programs: Defense Activity for Nontraditional Education Support (DANTES), including the College Level Examination Program (CLEP) and Defense

Subject Standardized Tests (DSST); American College Testing Proficiency Examination Program (ACTPEP); Graduate Record Examination (GRE); and Annenberg Project and Center for Public Broadcasting (AP/CPB).

The DANTES, CLEP, DSST, ACTPEP, GRE, and AP/CPB offerings all require independent study. Many subject packets include texts, workbooks, and audio- or videotapes that are used in conjunction with the paper materials. Most of the for-credit tests offered by these programs and agencies are each worth three or four semester hours of credit. The GRE, which includes a general exam and subject exams, is worth much more credit. The GRE sociology examination, for example, is worth thirty semester hours of undergraduate credit—fifteen lower division (100 and 200 level), and fifteen upper division (300 and 400 level).

DANTES independent study and examination program services are available to all eligible active-duty soldiers. One important aspect of the DANTES is the CLEP, which also enables students to earn credit by examination. The examinations measure knowledge of the basic concepts and applications involved in courses that have the same or similar titles. They are divided into two types: general examinations and subject examinations.

The general examination measures college-level achievement in five basic areas of the liberal arts: English composition, social sciences and history, natural sciences, humanities, and mathematics. Test material covers the first year of college, often referred to as the general or liberal education requirement. Subject examinations measure achievement in specific college courses and are worth course credit. Examples of test titles include Introduction to Business Management, General Psychology, Western Civilization, and American Literature.

Each civilian educational institution has its own criteria for using CLEP test scores to determine credit. You should have official transcripts forwarded to the registrar of the college or university at which you desire to receive credit (some institutions require that a minimum number of semester hours of classwork be completed before CLEP credit will be accepted). Another subject test that, like CLEP, substitutes for college classroom work is the DANTES Subject Standardized Tests.

GI BILL
Valuable educational benefits offered under the GI Bill are available today for would-be college graduates and for those soldiers who wish to pursue certain kinds of training. Originally named the Servicemen's Readjustment Act of 1944, the GI Bill was signed into law by Pres. Franklin D. Roosevelt on June 22, 1944. The bill, now called the Montgomery GI Bill after its latest champion, Congressman G. V. Montgomery, takes the form of the Montgomery Active Duty GI Bill and the Montgomery Selected Reserve GI Bill. The post-Vietnam Veterans Educational Assistance Program (VEAP) is also covered by the Montgomery GI Bill. A wide range of benefits valued at hundreds of dollars per month for up to thirty-six months is available. I cannot stress strongly enough that you should take full advantage of the benefits to which you are entitled.

Montgomery Active Duty GI Bill

The Montgomery Active Duty GI Bill (chapter 30, U.S. Code) provides up to thirty-six months of benefits. Soldiers covered by Category I of this program are those who first entered active duty after June 30, 1985, and who contributed a nonrefundable $100 a month for the first twelve months of service. Active-duty members may begin using their benefits after completing two years of service. Members of the National Guard who are in the Active Guard and Reserve Program also are covered by this contributory program, but they must have entered service after November 29, 1989, and must not have previously served on active duty.

Montgomery Selected Reserve GI Bill

The Montgomery Selected Reserve GI Bill (chapter 106, U.S. Code) is available to members of the Army Reserve and the Army National Guard. It applies to members who entered selected reserve status after June 30, 1985. To receive up to thirty-six months of entitlements under this program, members must have made a six-year commitment that began after September 30, 1990. Members also must have completed Initial Active Duty for Training, be high school graduates or have equivalent certificates, and serve in an active reserve or National Guard unit and remain in good standing. Soldiers entering the National Guard or Army Reserve on or after October 1, 1992, have their eligibility end fourteen years from your beginning date of eligibility, or on the day they leave the Selected Reserve. Soldiers entering service prior to October 1, 1992, have either ten years from beginning date of eligibility, your period of eligibility ends ten years from your beginning date of eligibility or on the day you leave the Selected Reserve.

Monetary Value of the GI Bill

As indicated above, the monetary value of the benefit program you qualify for will depend on various factors, including the date you entered the military, your status in the military, how long you have been or were in service, and the character of a previous discharge or separation. Also, if you are in a contributory program, the amount of money the government will contribute depends on how much you contribute, up to a maximum matching contributory amount.

In-service benefits are worth less, monetarily, than postservice benefits and normally cover only tuition and fees. But here is a kicker: Under current federal law, if you receive a college or university assistantship, fellowship, or grant that pays or offsets part or all of your tuition and fees or research expenses, you may still be entitled to receipt of education benefits—meaning that monthly entitlements received from the DVA are yours to keep.

Various rules and certain service- or usage-oriented restrictions cover the programs and situations described above. Visit your Army Education Center or local DVA office, obtain counseling, and get the most recently published copies of the following:

- Pamphlet 27-82-2, *A Summary of DVA Benefits.*
- Pamphlet 22-90-2, *Summary of Educational Benefits.*
- Pamphlet 22-90-1, *Avoiding VA Education Overpayments.*

When you decide to apply for benefits, first make sure that the education or training program you choose is approved by the Department of Veterans Affairs (DVA). Then complete and submit DVA Form 22-1990 at least two months before the beginning of the program. If you choose to use some of your benefits while in service, your commander and local education assistance officer must sign the form. Depending on your personal situation, you also may need to provide a copy of your marriage license, divorce decrees from any previous marriages, and children's birth certificates. The level of your educational benefits may be increased according to the number of legal dependents you have.

Except for the Selected Reserve program, educational benefits expire ten years from the date of your last discharge or release from active duty. The DVA can extend the ten-year period by the amount of time you were prevented from training during the period because of a certified disability, being recalled to active duty or detention by a foreign government power. Certain other exceptions apply as well and are covered in DVA Pamphlet 22-90-2.

You may use GI Bill benefits for the following purposes:

- To seek an associate's, bachelor's, master's, professional, or doctoral degree at a college or university.
- To participate in a cooperative training program.
- To participate in an accredited independent study program leading to a college degree.
- To take courses leading to a certificate or diploma from a business, technical, or vocational school.
- To work and train in an apprenticeship or job-training program offered by a company or union.
- To take a correspondence course.
- To participate in a program abroad that leads to a college degree.
- To take remedial, deficiency, and refresher courses, under certain circumstances.
- To receive tutorial assistance for a deficiency (such as in math), if you attend school at least half-time.
- To participate in the DVA work-study program, provided you attend school or train three-quarters or full-time.

Soldiers with private pilot's licenses are entitled to benefits leading to more advanced flying certification. This program has been extended indefinitely.

You may be entitled to benefits under more than one program, or you may be eligible for vocational rehabilitation if you have a service-connected disability. In either case, you are strongly encouraged to discuss your educational plans with a local DVA counselor. If local counselors are unavailable, contact DVA regional

offices. DVA toll-free telephone service is available in all fifty states, Puerto Rico, and the U.S. Virgin Islands. Call (800) 827-1000.

OTHER FINANCIAL AID

The U.S. Department of Education (DOE), in *The Student Guide*, informs you and your family members about federal student aid programs and how to apply for them. The department advises you to contact the financial aid administrator at the school that you, your spouse, or your children are interested in and ask about the total cost of education. Ask the state higher education agencies about state aid. Check the local library for state and private financial aid information. Check with companies, foundations, religious organizations, fraternities or sororities, and civic organizations such as the American Legion. Also ask about aid through professional associations.

The *Student Guide* is free and may be available at the local Army Education Office.

A FINAL THOUGHT ON EDUCATION

Buy bonds. Series EE savings bonds may be entirely tax free when used for education. If you have children and are worried about the rising cost of education, purchasing bonds on a regular basis is a smart way to invest in their future and protect your financial security. For example, assuming an annual interest rate of 6 percent, putting just $50 a month into bonds for a one-year-old child who will begin college at age eighteen will yield $17,356. Investing $100 a month will yield $34,712. If you are a soldier with a twelve-year-old who will begin college in six years, putting $50 a month into bonds will provide $4,227; $100 a month will yield $8,454—minimum.

If you are a young soldier, you may purchase bonds for yourself, hold them five years or so, then use them to augment other financial aid you will apply toward a bachelor's or master's degree.

Beginning with Series EE bonds purchased in 1990, the interest earned can be excluded from federal income tax if you pay tuition and fees at colleges, universities, and qualified technical schools during the same year the bonds are cashed. The exclusion applies not only to your own educational expenses but also to those of your spouse and any other dependents, according to the Savings Bonds Public Affairs Office in Washington, D.C. Some restrictions apply. Contact your unit savings bond coordinator for more information.

9

Leadership Competencies

It is perfectly reasonable and possible for a soldier to aspire and be promoted to the rank of corporal or sergeant during his or her first term of enlistment. Such a promotion, however, requires that the soldier possess certain leadership competencies—that is, be competent to lead.

The Army defines leadership as "the process of influencing people by providing purpose, direction, and motivation while operating to accomplish the mission and improve the organization." Leadership, despite the great strides in technology, remains the same—influencing and motivating people to get a job done. The new FM 6-22 (FM 22-100), *Army Leadership*, consolidates five current manuals and one Department of the Army pamphlet on various aspects and levels of leadership. The new manual discusses character-based leadership, clarifies values, establishes attributes as part of character, and most importantly focuses on improving people and organizations for the long term. Rather than provide a one-size-fits-all leadership model, Army leadership doctrine now outlines three levels of leadership—*direct*, *organizational*, and *strategic*; and it identifies four skill domains that apply at all levels: *interpersonal*, *conceptual*, *technical*, and *tactical*. The discussion on actions outlines for each level what leaders do—what turns character into leadership.

Although the concept "be, know, do" remains the centerpiece of the 1999 edition of *Army Leadership* by providing a specific framework with twenty-three dimensions that describes a leader of character and competence, leadership doctrine now flows from the axiom: *Leaders of character and competence act to achieve excellence by providing purpose, direction, and motivation.* Above all, the new doctrine anchors leaders of character and competence in moral bedrock—the Army values.

LEADERSHIP CHARACTER
Character describes who a person is inside, and at the core of Army leaders are Army values. Those values—*loyalty, duty, respect, selfless service, honor, integrity,* and *personal courage* (LDRSHIP)—capture the professional military ethos and describe the nature of our soldiers. Our common values help us understand the purpose of our missions and devise appropriate methods to accomplish them. Values are the foundation of all that we are and do.

Added to Army values is the practice of leadership, which involves exercising *will, initiative, self-discipline, intelligent judgment,* and *cultural awareness.* These

mental attributes combined with physical attributes (*military and professional bearing*, *physical and health fitness*, and *emotional self-control's balance* and *stability* components), when put into practice, form a leader's behavior.

The new definition of leadership focuses on *behavior,* something that can be seen and evaluated. *Influencing, operating*, and *improving* are basic leadership actions. Leaders demonstrate influence through communicating, decision making, and motivating. A leader's influence obviously applies in the day-to-day business of operating—accomplishing missions. As part of operating, a leader is responsible for detailed, suitable planning; careful, proficient executing; and continual assessing and adjusting. Assessing change is essential to improving an organization. This new doctrinal emphasis means that a leader's influence today involves preparing for tomorrow. The traditional measure of leadership is whether an organization performed its tasks, fulfilled its obligations, and accomplished its missions—all short-term goals.

The Army has identified three areas of leadership competency. The first area deals with the *behavior* of the leader: the traits the leader must have. The second area is *knowledge*: what the leader must know. The third area is *skills*: how a leader must do the job of leading. Together these areas are known as skills, knowledge, and behavior (SKB), or "be, know, do."

Within the area of skills and knowledge, there are nine further competencies: *communication, supervision, teaching, counseling, soldier team building, technical and tactical proficiency, decision making, planning, use of available systems*, and *professional ethics*.

The necessary behavior, skills, and knowledge of leaders in the grades of corporal and sergeant are shown in the following lists. Use them as the basis for your preparation for promotion, as well as when acting in a leadership position.

BEHAVIOR (BE)

To be a leader in today's Army means that you must be a soldier who behaves like a leader—one who:

- Enforces standards.
- Sets the example.
- Accomplishes the mission.
- Takes care of soldiers.
- Is dedicated and selfless.
- Accepts responsibilities for self and subordinates.
- Obeys lawful orders.
- Is honest and courageous.
- Maintains physical and mental toughness.
- Shows competence and self-confidence.
- Acts fairly and equitably with subordinates.
- Is loyal to the nation and the Constitution.
- Is loyal to superiors and subordinates.
- Shows initiative and motivation.

KNOWLEDGE (KNOW)
Leaders must *know* or learn the principles and/or policies in each leadership competency.

Communication
- Listening and watching principles (FM 6-22 [FM 22-100]).
- Speaking principles (Training Support Package [TSP], Noncommissioned Officer Education System [NCOES], and U.S. Army Sergeants Major Academy [USASMA] Reference Book 350-25).
- Reading level—grade 10 (Test for Adult Basic Education [TABE] and AR 25-30).
- Writing level—grade 10 (TABE and AR 25-30).

Supervision
- Duties, responsibilities, and authority of NCOs (FM 7-27.7 [TC 22-6]).
- Wear and appearance, drill and ceremony (AR 670-1 and FM 3-21.5 [FM 22-5]).
- Unit standing operating procedure.
- Army Training System and responsibilities of trainers (FM 7-0 [FM 25-100] and FM 7-10 [FM 25-101]).
- Operator's manuals for equipment (Technical Manual [TM] 10 series).
- Unit supply procedures (AR 735 series).
- Army safety program (AR 385 series).
- Equal opportunity (EO)/sexual harassment policy (AR 600-20).

Teaching and Counseling
- Common tasks skill levels (Soldier Training Publication [STP] 21-1).
- Common leader combat skills.
- Army training system and responsibilities of trainers (FM 7-0 [FM 25-100] and FM 7-10 [FM 25-101]).
- Performance counseling of individuals (FM 6-22 [FM 22-100]).
- After-action review techniques (FM 7-10 [FM 25-101] and Training Circular [TC] 25-20).
- Individual Training Evaluation Program (AR 350-37).

Soldier Team Development
- Concept of team building (FM 6-22 [FM 22-100]).
- Principles of leadership (FM 6-22 [FM 22-100]).
- Factors of leadership (FM 6-22 [FM 22-100]).
- Human stress factors (FM 6-22 [FM 22-100]).
- Customs and traditions of unit.
- Army enlisted promotion system (AR 600-20 and AR 600-8-19).
- Noncommissioned Officer Education System (AR 351-1).
- Disciplinary actions (UCMJ).
- Physical fitness training (FM 3-22-20 [FM 21-20]).

Technical and Tactical Proficiency
- Marksmanship training (FM 3-22.9 [FM 23-9]).
- Operation, characteristics, and employment of weapons and equipment.
- Appropriate MOS skill level tasks and standards (*Soldier's Manual* and AR 611-201).
- Appropriate common tasks skill level (STP 21-1 and STP 21-24).
- Land navigation/map reading (FM 3-22.26 [FM 21-26]).
- Movement techniques (FM 3-21.75 [21-75], FM 3-21.8 [7-8], FM 3-21.10 [7-10], 3-21.20 [7-20]).
- Operation of Multiple Integrated Laser Identification System (MILES) in tactical training (TC 25-6.)
- Equipment operator's manuals (Technical Manual [TM] 10 series).
- Unit collective tasks Army Training and Evaluation Program/Army Mission Training Plan (ARTEP/AMTP).
- Common leader combat skills.

Decision Making
- Problem-solving process (FM 6-22 [FM 22-100]).
- Ethical decision-making process (FM 6-22 [FM 22-100]).
- Military decision-making process (FM 101-5).

Planning
- Planning principles (FM 7-0 [FM 25-100]).
- Training schedules and event plans (FM 7-10 [FM 25-101]).
- Higher headquarters training objectives.
- Backward planning process (FM 6-22 [FM 22-100]).

Use of Available Systems
- Computers, automated systems, information management, and analytical techniques affecting battalions and higher-level commands.

Professional Ethics
- Soldierly qualities (FM 1 [FM 100-1]).
- Professional Army ethics (FM 1 [FM 100-1]).

SKILLS (DO)
In each of the nine competencies, a leader in the grade of corporal or sergeant must be able to do the tasks listed.

Communication
- Receive and interpret information from superiors and subordinates.
- Issue clear and concise oral and written orders.
- Write performance counseling statements.

- Provide input on personnel matters affecting subordinates.
- Participate in after-action reviews.

Supervision
- Enforce Army standards of appearance and conduct.
- Control and account for individuals and units.
- Supervise collective training.
- Supervise and/or lead and evaluate individual training.
- Lead team in performance of collective tasks.
- Supervise maintenance of equipment, living areas, and workplaces.
- Enforce the Army Safety Program.
- Enforce the Army equal opportunity and sexual harassment policies.

Teaching and Counseling
- Teach and coach common task training (CTT)—SGT.
- Teach and coach MOS skill level 1 tasks.
- Teach common leader combat skills.
- Teach performance-oriented training.
- Coach subordinates in proper execution of tasks.
- Evaluate tasks to standards.
- Provide feedback through performance counseling and after-action reviews (AARs).

Soldier Team Development
- Develop cohesion at appropriate level.
- Foster loyalty and commitment.
- Build spirit and confidence.
- Instill discipline.
- Take care of subordinates.
- Lead physical fitness training.
- Develop and mentor subordinate NCOs.

Technical and Tactical Proficiency
- Qualify with weapon; train and supervise or direct marksmanship training.
- Be proficient with mission-essential weapons and equipment.
- Perform MOS skill levels 1 and 2 tasks to standard—SGT.
- Perform MOS skill level 1 tasks to standard—CPL.
- Navigate and lead appropriate echelon movement.
- Employ multiple integrated laser engagement simulation (MILES) equipment.
- Perform preventative maintenance checks and services (PMCS) on individual and platoon/section/squad weapons and equipment.
- Train and lead collective tasks for element.

Decision Making
- Interpret information and make decisions affecting subordinates.
- Use problem-solving process.
- Use ethical decision-making process.
- Exercise initiative in tactical situations.

Planning
- Plan METL-based individual and collective training.
- Use backward planning process.

Use of Available Systems
- Use and control automated systems and information management at different echelons.

Professional Ethics
- Lead by example.
- Practice professional Army ethics.
- Demonstrate high moral standards.

Soldiers learn leadership every day. Simply by watching other leaders and performing their duties, they will learn leadership. Those who deliberately apply the process—study examples of leadership, reflect on their own experiences, apply lessons learned, and seek comments—become better leaders now and for the future.

Leadership skills are one of the lifelong benefits of military service. The skills are worth learning well. They are indispensable while on active duty and invaluable when you return to civilian life.

Additional information on leadership is found in FM 6-22 [FM 22-100] *Army Leadership.*

10

Career Decisions

Just as one day you enlisted, someday you will face separation. So what you do in the meantime is vital to your future (and, if you are married, your family's future). Have you remained qualified to reenlist? What are your "re-up" options? Do you want to reenlist? What if you choose not to re-up? Whatever you do, begin considering your options at least a year out—even though you may change your mind at the last minute.

If you separate, you will most certainly need to go to work unless a lottery jackpot or some other bonanza drops in your lap. If you choose not to re-up but have a remaining service obligation, you still have military career decisions to make about joining the Army Reserve or the Army National Guard. If you choose to remain in service to the nation full-time, do you have what it takes to become a senior NCO, warrant or commissioned officer?

If you enlisted when you were eighteen or nineteen years old, and you continue your Army career, you will be only thirty-eight or thirty-nine when you become eligible for retirement. Would you like to draw an Army retirement check before age forty, knowing that that check will arrive monthly for the rest of your life?

Soldiers must be in the grade of promotable sergeant or higher to be eligible to serve twenty years. Soldiers not promoted beyond the grade of sergeant may serve only fifteen years. And promotable corporals and specialists—those who do not get promoted before their separation dates—may serve no more than fifteen years.

THE REENLISTMENT DECISION

If you decide that the Army is right for you, you should consider all options when reenlisting. Begin early. Visit your unit retention office. Discuss your decision with your fellow soldiers. Seek counseling from your immediate supervisor and others in your chain of command. Talk to your family. Consider at least the following:

- Why you are reenlisting.
- How reenlisting can enhance your career.
- Whether you will receive a Regular or Selective Reenlistment Bonus.
- MOS training and schooling, or MOS reclassification options.
- Travel and assignment options.
- Your promotion potential.
- The needs of the Army and the nation.

Soldiers Reenlisting at the World Trade Center

Reenlistment Bonuses

The Army offers reenlistment bonuses as a means of encouraging soldiers in certain critical MOSs to reenlist or extend their current enlistments. Critical MOSs are determined by the needs of the Army. The Army updates the list of critical MOSs regularly and publishes it through the DA Circular 611 series. Your unit's retention NCO should be able to provide you with the list.

The Selective Reenlistment Bonus (SRB) Program is available to all soldiers, regardless of rank, who hold a primary MOS designated as critical. Soldiers reenlisting through the SRB Program are eligible for reenlistment bonuses up to $40,000 if they reenlist or extend for a minimum of three years. They may receive a maximum of three such SRBs during their military careers, and only one in each established time zone. The zones, based on time of active military service, are zone A, extending from twenty-one months to six years; zone B, from six to ten years; and zone C, from ten to fourteen years of active military service.

The actual amount of the SRB is determined by a formula based on the soldier's monthly basic pay. The bonus cannot exceed six times the monthly pay, multiplied by the number of years of additional obligated service, nor can the bonus exceed $40,000. The SRB is based on the current needs of the Army and on current reenlistment trends in specific MOSs. The more critical the Army's need, the higher the SRB. Consequently, sometimes no MOS qualifies for the maximum rate.

The following examples illustrate how the program operates: A soldier receiving basic pay of $800 a month reenlists under the SRB Program for four years; the bonus amount for his MOS is the maximum, six times the monthly basic pay. The SRB

bonus would be ($800 × 6) × 4 = $19,200. If, however, the soldier was receiving a basic pay of $1,000 a month, the SRB would not be ($1,000 × 6) × 4 = $24,000; instead, this soldier would receive the maximum allowable bonus—$20,000. Since qualifying MOSs and their SRB rates fluctuate based on the needs of the Army, interested soldiers should contact their retention office to obtain current information. The SRB is paid in addition to any other pay and allowance to which the soldier is already entitled.

Training and Duty Station Options

If you decide to remain on active duty, you have a number of options. Upon reenlistment, you can elect additional training, a particular duty station elsewhere, or current duty station stabilization.

Options for the first termer include airborne training, U.S. Army Intelligence and Security Command electronic warfare training, U.S. Army Information Systems Command training, language training, and other MOSs that have openings for new soldiers who qualify. Other options include volunteering for Special Forces, a combat arms unit of choice, and the U.S. Army 3rd Infantry (Old Guard).

Soldiers willing to reenlist or extend their enlistment can also apply for a number of interesting career development programs: explosive ordnance disposal (EOD), presidential support activities (working at the White House), technical escort (for chemical, ammunition, and EOD specialists), Army bands, instructors at service schools, drill sergeants, and recruiters. Selection of a new duty station may also be an option for your reenlistment. You may be eligible for the overseas area option; the CONUS-to-CONUS station option; or, if overseas, the CONUS station of choice option.

Information and requirements for each career program are contained in AR 614-200; reenlistment NCOs and career counselors can also be of assistance to the soldier who wishes to explore some of the more unusual career options in the Army.

OTHER MILITARY OPPORTUNITIES

Your career choices at the end of your first term are not limited to reenlisting in the Army or returning to civilian life. You may elect to serve in the Army Reserve or Army National Guard while pursuing a civilian career. Or you may decide to seek a commission or a warrant through Officer Candidate School, Warrant Officer Entry Courses, the U.S. Military Academy, or an ROTC program. All Army installations have reenlistment NCOs and in-service recruiters who can provide more detailed information about these options.

Army Reserve

The Army Reserve is a federal military force composed of the Ready Reserve and the Standby Reserve. The Ready Reserve is made up of combat support and combat service support units available for quick mobilization in times of national emergency or war. The Standby Reserve is a pool of soldiers who have a remaining military obligation and are eligible for recall to active duty.

Through the Ready Reserve, a former soldier can supplement his or her civilian income while taking full advantage of the leadership training he or she received while on active duty. Reservists receive four days' pay for each weekend of reserve training, which is usually held monthly. An additional requirement is a two-week annual training session. Salary ranges depend on time in service and pay grade.

Each soldier leaving active duty who enlists in the Ready Reserve within sixty days of discharge from the Army retains his or her active rank, pay grade, and time-in-grade status. Privileges include $400,000 Servicemen's Group Life Insurance (SGLI), space-available dental care, and commissary and post exchange privileges.

Army National Guard
The Army National Guard is a federal-state military force. Its primary mission is to maintain combat divisions and support units available for active duty in time of national emergency or war. Under its state mission, the Guard protects life and property and preserves state internal security.

Pay and benefits are essentially the same for the Guard as for the Army Reserve. One unique feature of the Guard is its Officer Candidate School (OCS) program. This one-year program provides training on weekends through the state OCS. Guard members can also attend the active Army OCS and earn a commission in fourteen weeks.

Officer Candidate School
Enlisted personnel who elect to remain on active duty may be eligible to apply for OCS training. Applicants must meet the following basic criteria:
- Be at least eighteen but less than thirty years of age upon enrollment.
- Have completed at least ninety semester hours of college.
- Have at least an 850 on the Scholastic Assessment Test (SAT) or 19 on the American College Testing Program Assessment (ACT).

During their assignment at OCS, candidates are paid at the E-5 level unless they previously held higher rank.

The fourteen-week program is rigorous and requires a high level of physical fitness, mental fortitude, and dedication to succeed. Upon completion of the course, graduates are commissioned as second lieutenants.

Warrant Officer Entry Course
Warrant officers are highly specialized experts and trainers who operate, maintain, administer, and manage the Army's equipment, support activities, and technical and tactical systems for their entire careers. The career progression of warrant officers is designed to encourage them to seek in-depth knowledge of particular systems and activities and maintain proficiency in their particular skills.

The Warrant Officer Entry Course, located at Fort Rucker, Alabama, trains selected enlisted personnel in the fundamentals of leadership, ethics, personnel management, and tactics. Following completion of the rigorous six-week course, warrant officers go on to additional specialized training in their particular MOSs.

To qualify for entry to the Warrant Officer Entry Course, a soldier must fit the following criteria:
* Be a sergeant or higher rank.
* Have earned a high school diploma or general education development (GED) equivalency.
* Have served three years' active enlisted service prior to appointment—unless applying as a warrant officer aviator.

Warrant officers may serve in a variety of MOSs, but there is an emphasis on maintenance and aviation specialties. For additional information, check the warrant officer recruiting team Web site at *usawocc.army.mil/warrant_off/howtowo.htm*

U.S. Military Academy

Soldiers wishing to attend the U.S. Military Academy at West Point may seek direct nomination under the provisions of AR 351-12 if they meet the entrance requirements without further study. The easiest way is to complete it online at *secwww.admissions.usma.edu/forms/apply/* or you can request one from the USMA admissions office at (800) 822-2769, ext. 5780, or DSN 688-5780.

Basic prerequisites are to be:
* A U.S. citizen.
* Unmarried with no legal obligation to support dependents.
* Under twenty-three years of age prior to July 1 of the year entering USMA (under twenty-two prior to July 1 of the year entering the Prep School).
* A high school graduate or have a GED.
* Of high moral character.

All applications are made directly to West Point. Soldiers not directly admitted to West Point will be automatically considered for admission to the Prep School. Soldiers who meet the basic eligibility requirements, have achieved SAT scores greater than 1000 or ACT composite score of 20 or higher, and achieved average grades or better in their high school curriculum are especially encouraged to apply. Soldiers must obtain an endorsement from their company or lowest-level unit commander. While this endorsement constitutes a nomination, soldiers are also strongly encouraged to obtain additional nominations from their congressional nomination sources. More information can be found at the USMA Admissions Web site: *admissions.usma.edu/Soldiers/*.

ROTC

One other option for the soldier is to separate from the service under a special ROTC scholarship program. In this program, the soldier may earn a degree, be commissioned a second lieutenant, and return to active duty. Through the "Green to Gold" program, these soldiers become civilians specifically to enter the ROTC program, complete a baccalaureate program, and then be commissioned as officers in the Regular Army or the Army Reserve. Once discharged, the soldier forfeits the pay and benefits of active duty, but he or she may still use any veterans' educational benefits earned while on active duty.

The ROTC cadet is not a soldier in civilian clothes. The former soldier leads the life of a normal college student with few additional responsibilities. Cadets must complete prescribed military science courses, a minimum of one semester of foreign language, Leader Development and Assessment Course (LDAC—a paid six-week training program between the junior and senior years), and any other training identified by the secretary of the Army as a requirement for commissioning.

Returning to active duty as a Regular Army second lieutenant is not a guarantee. Based on the needs of the Army, some cadets are commissioned as second lieutenants in the U.S. Army Reserve instead. Cadets select the branch of service in which they would prefer to serve, but branch selection is also not guaranteed; again, the needs of the Army must take precedence. Active-duty service can sometimes be delayed up to two years at the request of the individual in order to complete postgraduate studies; educational delays are also based on the needs of the Army at the time of commissioning.

Basic Requirements
The Green to Gold Scholarship Basic Eligibility Requirements are to:
- Be a U.S. citizen (nonwaiverable).
- Be under thirty years of age on December 31, of the year you complete all requirements for a commission and a college baccalaureate degree. (This is a statutory requirement and there are no waivers authorized.)
- Have a minimum of two years Active Duty.
- Have a general technical (GT) score of 110 or greater.
- Pass the APFT within the last six months.
- Be a high school graduate or equivalent.
- Have a cumulative high school or college GPA of 2.5.
- Have a letter of acceptance to school of choice offering Army ROTC.
- Have a letter of acceptance from the PMS of that Army ROTC battalion.
- Have no more than three dependents including spouse (waiverable).

Green to Gold Scholarship Option Program
The Green to Gold Scholarship provides scholarship funding for up to four years depending on degree requirements. The scholarship will provide up to $20,000 per year for tuition and fees, an annual $900 book allowance, and a monthly stipend that starts at $250 and ramps up to $400 and pay for attending the Leader Development and Assessment Course (LDAC) between the junior and senior years of college. Soldiers will be discharged in accordance with (IAW) AR 635-200, chapter 16. Soldiers will be able to use the Montgomery GI Bill and College Fund benefits in addition to the scholarship.

Green to Gold Active-Duty Option Program
This is different than above; this two-year program provides eligible, active duty enlisted soldiers an opportunity to complete a baccalaureate degree or graduate degree and be commissioned as an Army officer upon receiving the appropriate

degree. Soldiers selected to participate in this program will continue to receive their current pay and allowances while in the program (up to a maximum of twenty-four consecutive months), as well as permanent change of station (PCS) entitlements and if qualified, Montgomery GI Bill/Army College Fund benefits.

Green to Gold Nonscholarship Option Program

The Green to Gold Two-Year Nonscholarship Option Program is available to soldiers who have completed two years of college, and who can complete their college degree requirements in two years. Upon graduation, participants receive commissions as second lieutenant. While undergoing ROTC instruction, students receive a monthly stipend for up to ten months each school year that increases each year based on their Military Science Class; pay for attending the Leader Development and Assessment Course (LDAC) between the junior and senior years of college; and if qualified, Montgomery GI Bill/Army College Fund (MGIB/ACF) benefits. Green to Gold Nonscholarship Option members can also participate in the Simultaneous Membership Program (SMP). As SMPs, soldiers are members of either a drilling Reserve or Guard unit and ROTC. SMPs are entitled to Reserve Component pay of E-5 under this program. Also, many states offer tuition assistance to Reserve and National Guard soldiers.

You can request an application packet U.S. Army ROTC Cadet Command, ATTN: ATCC-C. Fort Monroe, VA 23651-5000, or you can apply online at *www.rotc.monroe.army.mil/scholarship_HPD2/green/index.asp.*

For the soldier interested in a possible career as an Army officer, or for the soldier who simply wants to make the road toward the baccalaureate degree shorter by attending college full-time, the ROTC Scholarship Program offers a viable alternative.

THE SEPARATION DECISION

Whether you decide on an Army career or separation after your first enlistment, sooner or later you must quit the service. In this section, we consider the various types of discharges, the operation of the U.S. Army Transfer facilities, and veterans' rights.

Separations

How and why a soldier is separated from the Army depends on many factors, according to AR 635-200, *Enlisted Personnel.* Separation policies in AR 635-200 promote readiness of the Army by providing an orderly means to accomplish the following:

- Ensure that the Army is served by individuals capable of meeting required standards of duty performance and discipline.
- Maintain standards of performance and conduct through characterization of service in a system that emphasizes the importance of honorable service.
- Achieve authorized force levels and grade distribution.
- Provide for the orderly administrative separation of soldiers in a variety of circumstances.

AR 635-200 provides the authority for separation of soldiers upon expiration of term of service (ETS); the authority and general provisions governing the separation of soldiers before ETS to meet the needs of the Army and its soldiers; the procedures to implement laws and policies governing voluntary retirement of soldiers for length of service; and the criteria governing uncharacterized separations and the issuance of honorable, general, and under other than honorable conditions discharges.

The following are the authorized types of separation under the provisions of AR 635-200:

Chapter 4—Separation for Expiration of Service Obligation. A soldier will be separated upon expiration of enlistment or fulfillment of service obligation.

Chapter 5—Separation for Convenience of the Government. A chapter 5 separation covers the following: involuntary separation due to parenthood; lack of jurisdiction as ordered by a U.S. court or judge thereof; aliens not lawfully admitted to the United States; personnel who did not meet procurement medical fitness standards; failure to qualify medically for flight training; personality disorders; concealment of arrest record; and failure to meet Army body composition and weight-control standards.

Chapter 6—Separation Because of Dependency or Hardship. Soldiers of the active Army and the reserve components serving on active duty or active duty for training may be discharged or released because of genuine dependency or hardship. Dependency exists when death or disability of a member of a soldier's (or spouse's) immediate family causes the family or one of its members to rely on the soldier for principal care or support. Hardship exists when in circumstances not involving death or disability of a member of the soldier's (or spouse's) immediate family, separation from the service will materially affect the care or support of the family by alleviating undue and genuine hardship.

Chapter 7—Defective Enlistments, Reenlistments, and Extensions. This chapter provides the authority, criteria, and procedures for the separation of soldiers because of minority, erroneous enlistment or extension of enlistment, defective enlistment agreement, and fraudulent entry.

Chapter 8—Separation of Enlisted Women for Pregnancy. Chapter 8 provides authority for voluntary separation of enlisted women because of pregnancy. A pregnant soldier is faced with a number of choices, the most basic of which is whether to separate from the Army. This decision can be very difficult because of its far-reaching ramifications. Once the soldier has decided to be retained on active duty, she will be expected to complete her full enlistment before she is again give the choice of continuing in the military or returning to civilian life.

Being the mother of a newborn child does not afford the soldier special privileges, but normally she will not receive PCS orders for an overseas assignment during the pregnancy. Such orders can often be deferred or deleted (for up to one year) if they should be issued. After the child is born and the mother is released from normal postnatal care, however, the military mother is given no unique consideration for assignments. She is expected to fulfill the needs of the Army just like any other

soldier. This means that she could receive orders for worldwide assignments, including to dependent-restricted overseas areas.

The Army is concerned for the welfare of the child, but it does not adjust the assignment process to accommodate the new mother. Instead, the Army requires each soldier with dependents who are unable to care for themselves to file an approved Family Care Plan. Failure to complete an adequate plan will result in a bar to reenlistment. The plan specifies what actions the soldier has taken to ensure care for her dependents in the event she is assigned to an area where dependents are not authorized. In addition, she is expected to make provisions for the care of her dependents while she is away or on military duty (both on a daily basis and in the event of a necessary temporary duty).

One other consequence of the pregnant soldier's decision to continue in the military is the possibility of involuntary separation. If the soldier cannot handle her normal duties during the pregnancy or once she is a new mother, she may be separated from the service involuntarily. Such decisions are made on the grounds of unsatisfactory performance of duty or misconduct, whichever is appropriate. Involuntary separation is covered by AR 635-200, paragraphs 5-8 and 13-2, in addition to chapter 14. If a soldier in an entry-level status becomes pregnant, she will be evaluated by a medical officer to determine whether she can fully participate in the training required for the MOS. If it is determined that she cannot participate in the training, she will be involuntarily discharged. Otherwise, the soldier will be retained unless she specifically requests discharge under AR 635-200, chapter 8.

The soldier will be provided medical care during and after the pregnancy. Again, she has a choice. She may remain at her present duty assignment and receive care through a military facility within thirty miles of that location; if such care is not available, she will be treated through a civilian doctor and civilian facilities. Or she may choose to take ordinary leave, advance leave, and excess leave so that she may return to her home or other appropriate and desired location for her maternity care and the birth of her child. Once labor begins, her leave status changes to convalescent leave for the period of labor, hospitalization, and postpartum care. Convalescent leave for postpartum care is limited to the amount of time the doctor specifies as essential for the medical needs of the mother. Generally, postpartum convalescent leave does not exceed forty-two days. Leave status and the pregnant soldier are covered in AR 630-5, chapter 9, section II.

If the soldier decides to return home to deliver the baby, it is her responsibility to first ensure that military facilities near her home have obstetrical care available. Many military facilities do not provide such care. The soldier cannot choose to return home for maternity care and have the government pay for that care at a civilian facility. This is prohibited in AR 40-3, except for bona fide medical emergencies that justify the use of a civilian facility. Using civilian facilities away from the duty location means that the soldier, not the government, is normally responsible for the medical bills. The health benefits adviser at the nearest military medical facility is the best source for further information on this matter.

If the pregnant soldier chooses to separate from the Army, she receives an honorable discharge and any benefits applicable to soldiers with the amount of time in service she has at the time of separation. Separation due to pregnancy is authorized under chapter 8 of AR 600-200.

Unit commanders must counsel women who are eligible for pregnancy separation. Army chaplains and the American Red Cross also offer counseling, and the judge advocate general's (JAG) office can instruct the soldier in legal matters regarding the birth and care of her child. The soldier will have at least a week to consider her options but must indicate her choice of either separating or remaining on active duty in writing.

Whether the soldier is allowed to reconsider her choice depends on the choice she initially made. If she originally chose to stay on active duty but then decides to separate, the Army must separate her. If she originally elected to separate and then decides she wants to remain in the Army, the case will be reviewed, and a decision whether to retain her will be made based on the best interests of the Army.

An abnormal pregnancy places a difficult burden on the woman involved. The Army allows a woman the option of seeking a discharge in the event of a miscarriage, abortion, or premature delivery if she had been pregnant for at least sixteen weeks at the time the pregnancy terminates.

Medical treatment for obstetrical and postpartum care is provided at government expense through a military medical facility. The separating soldier may not use TRICARE or civilian medical facilities at government expense. In fact, the pregnant soldier is required to sign a statement before she decides to separate from the military, clearly stating that she understands that under no circumstance can TRICARE, any military department, or the DVA reimburse her civilian maternity care expenses; the statement further clarifies that she understands that any costs for civilian care will be her personal financial responsibility. Therefore, careful planning must be made to ensure that she settles in an area where military medical facilities provide maternity care. The separating pregnant soldier will be authorized postpartum care for up to six weeks after the birth of the child.

Chapter 9—Alcohol or Other Drug Abuse Rehabilitation Failure. A soldier who is enrolled in the Alcohol and Drug Abuse Prevention and Control Program (ADAPCP) for substance abuse may be separated because of inability or refusal to participate in, cooperate in, or successfully complete such a program.

Chapter 10—Discharge for the Good of the Service. A soldier who has committed an offense or offenses punishable by a bad conduct discharge or dishonorable discharge under the provisions of the UCMJ and the *Manual for Courts-Martial* may submit a request for discharge for the good of the service. The request does not prevent or suspend disciplinary proceedings. (See AR 635-200, pages 43–45 for details.)

Chapter 11—Entry-Level Status Performance and Conduct. This chapter provides guidance for the separation of personnel because of unsatisfactory performance or conduct (or both) while in entry-level status. It covers inability, lack of reasonable effort, or failure to adapt to the military environment.

Chapter 12—Retirement for Length of Service. A soldier who has completed twenty years' active federal service and who has completed all required service obligations is eligible to retire. Upon retirement, the soldier is transferred to the U.S. Army Reserve Control Group (Retired) and remains in that status until active service time plus control group time equals thirty years, and then is placed on the retired list. A Regular Army soldier who has completed at least thirty years of active federal service will, upon request, be placed on the retired list.

Chapter 13—Separation for Unsatisfactory Performance. A soldier may be separated per this chapter when unqualified for further military service because of unsatisfactory performance, under the following circumstances: (1) the soldier will not develop sufficiently; (2) the seriousness of the circumstance is such that retention would have an adverse impact on military discipline, good order, and morale; (3) it is likely that the soldier will be a disruptive influence; (4) it is likely that the circumstances will continue to recur; (5) the ability of the soldier to perform duties, including potential for advancement or leadership, is unlikely; (6) the soldier meets retention medical standards.

Chapter 14—Separation for Misconduct. This chapter establishes procedures for separating personnel for misconduct because of minor disciplinary infractions, a pattern of misconduct, commission of a serious offense, conviction by civil authorities, desertion, and absence without leave. A discharge under other than honorable conditions is normally appropriate for a soldier discharged under this chapter.

Chapter 15—Discharge for Homosexual Conduct. Homosexual conduct is grounds for separation from the Army. This includes preservice, prior service, or current service homosexual conduct.

Chapter 19—Qualitative Management Program. This chapter contains policies and procedures for voluntary and involuntary separation, for the convenience of the government, of Regular Army (RA) NCOs and U.S. Army Reserve (USAR) NCOs serving in Active Guard and Reserve (AGR) status, under the qualitative management program (QMP). Soldiers separating under this chapter have their discharges characterized as honorable.

Types of Discharge

Honorable Discharge
An honorable discharge is given when an individual is separated from the military service with honor. An honorable discharge cannot be denied to a person solely on the basis of convictions by courts-martial or actions under Article 15 of the UCMJ. Denial must be based on patterns of misbehavior and not isolated instances. An honorable discharge may be awarded when disqualifying entries in an individual's service record are outweighed by subsequent honorable and faithful service over a greater period of time during the current period of service. Unless otherwise ineligible, a member may receive an honorable discharge if he or she has, during the current enlistment or extensions thereof, received a personal decoration or is separated by reason of disability incurred in the line of duty.

General Discharge

A general discharge is issued to an individual whose character of service has been satisfactory but not sufficiently meritorious to warrant an honorable discharge. Such persons would have, for example, frequent punishments under article 15 of the UCMJ or be classified as general troublemakers.

Other Than Honorable Discharge

Discharges that fall within this category are given for reasons of misconduct, homosexuality, security, or the good of the service and are covered by AR 635-200. No person shall receive a discharge under other than honorable conditions unless afforded the right to present his or her case before an administrative discharge board with the advice of legal counsel.

Uncharacterized Separations

There are two types of uncharacterized separations: those given when a soldier is in entry-level status and those given because of void enlistments or inductions.

Bad Conduct or Dishonorable Discharge

A soldier will be given a bad conduct discharge pursuant only to an approved sentence of a general or special court-martial. A soldier will be given a dishonorable discharge pursuant only to an approved sentence of a general court-martial. The appellate reviews must be completed and the affirmed sentence duly executed. Dishonorable and bad conduct discharges result in expulsion from the Army.

TRANSITION ACTIVITIES

U.S. Army transfer facilities provide an informal, quiet atmosphere centrally located at a post where personnel being separated may be processed within acceptable time limits. AR 635-10 prescribes that overseas returnees, except retirees, be separated on the first workday after their arrival at the separation transfer point, when possible. Personnel being released from active duty who are discharged before expiration, term of service (ETS), or the period for which ordered to active duty are separated by the third workday after approved separation. All others are separated on their scheduled separation dates, except for those individuals who elect to be separated on the last workday before a weekend or a holiday.

Medical Examination

There is no statutory requirement for soldiers to undergo a medical exam incidental to separation. It is Army policy, however, to accomplish a medical examination if a soldier is active Army and retiring after twenty or more years of active duty. An examination is also required if a soldier is being discharged or released and requests a medical examination, if review of the soldier's health record by a physician or physician's assistant warrants an exam, or if an examination is required by AR 40-501.

Each soldier undergoing separation processing will have his or her medical records screened by a physician, regardless of whether a separation physical has been requested. *A separation physical may be one of the most important medical examinations of your life.* Separation physicals end in a personal interview with a doctor. That interview is the proper time to bring up every single medical fact incident to military service. This interview substantiates service connection should a soldier, after discharge, request disability compensation from the DVA based on military service. Above all, each soldier being separated from the service should make a copy of his or her medical and dental records and keep them after discharge.

Army Career and Alumni Program

The Army Career and Alumni Program (ACAP) is a transition and job assistance initiative located at military sites worldwide. Each ACAP site includes a transition assistance office (TAO) and a job assistance center (JAC), which are available for active and reserve component soldiers, Army civilians, and military and civilian family members. Additional information can be found at the ACAP Web site: *www.acap.army.mil/.*

Transition Assistance. The transition assistance office (TAO) is the first step in the transition process. It synchronizes current pre-severance transition services on an individual basis to help personnel leaving the Army. The office staff provide eligible clients with transition advice and serve as a focal point for problems.

Job Assistance. The JAC provides clients with job search training, individual assistance and counseling, and a referral service. It conducts individual, small-, and large-group workshops to help soldiers prepare for interviews, evaluate job offers, track job leads, and develop their résumés.

Ideally, the TAO and JAC like to see you 180 days before your separation or retirement date. If that is not possible, you are eligible to be seen at the ACAP office until you are discharged from the Army.

Army Employment Network

The Army Employment Network (AEN) is an ACAP database that contains information about companies that are committed to considering Army personnel for employment. The AEN provides the company name, location of all branches of the company, total number of personnel hired annually, types of positions for which a company hires, points of contact, and, in some cases, a listing of currently available positions. The network is linked to regional and federal Office of Personnel Management computers that list federal jobs and is also tied to the DVA.

For more information about the ACAP, call toll-free in the continental United States (800) 445-2049. If you are stationed overseas, call DSN 221-0993.

Terminal Leave

Deciding whether to take terminal leave may not be an easy decision; it depends on how much leave a soldier has accrued at the time of separation, how much leave he

or she may have previously cashed in for pay, and what plans the servicemember has for job-hunting activities, travel, or vacation.

Personnel taking terminal leave will be allowed to finish processing at the local transfer activity before departure on leave. On the day of separation, a telephone call from the soldier, verifying his or her status and whereabouts, is all that is needed to finish the outprocessing procedure.

Discharge Certificates

Your DD Form 214, *Certificate of Release or Discharge from Active Duty*, is the most important document you will receive during your outprocessing and is one of the most important documents you will ever receive during your military career. At the time of your separation, you will receive copies one (original) and four (carbons) of DD Form 214. Be sure to make copies of these forms and protect the originals. Do not let the originals out of your possession.

Travel and Transportation Allowances

Soldiers are authorized travel allowances from their last duty station to their home. Shipment and storage of household goods incident to retirement is authorized on a one-time basis, subject to weight limitations and other controls. Specific information relative to shipment and storage of household goods is contained in DA Pam 55-2, *Personal Property Shipping Information.*

Wearing the Uniform

Wearing of the uniform by separated soldiers is a privilege granted in recognition of faithful service to the country. Former members of the Army who served honorably during a declared or undeclared war and whose most recent service was terminated under honorable conditions may wear the Army uniform in the highest grade held during such war service. The uniform may be worn only for the following ceremonies and when traveling to and from such ceremonies:

- Military funerals, memorial services, weddings, inaugurals, and other occasions of ceremony.
- Parades on national or state holidays, or other parades or ceremonies of a patriotic nature in which any active or reserve U.S. military unit is taking part.

Wearing of the Army uniform at any other time or for any other purpose is prohibited.

VETERANS' RIGHTS AND BENEFITS

The benefits discussed in this section are available to all veterans regardless of status. All Veterans Administration (VA) benefits (with the exception of insurance and certain medical benefits) payable to veterans or their dependents require that the particular period of service on which the entitlement is based be terminated under certain conditions. Honorable and general discharges qualify the veteran as eligible for benefits; however, dishonorable discharges and bad conduct discharges issued

by general courts-martial are a bar to VA benefits. Other bad conduct discharges and discharges characterized as other than honorable may or may not qualify. Qualification depends on a special determination made by the VA and is based on the facts of each case.

In order to prove your eligibility for VA benefits, you must have the following:
- A complete copy of your medical records.
- DD Form 214, *Discharge Certificate.*

Conversion of SGLI to VGLI

A servicemember has 120 days after separation to apply for Veterans Group Life Insurance (VGLI), with no medical examination requirements. Beyond the 120 days, a soldier has one year to apply, with exam requirements. During the 120 days after separation, the SGLI coverage continues without premiums.

You can keep your VGLI coverage for your lifetime, as long as you continue paying premiums. At any time, however, you may convert your VGLI coverage to an individual policy of life insurance with a commercial company that participates in the program at the company's standard premium rate regardless of your health. No disability or other supplemental benefits will be provided on converted policies. You may convert up to the amount of VGLI coverage you hold. The link at *www.insurance.va.gov/sgliSite/conversion/conversion.htm* provides information on how to convert to an individual policy with a list of participating companies.

Employment

Priority referral for job openings and training opportunities is given to eligible veterans, with preferential treatment for disabled veterans. In cooperation with VA regional offices and Veterans Outreach Centers, the job service assists veterans who are seeking employment by providing information about such opportunities as job marts, on-the-job training, and apprenticeship training.

Veterans seeking employment with the federal government may receive special opportunities, such as the following:
- A five-point preference is given to those who served during any war, in any campaign, in an expedition for which a campaign medal has been authorized, or for 180 consecutive days between January 31, 1955, and October 15, 1976.
- A ten-point preference is given to those who were awarded the Purple Heart, have a current service-connected disability, or are receiving compensation, disability retirement benefits, or pension from the VA.
- A veteran with a 30 percent or more disability may receive appointment without a competitive examination—with a right to be converted to a career appointment and with retention rights during reductions in force.

Educational Benefits

See your ACES counselor for details on the GI Bill (also covered in chapter 8), Veterans Educational Assistance Program (VEAP), and other educational benefits programs. For more information visit the GI Bill Web site at *www.gibill.va.gov/.*

GI Loans

The purpose of VA GI loans is to buy a home; to buy a residential unit in certain condominium projects; to build a home; to repair, alter, or improve a home; to refinance an existing home loan; to buy a manufactured home (with or without a lot); to buy a lot for a manufactured home that you already own; to improve a home through installation of solar heating and/or cooling system or other weatherization improvements; to purchase and simultaneously improve a home with energy-conserving measures; to refinance an existing VA loan to reduce the interest rate; to refinance a manufactured home loan in order to acquire a lot; and to simultaneously purchase and improve a home. Eligibility requirements vary, based on period of service with the exception that all eligible veterans must have been discharged under conditions other than dishonorable.

The loan terms are subject to negotiation between the veteran and the lender. The repayment period or maturity of GI home loans may be as long as thirty years. Newly discharged veterans are mailed certificates of eligibility shortly after discharge. Other veterans may secure their certificates by sending VA Form 26-1880, *Request for a Certificate Of Eligibility for VA Home Loan Benefits,* along with the required supporting documents, to the VA regional office nearest them. Active-duty personnel may also take advantage of these loans.

Unemployment Compensation

The purpose of unemployment compensation for veterans is to provide income for a limited time to help meet basic needs while employment is sought. The amount and duration of payments vary because they are governed by state laws, although benefits are paid from federal funds. Veterans should apply immediately after discharge at the nearest state employment service, not at the VA. A copy of DD Form 214 is needed to establish the type of separation from the service.

One-Time Dental Treatment

In addition to dental conditions that qualify for treatment because of service connection, veterans are entitled to a one-time dental treatment without review of service records to establish service connection. This treatment must be applied for within ninety days of separation. Do not fail to take advantage of this important benefit. Contact the local VA office for a copy of VA Form 10-10, *Application for Medical Benefits.*

Department of Veterans Affairs (Disability) Compensation

If you believe that you have a condition that may entitle you to VA compensation, file your claim at the time of separation. If the VA, upon reviewing your medical records, finds that you do have grounds for seeking compensation, an appointment for a physical exam will be made for you at the Department of Veterans Affairs hospital closest to your retirement home. Your claim will be processed based upon the examination results.

Medical Benefits

The Department of Veterans Affairs provides a Medical Benefits Package, a standard enhanced health benefits plan available to all enrolled veterans. Through it the VA offers the whole spectrum of medical benefits to qualified veterans: aids and services for the blind, alcohol treatment, domiciliary care, drug treatment, hospitalization care for dependents or survivors, nursing home care, outpatient dental treatment, outpatient medical treatment, and prosthetic appliances.

The VA maintains an annual enrollment system to manage the provision of quality hospital and outpatient medical care and treatment to all enrolled veterans. A priority system ensures that veterans with service-connected disabilities and those below the low-income threshold are able to be enrolled in VA's health-care system. Veterans who are receiving compensation or who would be eligible to receive compensation (except for retirement pay) who need treatment for an ailment connected with their service are admitted as beds are available. Under certain circumstances, veterans who were not discharged or retired for disability or who are not receiving compensation and who apply for treatment of a non-service-connected disability may be admitted to a VA hospital. Any veteran with a service-connected disability may receive VA outpatient medical treatment.

Vocational Rehabilitation

Generally, a veteran is eligible for vocational rehabilitation for twelve years following discharge or release from active service. A four-year extension is possible under certain circumstances, and further extensions may be granted for veterans who are seriously disabled, as determined by the DVA. Eligible disabled veterans may receive training up to a total of four years or the equivalent in part-time or a combination of part-time and full-time training. Eligibility for this training is determined by the VA.

Correspondence and Records

Keep a file of every paper the VA sends you. Your dealings with the VA will require patience and persistence; the required degree of each will depend to a large extent on how busy your local VA office is. Invariably, VA personnel are courteous, and they try to be helpful, but processing your claim may take some time.

Burial

Burial is available to any deceased veteran of wartime or peacetime service (other than training) at all national cemeteries having available grave space, except Arlington Cemetery. The veteran must have been discharged under conditions other than dishonorable.

Eligible veterans' dependents may receive a headstone or grave marker without charge, shipped to a designated consignee. The cost of placing the marker in a private ceremony must be borne by the applicant. The VA may partially reimburse (up to the average actual cost of a government headstone or marker) costs incurred by

an applicant acquiring a nongovernment headstone or marker for placement in a cemetery other than a national cemetery.

References

AR 612-10, *Reassignment Processing and Army Sponsorship (and Orientation) Program*

AR 614-30, *Overseas Service*

AR 635-10, *Processing Personnel for Separation*

AR 635-200, *Active Duty Enlisted Administrative Separations*

DA Pamphlet (Pam) 600-5, *Handbook on Retirement Services*

DA Pam 600-8, *Management and Administrative Procedures*

VA Fact Sheet (FS) 1S-1, *Federal Benefits for Veterans and Dependents*

PART III

Quick Reference

11

Army Traditions

Traditions are tied directly to Army history, dating to June 14, 1775, when the Army began to take shape in Pennsylvania, Maryland, and Virginia. In 1776, the Continental Congress established the Board of War and Ordnance, which later became the War Department, now called the Department of the Army. Soldiers are the defenders of the Constitution, and Army traditions, customs, and courtesies are based on this role.

The men and women serving in today's Army are members of a proud profession long in history and rich in heritage and tradition. Soldiers perpetuate Army traditions by being model citizens, by respecting one another, and by showing symbols of national unity such as the U.S. flag.

MILITARY COURTESY

Military courtesy is the respect shown to superiors by subordinates and the mutual respect demonstrated between senior and subordinate personnel. It is basic to military discipline and founded on respect for and loyalty to authority. Military courtesy has an effect on every aspect of military life.

The Salute

The most common military courtesy is the salute. Although many forms of salutes are authorized, depending on the arms you may be carrying and the situation involved, the most common salute is the hand salute. A sharp, crisp salute shows pride in recognizing the comrade in arms; conversely, a sloppy or halfhearted salute shows a lack of pride and is a poor reflection on the soldiers rendering it.

The hand salute is required whenever you recognize an officer. Exceptions are made when the situation so requires—in public transportation (such as buses and planes) or in public places (such as theaters), or when the salute would be impractical (at work, when driving a vehicle, or when actively engaged in athletics). Even though saluting an officer is not required by military regulation when both soldier and officer are in civilian clothes, the soldier who renders this courtesy is following long-standing military tradition.

Every soldier should learn the following guidelines:
- If running, slow to a walk before saluting.
- Always hold your salute until it is returned by the officer.

When the overseas cap, cold weather cap, or beret is worn, the hand salute is to the forehead—except when wearing glasses, when the tip of the fingers should touch the corner of the frame. When the utility cap, camouflage cap, or helmet is worn, the salute is to the visor.

- Never salute while holding an object in your right hand.
- Render the greeting of the day in a firm, crisp voice. A confident "Good morning, sir (or ma'am)" demonstrates pride in yourself.
- In formation, salute only on the command "Present arms." Keep in mind that if you are in charge of a fatigue detail or formation, you are responsible for rendering the courtesies for the group.

The salute itself should be made in one movement, raising the right arm so that the upper arm is horizontal and bending the elbow so that the tip of the forefinger touches the forehead slightly to the right of the right eyebrow. The fingers and thumb should be extended, with the fingers "joined," or touching one another. Neither the palm nor the back of the hand should be visible from a front view.

If you wear eyeglasses, the fingertip of your right hand should touch the point on the glasses where the front frame joins the temple or earpiece. When you are wearing a utility cap or a helmet, your fingertip should touch the visor of the headgear.

On some occasions, you should salute the officer twice. Specifically, if you salute an officer and the officer stays in your general vicinity but does not converse directly with you, all military courtesies have been fulfilled. When the officer spends a few moments talking with you, however, you should salute a second time at the end of the conversation. This custom can be considered a preliminary greeting followed by a farewell.

When a vehicle passes carrying an officer that you recognize, you should render a salute. Likewise, if an official vehicle passes displaying vehicle plates or flags that depict the rank of the passenger, you should salute.

The salute is also used to show respect to the American flag, when the flag passes or during the retreat ceremony.

The best advice on saluting is to render the salute whenever any doubt exists as to whether the salute is actually required. Rendering the salute is a matter of pride.

Correct Use of Titles

Each member of the armed forces has a military rank: private to general in the Army and Marine Corps, airman to general in the Air Force, and seaman to admiral in the Navy. The accompanying chart shows the ranks used in the U.S. armed forces.

Rank becomes a soldier's military title by force of regulation and custom. In official documents, a member's rank or title always accompanies his or her name, and it is also used in conversation. By custom, military titles are used between civilians and the military, just as the custom has been established to use the title "doctor," "professor," or "governor." A person who has earned a military title carries it permanently and, if desired, into retirement.

When addressing another soldier, preface the soldier's last name with his or her rank. "Sergeant Jones," "Sergeant Major Smith," "Private Henderson," "Major Brown" are appropriate means of addressing soldiers conversationally.

When referring to persons not present, always use ranks and names. Use of last names only is disrespectful; use of pay grades (e.g., "I was talking to an O-4" or "It

ENLISTED INSIGNIA OF GRADE

AIR FORCE	ARMY	MARINES	NAVY
Chief Master Sergeant of the Air Force (CMSAF)	Sergeant Major of the Army (SMA)	Sergeant Major of the Marine Corps (SgtMajMC)	Master Chief Petty Officer of the Navy (MCPON)
Chief Master Sergeant (CMSgt) — Command Chief Master Sergeant	Command Sergeant Major (CSM) — Sergeant Major (SGM)	Sergeant Major (SgtMaj) — Master Gunnery Sergeant (MGySgt)	Fleet/Command Master Chief Petty Officer — Master Chief Petty Officer (MCPO)
Senior Master Sergeant (SMSgt) — First Sergeant (E-8)	First Sergeant (1SG) — Master Sergeant (MSG)	First Sergeant (1stSgt) — Master Sergeant (MSgt)	Senior Chief Petty Officer (SCPO)
Master Sergeant (MSgt) — First Sergeant (E-7)	Platoon Sergeant (PSG) or Sergeant First Class (SFC)	Gunnery Sergeant (GySgt)	Chief Petty Officer (CPO)
Technical Sergeant (TSgt)	Staff Sergeant (SSG)	Staff Sergeant (SSgt)	Petty Officer First Class (PO1)
Staff Sergeant (SSgt)	Sergeant (SGT)	Sergeant (Sgt)	Petty Officer Second Class (PO2)
Senior Airman (SrA)	Corporal (CPL) — Specialist (SPC)	Corporal (Cpl)	Petty Officer Third Class (PO3)
Airman First Class (A1C)	Private First Class (PFC)	Lance Corporal (LCpl)	Seaman (Seaman)
Airman (Amn)	Private E-2 (PV2)	Private First Class (PFC)	Seaman Apprentice (SA)
Airman Basic (AB) (no insignia)	Private E-1 (PV1) (no insignia)	Private (Pvt) (no insignia)	Seaman Recruit (SR)

OFFICER INSIGNIA OF GRADE

AIR FORCE	ARMY	MARINES	NAVY
General of the Air Force	General of the Army	(None)	Fleet Admiral
General	General	General	Admiral
Lieutenant General	Lieutenant General	Lieutenant General	Vice Admiral
Major General	Major General	Major General	Rear Admiral (Upper Half)
Brigadier General	Brigadier General	Brigadier General	Rear Admiral (Lower Half)
Colonel	Colonel	Colonel	Captain
Lieutenant Colonel	Lieutenant Colonel	Lieutenant Colonel	Commander
Major	Major	Major	Lieutenant Commander

OFFICER INSIGNIA OF GRADE

AIR FORCE	ARMY	MARINES	NAVY
Captain	Captain	Captain	Lieutenant
First Lieutenant	First Lieutenant	First Lieutenant	Lieutenant Junior Grade
Second Lieutenant	Second Lieutenant	Second Lieutenant	Ensign

(None)	SILVER AND BLACK	SCARLET AND SILVER	
	W-5 · W-4 · W-3 Chief Warrant Officer · Chief Warrant Officer · Chief Warrant Officer	W-5 · W-4 · W-3 Chief Warrant Officer · Chief Warrant Officer · Chief Warrant Officer	W-4 · W-3 Chief Warrant Officer · Chief Warrant Officer
	SILVER AND BLACK	SCARLET AND GOLD	
	W-2 · W-1 Chief Warrant Officer · Warrant Officer	W-2 · W-1 Chief Warrant Officer · Warrant Officer	W-2 · W-1 Chief Warrant Officer · Warrant Officer

COAST GUARD

Coast Guard officers use the same rank insignia as Navy officers. Coast Guard enlisted rating badges are the same as the Navy's for grades E-1 through E-9, but they have silver specialty marks, eagles and stars, and gold chevrons. The badge of the Master Chief Petty Officer of the Coast Guard has a gold chevron and specialty mark, a silver eagle, and gold stars. For all ranks, the gold Coast Guard shield on the uniform sleeve replaces the Navy star.

was an E-7") is unmilitary and degrading. All soldiers have earned their ranks, from the newest private first class to the most senior general; use them accordingly.

Titles of Commissioned Officers

Lieutenants are addressed officially as "Lieutenant." This applies to both first lieutenants and second lieutenants. The same applies to colonels and lieutenant colonels, both of which are addressed officially as "Colonel." Likewise, all generals are addressed as "General," regardless of whether they are brigadier, major, or lieutenant generals.

When not using the rank title, "Sir" is used for all officers. "Ma'am" is used to address women officers when "Sir" would be used with male officers. All chaplains are officially addressed as "Chaplain," regardless of their military rank or professional title. Likewise, doctors are addressed as "Doctor."

Titles of Warrant Officers

The warrant officer (all five grades) officially ranks below second lieutenant and above cadet. He or she is extended the same privileges and respect as a commissioned officer and differs only in that there are certain regulated restrictions on command functions. The warrant officer is the Army's top-grade specialist and is addressed as "Mister" or "Miss," as appropriate. Under informal conditions, a chief warrant officer may be addressed as "Chief."

Titles of Cadets

Cadets of the U.S. Military Academy and the ROTC often serve summer internships with regular units where they experience military life during their training. In written communications and in conversations when they are not present, cadets are addressed as "Cadet." In direct conversation, they are addressed as "Mister" or "Miss."

Titles of Noncommissioned Officers

Sergeants major are addressed as "Sergeant Major." A first sergeant is addressed as "First Sergeant." Other sergeants, regardless of rank, are addressed as "Sergeant." Corporals and specialists are addressed with those titles. Privates first class are addressed with the abbreviation of their rank: PFC. Privates E-1 and E-2 are called "Private." The full titles of all enlisted members are used in official communications.

The Place of Honor

The place of honor is on the right. When a junior walks, rides, or sits with a senior, the junior takes position abreast and to the left of the senior. The junior should walk in step with the senior, step back and allow the senior to be the first to enter a door, and render similar acts of courtesy to the senior. The same applies when riding in a van or sedan. The junior enters the right door first and sits on the left seat; the senior enters second and sits to the right of the junior.

Courtesies to Officers

A number of customs and courtesies for showing respect to officers have evolved over the years. For instance, an officer entering a room is shown courtesy. The first soldier to recognize the officer calls the other personnel in the room to attention, but the soldier does not salute. A salute is rendered indoors only when the soldier is reporting. Soldiers should remain at attention until the officer gives an "at ease" command. Do not call the room to attention if the entering officer is junior in grade to an officer already in the room. Coming to attention in the work environment is required at the start of the day when the commander or senior person first enters the building. It is not required thereafter. If at all practical, however, when an officer not commonly working directly with a soldier is in the work environment and addresses the soldier directly, the soldier should stand.

Outside of the work environment, standing at attention is always expected of the soldier when he or she is talking with an officer. Frequently the officer will instruct the soldier to stand at ease. When the conversation is completed, the soldier should return to attention, salute, and voice an appropriate acknowledgment of the conversation, such as, "Yes, ma'am," or "Good afternoon, sir."

One final recommendation on rendering courtesies to officers: You should regard "requests," "desires," or "wishes" expressed by a commanding officer as orders. Frequently, the wording is softened as a courtesy to the subordinate, but the intent is the same as an order.

Appointments with Commanding Officers

Soldiers are authorized under the Army's "open-door policy" to speak with each commander in their chain of command. It is usually under the most serious conditions that this is done, when a soldier believes that he or she has been wronged or has some important information that the commander may need to know.

Soldiers are usually able to get help with difficulties from offices on post or from their NCO support channel, which is the squad or section leader, the platoon sergeant, or the first sergeant. It is essential, however, that each soldier knows that he or she has the right to appeal directly to the commander for redress of wrongs.

When a soldier believes that a matter requires a commander's attention, he or she should make an appointment to see the commander. The first sergeant can make appointments to see the company commander and can coordinate appointments with the battalion commander by going through the battalion command sergeant major. Just inquire, "May I see the commanding officer?" Often it is appropriate to state the reason, unless the matter is extremely private. Once an appointment is made with the commander, be sure to arrive promptly for the meeting, and render all military courtesies.

TABOOS

Do Not Defame the Uniform. When you wear your uniform, you are acting in a capacity of a member of the government of your country. Do not defame yourself, your uniform, your unit, or your country by behaving badly while wearing the uni-

form or by wearing the uniform in any manner other than as prescribed. Be especially strict with yourself when in foreign countries.

Never Slink Undercover to Avoid Retreat. Now and then, thoughtless people are observed ducking inside a building or undercover just to avoid a retreat ceremony and the moment of respect it includes. Never slink away from an opportunity to pay respect to our flag and our national anthem. The flag and anthem are the symbols of what soldiers and, indeed, the whole Army exist to protect.

Proffer No Excuses. Never make excuses or explain a shortcoming unless an explanation is demanded. The Army demands results. Soldiers of all grades make mistakes, and when that happens, admit the mistake, correct the error if possible, and find out how to do it right the next time. Admitting and bearing the consequences of a mistake will earn you the respect of colleagues and superiors alike.

Never Lie to a Superior. The fourth "rule" of the 1759 Standing Orders for Rogers Rangers says: "Tell the truth about what you see and do. There is an army depending on us for correct information. You can lie all you please when you tell other folks about the Rangers, but don't never lie to a Ranger or officer." This applies to noncommissioned, warrant, and commissioned officers.

Avoid Going over a Superior's Head. It is both a customary and a legal right for soldiers to discuss grievances with their chain of command. Except for the most exceptional cases, it is bad form for a soldier to take a problem or grievance to the battalion commander without first having sought relief with the platoon leader and platoon sergeant or the first sergeant and company commander.

Do Not Associate Inappropriately. It is a long-standing Army tradition that enlisted soldiers do not associate socially with officers. Enlisted soldiers do not gamble, borrow, or lend money, or drink intoxicants with officers. Dating is strictly forbidden. See chapter 4 for more details on this matter.

Never Lean on a Superior's Desk. When called before a senior commissioned or noncommissioned officer, avoid leaning or lolling against the senior's desk. Stand erect until offered a seat.

Never Keep Anyone Waiting. Report at once when notified to do so. Never keep anyone waiting unnecessarily. This is certainly an old Army tradition. The failure of a soldier to appear at his or her place of duty is a punishable offense.

Do Not Carry an Umbrella While in Uniform. There is a long-standing taboo against soldiers in uniform carrying umbrellas. Women soldiers, however, may carry and use umbrellas when in uniform and not in formation. The logic of this taboo for men has never been explained. Accept it on faith.

COURTESY TO THE FLAG
Four common sizes exist for the national flag. The garrison flag, flown on special occasions and holidays, measures 20 by 38 feet. The post flag, flown for general use, is 10 by 19 feet. The storm flag, used in inclement weather, is 5 by 9.5 feet. The last size is that of the grave-decorating flag, which measures 7 by 11 inches.

In addition to the national flag, we can speak of the national color, the national standard, and the national ensign. The national color, carried by dismounted units,

is a 3-by-4-foot flag trimmed on three sides by a golden yellow fringe measuring 2.5 inches in width. The national standard is identical to the national color, except that it is carried by a mechanized, motorized, or mounted unit. The national ensign is a naval term designating a flag of any size used to indicate the nationality of ship personnel. The term flag does not technically refer to colors, standards, or ensigns. Other terms associated with flags are also a part of military tradition. The hoist is the width, the fly is the length, and the truck is the ball at the top of the flagstaff.

Honor the Flag; Honor Yourself
Honoring the nation's flag is an integral part of military customs and courtesies. The hand salute is rendered to show respect when the flag passes in front of a soldier in uniform. You should initiate the salute when the flag is approaching and is within six paces, and then you should hold the salute until the flag has passed six paces. If you are walking past a stationary flag, the same six-pace rule applies. In addition, you should turn your head in the direction of the flag. Soldiers marching in formation render salute only on command. If you are indoors when the flag passes, do not render the hand salute.

A soldier in civilian clothes still honors the flag with a salute, but it is modified to a "civilian salute," with the right hand placed over the heart. If headgear is worn with civilian clothing by a male soldier, the headgear is removed with the right hand and held over the heart; a female soldier in civilian clothing wearing headgear does not remove the headgear but still places her right hand over her heart.

The national flag should never be dipped low as a means of salute or greeting. The only exception is made for military vessels under specific international courtesies. Organizational flags, including the U.S. Army flag, are dipped lower than the national flag during the playing of the national anthem, "To the Color," or a foreign national anthem.

Out of respect for the flag, you should never use it as part of a costume, on a float, or on a vehicle, unless it is displayed on a staff. No lettering of any kind should ever be added to the flag. When a flag is damaged, soiled, or weathered, it should be burned or disposed of in a dignified manner. No portion of the flag should ever be allowed to touch the ground; if it does, the flag is considered soiled. The proper way of folding the flag should be followed exactly (see illustration).

Another means of showing respect to the flag is the Pledge of Allegiance, first adopted by Congress in 1942. The tradition surrounding the pledge specifies that it should be said while standing at attention, with the right hand over the heart. The Pledge of Allegiance is normally not recited in military formations or in military ceremonies.

Raising and Lowering the Flag
Military customs and traditions govern the raising and lowering of the flag, as well. Reveille is the daily military ceremony honoring the flag at the beginning of the day. Retreat is the counterpart when the flag is lowered at the end of the day. Reveille is a bugle call, often recorded and played over a public-address system on

FOLD THE LOWER STRIPED SECTION OF THE FLAG OVER THE BLUE FIELD.

FOLD THE FOLDED EDGE OVER TO MEET THE OPEN EDGE.

START A TRIANGULAR FOLD BY BRINGING THE STRIPED CORNER
OF THE FOLDED EDGE TO THE OPEN EDGE.

FOLD THE OUTER POINT INWARD PARALLEL WITH THE
OPEN EDGE TO FORM A SECOND TRIANGLE.

CONTINUE FOLDING UNTIL THE ENTIRE LENGTH OF THE FLAG IS FOLDED
INTO A TRIANGLE WITH ONLY THE BLUE FIELD AND MARGIN SHOWING.

TUCK THE REMAINING MARGIN INTO THE POCKET FORMED BY THE
FOLDS AT THE BLUE FIELD EDGE OF THE FLAG.

THE PROPERLY FOLDED FLAG SHOULD RESEMBLE A COCKED HAT.

Folding the American Flag

military installations today. The flag is hoisted quickly to the top of the flagpole, beginning on the first note of reveille. Retreat ceremonies, full of traditions, are discussed in the following section.

The flag is sometimes flown at half-staff as a salute to the honored dead. Memorial Day, the last Monday in May, is one occasion when the flag is flown at half-staff from reveille to 1200 hours. A twenty-one-gun salute is then fired before the flag is raised to the top of the staff until retreat. Whenever the flag is to be flown at half-staff, it should first be hoisted to the top of the staff and then lowered to the midpoint. Likewise, before lowering the flag, it should be hoisted the full height of the staff and then lowered and properly folded.

Full details on flag courtesies can be found in AR 840-10.

CUSTOMS

The customs of the service make up the unwritten "common law" of the Army. These customs are rich in tradition, and every soldier should know and observe them.

Retreat Ceremony

The purpose of the retreat ceremony is to honor the national flag at the end of the day. Often the evening gun is fired at the time of retreat so that soldiers throughout the installation will be aware of the ceremony even if they are outside the range of the bugle. The evening gun is also used to mark the end of the work day.

Retreat is not necessarily observed at the same time at each installation. The post commander sets the time of the sounding of both reveille and retreat.

During the retreat ceremony, the evening gun is fired at the last note of retreat. At that time a band, a bugler, or recorded music plays the national anthem or sounds "To the Color." Soldiers begin lowering the flag on the first note of the national anthem or "To the Color" at a rate that ensures that the lowering is completed with the last note of music. Then, following strict customs, the flag is folded and stored until reveille the next morning.

Special respect is rendered to the flag and to the national anthem during retreat by soldiers all across the installation, not merely by those participating directly in the ceremony. Under no circumstances should a soldier run into a building to avoid rendering this courtesy to the flag.

During the playing of the national anthem, soldiers in uniform should stand at attention, facing the flag if visible or the music if the flag is not visible. A salute should be rendered on the first note and held until the final note. The same courtesy applies to "To the Color." When indoors, the salute is omitted. Soldiers in civilian clothing render the "civilian salute" in the same manner as to the flag. Women never remove headgear.

All vehicular traffic should stop during the retreat ceremony. For cars and motorcycles, the driver and passengers should get out of the vehicle and show proper respect. For other vehicles, such as buses or armored vehicles, the ranking

soldier should get out and render the appropriate salute. All other passengers should sit quietly at attention inside the vehicle. Commanding officers of tanks or armored cars can salute from the vehicle.

The same respect should be rendered to the national anthems of friendly nations when they are played during official occasions.

Bugle Calls

In addition to reveille and retreat, several other bugle calls play important roles in military tradition. In general, bugle calls can be divided into four categories: alarm, formation, service (which includes reveille and retreat), and warning.

First call is the first bugle of the day. Considered a warning call, it alerts you that reveille is about to take place and that you will be late if you're not ready within the next few minutes.

The last bugle call of the day is taps, a service call dating back to Civil War days. Taps is traditionally used at military funerals as well, giving the final bugle call for the fallen soldier.

"*To the Color*" is the alternative music used during the retreat ceremony. It signals that the flag is being lowered. You should render the salute during "*To the Color*," as you would during the national anthem. Both are meant to honor the flag.

Tattoo is usually played near 2100 hours and has traditionally been the call for lights-out in fifteen minutes.

Unit Customs

Individual units foster pride and esprit de corps by observing a variety of customs that set them apart from the rest of the Army. Since it is a matter of personal honor for a soldier to know in which battles his or her unit took part, soldiers joining a new unit should learn its history. A quick check with the post library is often the best way to start.

Units perpetuate their history through their organizational properties, mottoes, and insignia. A unit's organizational properties include flags and standards (including battle honors and campaign streamers) and other physical representations of its heritage. Many units claim regimental silver with a unique history as part of their organizational property. For example, the 23rd Infantry's silver bowl was made from the metal of 5,610 combat infantrymen's badges earned by the 23rd's infantrymen during the first eighteen months of combat in Korea. Perhaps the most famous regimental silver property is the 31st Infantry's "Shanghai Bowl," which was presented to the regiment by the citizens of Shanghai after the Boxer Rebellion.

Unit mottoes provide another link with the past. The 19th Infantry's motto, "The Rock of Chickamauga," recalls the regiment's service at the battle of Chickamauga. The 7th Cavalry's motto and song, "Garry Owen," was brought to the regiment in the 1860s by Irish immigrants. The 22nd Infantry's motto "Deeds, Not Words" speaks for itself.

Many units have acquired Infantry's nicknames as a result of past service. The 31st Infantry is known as the "Polar Bears" as a result of duty in northern Russia

after the end of World War I. The 28th Infantry's "Lions of Cantigny" recalls the regiment's service at the first American offensive battle in World War I.

Unit insignia also embody unit traditions. For example, shoulder-sleeve insignia, first authorized during World War I, were originally conceived to foster esprit de corps and heighten the individual soldier's identification with his unit. The 81st Infantry Division was the first division to develop a sleeve insignia, that of a black wildcat on a circular path. The idea was so well received by the headquarters of the American Expeditionary Force that Gen. John J. Pershing directed the other divisions to develop their own distinctive cloth patches.

The Army Song

Another tradition that literally brings soldiers to their feet is the Army song. When you hear it being sung or being played, the appropriate action is to stand at attention. The melody is that of the "Caisson Song," composed in the early 1900s by then Lt. Edmund L. Gruber, who later was promoted to brigadier general. But the words for "The Army Goes Rolling Along" were selected much later. The eight-year process began in 1948 with a nationwide contest to create an official Army song. Within four years, the Army had also enlisted the aid of several music composers, publishers, and recording studios. Their joint efforts produced the new lyrics, set to the music of the old "Caisson Song." "The Army Goes Rolling Along" became the official Army song when it was dedicated on Veterans Day, November 11, 1956, at Army installations throughout the world.

The Army Goes Rolling Along

Verse:	March along, sing our song with the army of the free. Count the brave, count the true Who have fought to victory. We're the Army and proud of our name! We're the Army and proudly proclaim:
1st Chorus:	First to fight for the right And to build the nation's might, and THE ARMY GOES ROLLING ALONG. Proud of all we have done, Fighting till the battle's won, and THE ARMY GOES ROLLING ALONG.
Refrain:	Then it's hi! hi! hey! The Army's on its way, Count off the cadence loud and strong: (two! three!) For where'er we go, you will always know That THE ARMY GOES ROLLING ALONG.

2nd Chorus: Valley Forge, Custer's ranks,
                 San Juan Hill and Patton's tanks,
                 And the Army went rolling along.
                 Minutemen from the start,
                 Always fighting from the heart,
                 And the Army keeps rolling along.

Refrain: Then it's hi! hi! hey!
                 The Army's on its way,
                 Count off the cadence loud and strong: (two! three!)
                 For where'er we go, you will always know
                 That THE ARMY GOES ROLLING ALONG.

3rd Chorus: Men in rags, men who froze,
                 Still that Army met its foes,
                 And the Army went rolling along.
                 Faith in God, then we're right
                 And we'll fight with all our might
                 As the Army keeps rolling along.

Refrain: Then it's hi! hi! hey!
                 The Army's on its way,
                 Count off the cadence loud and strong:
                 (two! three!)
                 For where'er we go, you will always know
                 That THE ARMY GOES ROLLING ALONG.
                 (Keep it rolling!)
                 And THE ARMY GOES ROLLING ALONG.

12

Assignments

For soldiers who read the *Army Times* or *Soldiers* magazine for any glimmer of changes to Army personnel policy while waiting for the new regulation updates to arrive in the mail, there is now a new Internet site at *www.hrc.army.mil/site/Active/ enlist/ENLIST.htm*. On the enlisted management Web page is everything an inquiring soldier wants to know in real time and up to date. Instead of waiting months to find out if your DA Form 4187, *Personnel Action Request*, for reassignment has gone through, call the IVRS, send an e-mail, use the fax, or, even better, sign on to the Assignment Satisfaction Key, all of which are explained below.

COMMUNICATING WITH HUMAN RESOURCES COMMAND

The U.S. Army Human Resources Command (HRC) continues a series of initiatives designed to increase enlisted soldiers' participation in managing their careers. What was once paper-intensive and not very responsive is now, with automation, very responsive to those soldiers who care about their assignments.

To help soldiers communicate better with their career managers, the Enlisted Personnel Management Directorate (EPMD) employs five tools. These initiatives include an Interactive Voice Response Telephone System (IVRS), expanded e-mail capabilities, high-speed fax machines, mail-grams, and a pocket reference information card that lists telephone numbers, e-mail addresses, and other data valuable to soldiers wanting to help manage their careers.

The cornerstone of the new system is the Web site on the Internet at *www.hrc .army.mil/indexflash.asp;* although IVRS, which is an automated voice response telephone system that provides soldiers with career information twenty-four hours a day, remains available for those without Internet access. Soldiers can activate the IVRS by dialing (800) FYI-EPMD or DSN 221-3763. The 800 number is available only in the continental United States. To use the IVRS system, enter your Social Security number and then follow the menu options that will let you know if you are on assignment or scheduled to attend an Army school. It will also provide topical information on retention, recruiting, drill sergeant, Special Forces, Ranger, compassionate reassignments, Married Army Couples Program, Exceptional Family Member Program, and separations.

EPMD also encourages you to use e-mail to contact your branch. Inquiries concerning the status of personnel actions, future schooling, or assignments are exam-

ples of typical information exchanges that can be conducted twenty-four hours a day. Soldiers can also correspond with their career managers by using fax machines. Soldiers and personnel service centers can save time by faxing communications directly to the desired career branch within EPMD for processing. The EPMD e-mail, fax, and mail addresses are shown below.

Points of Contact
You can contact the Enlisted Personnel Management Directorate in the following ways:

Telephone
> Interactive Voice Response System (IVRS)
> 1-800-FYI-EPMD (CONUS)
> 1-800-394-3763 (CONUS)
> (703) 325-3763 (Commercial)
> DSN 221-2763

Mail
> U.S. Army Human Resources Command
> Attention: Your branch office symbol (Column 2 in below table)
> 2461 Eisenhower Avenue
> Alexandria, VA 22331

e-mail
> Your branch e-mail ID (column 3 in below table) @*hoffman.army.mil*

Fax
> DSN 221-XXXX
> (703) 325-XXXX (commercial)
> Your branch fax extension (column 4 in below table)
> Fax
> DSN 221-XXXX
> (703) 325-XXXX (commercial)
> Your branch fax extension (column 4 in below table)

ASSIGNMENT SATISFACTION KEY (ASK)—SOLDIER ASSIGNMENT MODULE (SAM)
ASK—SAM provides virtually instant capability for your assignment manager and professional development NCO to identify all open requirements you may be eligible for, provides the capabilities to hone in on the most eligible soldiers, and also identifies all volunteers for a specific assignment location.

Accessible from the HRC Web site and/or a soldier's Army Knowledge Online (AKO) account, the futuristic vision of soldiers making all their own assignments is

ENLISTED ASSIGNMENT CONTACT INFORMATION

1 Assignment Branch	2 Office Symbol	3 E-mail ID	4 Fax Extension
Infantry	EPK-I	EPINF	4880
Air Defense Artillery	EPK-A	EPADA	4664
Field Artillery	EPK-F	EPFA	4533
Special Forces	EPK-S	EPSF	4510
Armor	EPK-R	EPAR	4683
Engineer	EPL-E	EPENGR	4307
MP	EPL-M	EPMP	4304
MI	EPL-M	EPINTELL	4304
Language	EPL-M	EPLANG	4304
Signal	EPL-S	EPSIG	4306
Aviation	EPL-T	EPAVN	4308
Transportation	EPL-T	EPTRANS	4308
Adjutant General	EPM-A	EPAG	5836
Health Services	EPM-H	EPHS	6402
QM/Chemical	EPM-L	EPQMC	4521
Ordnance	EPM-O	EPORD	6555
CSM/SGM Office	EPZ-E	EPCSMSGM	4694
Retention/Reclass	EPR	TAPCEPR	3565

slowly becoming a reality. This innovation provides the soldier with an automated tool to quickly update his or her preferences and contact information via the Internet through their respective AKO account. During the "dream sheet" days you had many assignment locations to choose from but little chance of being assigned to where you asked, unless you were able to correspond with your assignment manager. Today the majority of assignment locations are available to you to select, and those who decline to submit a preference will be assigned according to the needs of the Army. Bottom line, the ASK provides soldiers the capability to post assignment preferences directly onto the Total Army Personnel Database. This system is expected one day to eliminate the paper- and labor-intensive DA Form 4187. The Assignment Selection Key is available through the HRC Web site at *www.hrc.army.mil/indexflash.asp.* Use your Army Knowledge Online (AKO) account password to gain access, which will ensure that your personal data remains secure.

Plus 2 Personal Life Cycle Unit Selection System
Plus 2 supports life cycle management and unit-focused stability by providing a Web-based means for soldiers to volunteer for Units of Action (UAs). By using volunteers to maximize soldier and unit cohesion, this reduces requirements for

nonvolunteer permanent change of stations (PCSs). The Web site is at *isdrad16 .hoffman.army.mil/HRCSoldierPreferenceWeb/*. As above, log in using your AKO account password.

When you log into the system, you are shown requisitions for which you are eligible. From the list you select and reserve your unit and duty position. Although career managers still approve assignment requests based on professional development considerations, indications are that if you are able to make an assignment selection you are virtually assured of their desired assignment.

THE ENLISTED PERSONNEL ASSIGNMENT SYSTEM

The primary goal of the enlisted personnel assignment system is to satisfy the personnel requirements of the Army.

Secondary goals are to:

- To place soldiers in positions that require skills, knowledge, and abilities as shown by their primary military occupational specialty (PMOS), secondary military occupational specialty (SMOS), or additionally awarded military occupational specialty (AMOS).
- To provide policies on personnel utilization that will strengthen and broaden MOS qualifications and prepare soldiers for career progression, greater responsibility, and diversity of assignment.

First-term soldiers with initial enlistments of three years or less will receive only one assignment before expiration term of service (ETS) following basic and skill training. If required to serve in an unaccompanied hardship tour area outside the continental United States (OCONUS), they will then be given no more than two assignments in different locations. Those with enlistments of more than three but less than four years will receive, following basic and skill training, no more than one CONUS assignment or two OCONUS assignments. Soldiers with enlistments of four or more years, following basic and skill training, will serve no more than two assignments in different locations, regardless of the tour length.

Consistent with Army needs, soldiers will remain as long as possible at their Continental U.S. (CONUS) duty stations. The Army's time-on-station (TOS) requirement for CONUS is forty-eight months; for OCONUS it is the length of the prescribed tour. Soldiers complete the forty-eight-month TOS/tour requirement unless operational or training necessities are so overriding that they must be reassigned earlier. There is no statutory limitation on the amount of time soldiers may remain overseas, just as there is no statutory limit as to how long a soldier remain at a post. Except for CONUS requirements that are filled from OCONUS returnees who are immediately available, qualified volunteers are considered first for all assignments.

Soldiers may submit a request for reassignment before completion of TOS requirements, but they must complete minimum TOS requirements at their present duty station before movement. When possible, soldiers will remain on station for the maximum number of years possible consistent with Army requirements.

Civility in War

NEW MANNING STRATEGIES

During the next years, the Army will continue combat operations while transitioning to a unit-focused manning strategy. This unit-focused strategy is key to the Army as it transitions to an expeditionary force with combat readiness and unit cohesion in deploying forces as the primary objectives. The primary assumption is that soldiers and units will continue one-year assignments/rotations to Korea, Iraq, Afghanistan, and Kosovo for the near future. The foundation of the strategy is to retain unit integrity for the maximum period possible. Force stabilization will increase unit readiness and deployability by reducing turbulence and increasing stability so soldiers and units can train, deploy, fight, win, and return together.

Soldiers' assignment cycles will be aligned with the operational cycles of their units, making them more deployable and combat ready. The intent under the life cycle manning method is that all soldiers assigned to life cycle-manned units during the reset period will have thirty-six months' retainability with an NCO level fill of between 70 to 80 percent with the remaining 20 to 30 percent being filled using grade substitution. The Noncommissioned Officer Education System (NCOES) and other leader development opportunities and reenlistment options will occur only during their unit's reset period.

Stabilization

After units redeploy from operational deployments, soldiers will be stabilized for ninety days. Exceptions to the ninety-day period will be minimized and where possible be limited to soldiers volunteering for schools, reassignment, or separating from active service. At the conclusion of their initial stabilization period, unit personnel will begin a formalized reset period of sixty days, during which time they will be refitted and remanned.

The intent during the reset period of a life cycle–manned unit is to bring in new soldiers to replace soldiers scheduled to ETS, retire, or PCS; minimize HQDA directed departures; and retain as many soldiers already assigned to the unit as possible. Some soldiers with recent combat troop experience, however, will be transferred to fill other high priority assignments. Their knowledge and experience, as lessons learned and promulgated across the Army, will significantly enhance combat operations. Postdeployment assignments will be made with a view to future operations to minimize turbulence and maximize stability and predictability. The intent is to minimize use of "stop loss/stop move" for all operational missions. Stabilizing and retaining soldiers in their recently redeployed units is the optimal solution.

Under individual stabilization, soldiers assigned to selected installations in CONUS will serve extended tours at the same duty station. The majority of enlisted soldiers assigned to CONUS installations housing large combat formations such as brigades/regiments, divisions, support groups and corps, can expect to be assigned at the installation for extended periods. Soldiers will be reassigned based on the following prioritized criteria: needs of the Army, leader development, and soldier preference.

Stop Loss

The Stop Loss program is authorized by statute and allows the military services to retain trained, experienced, and skilled manpower by suspending certain laws, regulations, and policies that allow separations from active duty, including retirement. Those affected by the order generally cannot voluntarily retire or leave the service as long as Reserves are called to active duty or until relieved by proper authority. There are two types of Stop Loss that apply to soldiers in the reserve components: unit stop loss and skill-based stop loss. Currently, the only stop loss policy in effect is reserve component (RC) unit stop loss.

Normally, the local military personnel office (MILPO), in coordination with the unit, compares authorized and projected positions with current assigned strength and known or projected gains and losses to determine the requirements for assignments. Requisitions are then prepared for these requirements and submitted to the commanding general, Army Human Resources Command (HRC), in Alexandria, Virginia. On receipt, HRC edits and validates the requisitions. It is the responsibility of the requisitioning unit not to over- or under-requisition and to resolve any discrepancy before submitting the validated requisition for processing. Soldiers become available to be assigned against these requisitions for a variety of reasons. Soldiers

who enlist in the Army are available for assignment on completion of training and award of an MOS. Others are available when they have done one of the following:

- Volunteered for reassignment.
- Completed an overseas tour of duty.
- Completed schooling or training.
- Completed a stabilized tour of duty.
- Completed normal time on station in the continental United States (CONUS) for a given MOS ("turnaround time" varies by MOS).

Homebase and Advance Assignment Program

The Homebase and Advance Assignment Program (HAAP) is governed by AR 614-200-9-1 and AR 600-200, chapter 2, section VIII. Participation in the HAAP is optional. The HAAP is designed to reduce permanent change of station (PCS) costs and the number of PCS moves by soldiers and their families. The program has two options. Homebase assignment projects the enlisted soldier to return to the same installation upon completion of a twelve-month dependent-restricted short tour. Advanced assignment projects the enlisted soldier to be assigned to a new duty station upon completion of a twelve-month dependent-restricted short tour.

Only sergeants through master sergeants assigned to twelve-month dependent-restricted short tour areas are authorized to participate in the HAAP. The HAAPs will not be given to enlisted soldiers who voluntarily elect to serve a twelve-month "all others" tour when assigned to an accompanied tour area.

Compassionate Assignments

AR 614-200 establishes specific policies governing individual requests submitted by soldiers for a PCS or deletion from assignment instructions. A soldier may submit a request for any of the following reasons:

Extreme Family Problems

These are divided into problems that are temporary and can be resolved in one year and those that are not expected to be resolved in one year. Soldiers making compassionate requests are not exempt from PCS moves or temporary duty (TDY) while waiting for resolution.

Sole Surviving Son or Daughter

AR 614-200 S-7 and DA Pam 600-8 apply. The sole surviving son or daughter of a family that has suffered the loss of the father, mother, or one or more sons or daughters in the military service will not be required to serve in combat. Soldiers who become sole surviving sons or daughters after their enlistment may request discharge under AR 635-200. A soldier may waive entitlement to assignment limitations, whether entitlement was based on his or her own application or the request of his or her immediate family.

Married Army Couples Program
AR 614-209 and AR 614-30 apply. Army requirements and readiness goals are paramount when considering personnel for assignment. Married Army couples desiring joint assignment to establish a common household (joint domicile) must request such assignment. The assignment desires of soldiers married to other soldiers are fully considered. Married Army couples must be enrolled in the Total Army Personnel Database (TAPDB) to be considered for joint assignment. Enrollment is a simple process of verifying that two soldiers are married to each other and having this information transmitted from the servicing Personnel Service Center (PSC) to the TAPDB. A separate transaction is required for each spouse. Once enrolled, both soldiers will be continuously considered for joint assignments. In 2005, of the 20,000 plus enlisted soldiers enrolled in the program, approximately 75 percent of those enrolled in the Married Army Couples Program (MACP) were serving in joint domicile assignments

Army Exceptional Family Member Program (AR 608-75)
The Exceptional Family Member Program (EFMP) is based on Public Law 94-142, which entitles handicapped children to free education and all medically related services in pursuit of education. The EFMP includes all family members with special medical and educational needs.

Soldiers enroll through their local Army medical treatment facility. The military sponsor and the attending medical or educational specialist complete enrollment forms. When HRC nominates a soldier enrolled in the EFMP for assignment, the assignment manager coordinates with the gaining command to determine if needed medical services are available. When services are not available, HRC considers alternative assignment locations based on existing assignment priorities or sends the soldier in an unaccompanied status.

Assignment of Women Soldiers
Women are authorized to serve in all types of units except those battalion sized or smaller that have a routine mission to engage in direct combat or that collocate routinely with units assigned a direct combat mission. Female soldiers are assigned in accordance with Direct Combat Probability Coding (DCPC) and are restricted from filling a position with a DCPC of P1 (closed to women). All table of organizational elements (TOE) positions are assigned either a DCPC code of P1 or P2 (open to women). Table of distribution and allowance (TDA) positions are gender neutral.

Exchange Assignments
DA Pam 600-8 and AR 614-200-5-6 apply. For mutual convenience, CONUS-assigned soldiers may request an exchange assignment with a soldier within CONUS; a soldier assigned overseas may request an exchange assignment with a soldier within his or her same overseas command. DA Pam 600-8 contains detailed guidance for preparing and processing requests for an exchange assignment. The

Army Times publishes lists of soldiers who desire to contact others to arrange for exchange assignments.

Sometimes changes in enlisted assignments are necessary to meet the needs of the Army. When this occurs, HRC offers the enlisted soldier a selection of three locations for a new assignment.

CAREER DEVELOPMENT PROGRAM ASSIGNMENTS

A career development program is a system of intensive management of selected MOSs or CMFs. Career development programs are established to ensure that there are enough highly trained and experienced soldiers to fill positions that require unique or highly technical skills. To develop soldiers with the required proficiency, career fields within each program often require the following:

- Frequent movement from one job to another to gain required experience.
- An above-average frequency of advanced training.
- Lengthy or frequent training periods.

Unless otherwise stated in AR 614-200, volunteers for a career development program should submit applications on DA Form 4187, using DA Pam 600-8 for detailed application procedures. In applying for career programs and related training, applicants should consider the prerequisites listed in DA Pam 351-4 for the appropriate course of instruction.

Chapter 7 of AR 614-200 contains the minimum requirements (subject to change) for each career program. Attaining the prerequisites does not automatically ensure entry into a career program. The appropriate career management branch selects the best-qualified soldiers for a career program.

Waivers are not granted for remaining service requirements for formal training. Waivers for other eligibility requirements or selection standards are considered unless otherwise stated in AR 614-200. Waivers cannot be implied. Each must be specifically requested. In the application for entry into the program or training requested, the applicant must include the reason for the waiver.

Career development programs include the following:

- Intelligence Career Program.
- Explosive Ordnance Disposal Career Program.
- Technical Escort Career Program.
- Army Bandsman Career Program.

ASSIGNMENT TO SPECIFIC ORGANIZATIONS AND DUTY POSITIONS

AR 614-200 contains specific policies and procedures for nomination, evaluation, selection, and assignment of enlisted soldiers to the following:

- Presidential support activities.
- Observer controller at combat training centers.
- U.S. Military Entrance Processing Command.
- Enlisted aides to general officers.
- Inspector General positions.

- Drill Sergeant Program.
- Assignment as instructors at uniformed service schools.
- Assignment to international and overseas joint headquarters, U.S. Military Missions, Military Assistance Advisory Groups (MAAGs), and Joint U.S. Military Advisory Groups (JUSMAGs).
- Assignment to certain Defense and departmental-level organizations and agencies.
- Reserve component or ROTC duty.
- Food inspection specialists.
- Selection and assignment of first sergeants.

OVERSEAS SERVICE

Many Americans work very hard all their lives, and then in their declining years, when they at last have the leisure and money to travel, they see the world. Soldiers not only see the world when they are young, but they also have the unique opportunity to live among foreign peoples for extended periods and learn about their cultures from firsthand experience.

There are two ways that you can approach your first overseas tour. You can go kicking and screaming and spend your time isolated in the American community of some foreign country, never venturing very far outside the cocoon of familiar surroundings, counting the dreary days until you rotate; or you can approach foreign service as a thrilling adventure to be experienced to the fullest, and you can be a goodwill ambassador for the United States of America.

Running afoul of the law in a foreign country can be very dangerous. In countries where a Status of Forces Agreement (SOFA) exists between the U.S. government and the foreign government, soldiers may be tried for offenses under the laws of the country concerned.

Most major overseas commands operate orientation programs for newly arrived personnel in the command. These courses attempt to expose soldiers to the culture in which they will be living in order to lessen the effect of culture shock that some people experience the first time they encounter a foreign society. When you receive overseas assignment instructions, it would be a good idea for you (and your spouse, if you have one) to study the language of the country to which you will be going. Some special assignments require extensive formal language training, but most Army installations do provide some language instruction for soldiers and their dependents who are bound overseas. Learning the rudiments of a foreign language can be fun, and speaking a foreign language is a valuable skill to have once you arrive at your overseas duty station.

Standards of living overseas vary, depending on the country. Germany's standard of living is very high, and your money will not go far there; other countries are beset with substantial economic problems, and the standards of living in those places can sometimes be so low that only the very rich can afford luxuries that are considered common in the United States, and you won't be able to afford them at local prices.

As with everything else, what you get out of your situation is what you make of it. And remember that your overseas tour will not last forever; sooner or later, you must leave to come home. Emotional attachments are very hard to break off, so be warned if you establish any kind of relationship with a foreign man or woman. What usually starts as a casual, fun-filled lark, a pleasant way to pass the time, frequently develops into a serious involvement. If it is not consummated by marriage, its termination can be an emotional trauma that will be painful for both of you.

Policies

The chief consideration in selecting a soldier for service overseas is that a valid authorization exists for his or her military qualifications. Equitable distribution is made, within a given MOS and grade, of overseas duty assignments, considering both desirable and undesirable locations. All reasonable efforts are made to minimize periods of forced separations and any adverse effects of overseas service encountered by soldiers and their families.

Between overseas tours, with the exception of Hawaii, soldiers are assigned in their sustaining base for at least twelve months on station. Consistent with Army needs, soldiers are retained as long as possible in CONUS. Among individuals who have previous overseas service, those with the earliest date of return from overseas normally will be selected first. Subject to personnel requirements in short-tour areas, soldiers who have completed a normal overseas service tour in a short-tour area will not be assigned to another short-tour area on their next overseas assignment.

Kinds of Overseas Tours

Personnel accompanied or joined by their dependents at government expense must have enough remaining service to serve the tour prescribed for those "with dependents."

Army personnel married to each other and serving in the same overseas area serve tours in accordance with AR 614-30. They must extend or reenlist, if necessary, to have enough time in service to serve the tour prescribed by the table before compliance with orders directing movement.

The "all others" tour is served by soldiers who meet the following criteria:
- Elect to serve overseas without dependents.
- Are serving in an area where dependents are not permitted.
- Do not have dependents (this rule does not apply in areas where personnel who have dependents must serve "with dependents" tours).
- Are divorced or legally separated and pay child support.

Tours are normally the same for all personnel at the same station. Where there are personnel of more than one service, the service having the main interest (normally, the most personnel in the area) develops a recommended tour length that is coordinated with the other services. Tour length may vary within any given country or area, depending on the specific duty station. AR 614-30 lists overseas duty tours for military personnel.

Short-Tour and Long-Tour Eligibility

AR 614-30 chapters 2 and 9 apply. Personnel are assigned to short-tour overseas assignments according to the following priorities:

- Volunteers who have completed a minimum of twelve months' time on station or are not otherwise stabilized.
    (1) Intertheater consecutive overseas tour (COT) volunteers after completion of current outside continental United States (OCONUS) tour.
    (2) From CONUS
        (a) HQDA approved volunteers.
        (b) No previous OCONUS service.
        (c) No previous short tour and last outside continental United States (OCONUS) assignment was a "with-dependents" tour.
        (d) Last OCONUS assignment was a "with-dependents" tour in a long-tour area and has previously served a short tour.
        (e) Last OCONUS tour was a short tour in accompanied status.
        (f) No previous short tour and last assignment was an "all-others" tour.
        (g) Serving in a long-tour area of Alaska or Hawaii and completed the prescribed thirty-six-month tour.
        (h) In CONUS and last OCONUS tour was a short-tour in an unaccompanied status.

Deferments and Deletions

AR 614-30 chapter 6 applies. Because of the possible adverse effect on command operational readiness, granting of deferments for overseas service is strictly controlled and held to an absolute minimum. The need of the service is the major determining factor in granting deferments.

Normally, once an application has been submitted, the soldier will be retained at the home station, pending a final decision. When a soldier requests deferment and it results in his or her having less remaining time in service than the length of the prescribed tour, the individual will continue on the overseas assignment. Unless he or she voluntarily reenlists or extends to be eligible to complete the prescribed tour, the individual must sign a counseling statement, which is a bar to reenlistment. Applications are initiated by the individual concerned on DA Form 4187.

The following conditions normally warrant deferments or deletion from overseas assignment:

- A recent severe psychotic episode involving a spouse or child after a soldier receives assignment instructions.
- The soldier's children being made wards of the court or being placed in an orphanage or a foster home because of family separation. This separation must be because of military service and not because of neglect or misconduct on the part of the soldier.
- Adoption cases in which the home study (deciding whether a child is to be placed) has been completed and a child is scheduled to be placed in the soldier's home within ninety days.

- Illness of a family member (see AR 614-30 for details).
- Terminal illness of a family member where death is anticipated within one year.
- Death of a soldier's spouse or child after receipt of assignment instructions.
- Prolonged hospitalization of more than ninety days when the soldier's presence is deemed essential to resolve associated problems.
- Documented rape of the soldier's spouse or child within nintety days of the scheduled movement date, when the soldier's presence is deemed essential to resolve associated problems.
- Selection to attend the Basic or Advanced NCO Courses or OCS, where attendance will delay overseas travel more than ninety days.
- Enrollment in the Drug and Alcohol Abuse Residential Rehabilitation Treatment Program.
- Pregnancy or related complications exceeding ninety days.

Curtailment of Overseas Tours
AR 614-30, chapter 8, applies. Overseas commanders may curtail overseas tours when military requirements so dictate. They may also disapprove curtailment requests.

When curtailments of more than sixty days are considered, commanders must recommend curtailments and request reassignment instructions from HRC as early as possible, not later than forty-five days before the departure date. Curtailing a tour must not cause an emergency requisition to fill the vacated position.

Overseas commanders may, at any time, curtail the tour of a soldier who has discredited or embarrassed or may discredit or embarrass the United States or jeopardize the commander's mission. They may also curtail tours when family members are moved to the United States because of criminal activity, a health problem, or death in the immediate family living with the sponsor. In exceptional cases, the commander may waive advance Headquarters Department of the Army (HQDA) coordination and attach the soldier to the nearest personnel assistance point for issue of PCS orders. These exceptions are as follows: potential defectors, extreme personal hardship, and expeditious removal of a soldier in the best interests of the service (for example, when a soldier causes an embarrassment to the command in its relationship with a foreign government).

Pregnant soldiers are not curtailed from their overseas tours solely because of pregnancy. If noncombatant evacuation is ordered, however, pregnant soldiers who have reached the seventh month of pregnancy will be curtailed and evacuated. Such a curtailment does not, however, preclude the solder's being reassigned overseas again after completion of the pregnancy and discharge from inpatient status.

Change in Overseas Tour Status
Change of tour requests are normally approved, provided the government has not expended funds for shipment of household goods or movement of dependents, and the gaining command has concurred with the change. Additionally, a soldier may be

required to extend or reenlist to meet tour length requirements. Requests are normally not favorably considered if the government has expended funds for shipment of household goods or movement of family members. Exceptions to policy are considered under extenuating circumstances. Army Regulation 55-46, *Travel of Dependents and Accompanied Military and Civilian Personnel to, from, or between Overseas Areas*, the Joint Travel Regulation (JFTR), and AR 614-30, *Overseas Service*, are the applicable regulations.

Consecutive Outside Continental U.S. Tours

Regulatory guidance pertaining to consecutive overseas tours (COTs) is found in AR 614-30, *Overseas Service*, chapter 4. Soldiers who volunteer to serve two full consecutive OCONUS tours are authorized government-paid travel for themselves and command-sponsored family members to leave locations equal to the distance to the soldier's home of record. Soldiers may travel greater distances provided they pay the additional travel costs. The leave location is not restricted to CONUS and must normally be between the two tours. The government-paid travel is the only benefit associated with a COT; any leave used is chargeable to the soldier.

To be eligible for a COT, soldiers must complete their current prescribed tour plus any voluntary extensions and agree to serve another full tour plus leave and travel time between tours. COTs fall into two categories: OCONUS tours that involve a permanent change of station and OCONUS tours that do not involve a PCS.

Concurrent and Deferred Travel

Soldiers being transferred overseas should seek command sponsorship of their family members, as well as concurrent or deferred travel for family members. Sponsorship of soldiers' families is dependent upon the availability of government or economy housing, and, if housing will be available within 60 days, concurrent travel is normally authorized. If housing will not be available until between 61 days and 140 days, deferred travel is normally authorized.

SPONSORSHIP

Every new assignment raises questions and concerns for the soldier and his or her family. The sponsorship program (AR 600-8-8) assists soldiers and their dependents in establishing themselves at a new duty station and guides soldiers while they adjust to their new work environment.

A "sponsor" is an individual designated by name at a gaining organization to assist incoming members and their families in making a smooth transition into the unit and community environment. Sponsors should be a grade equal to or higher than that of the incoming soldier; be the same sex, marital status, and MOS; be familiar with the surrounding area; and not have received assignment instructions.

Commanders are responsible for ensuring that sponsors are provided enough time from their duties to help new soldiers. In addition, commanders arrange trans-

portation so that sponsors can meet new members and their dependents at the point of arrival and bring them back to the unit (overseas only).

The incoming soldier should answer the sponsor's letter immediately and do the following:

- Inform the sponsor of his or her time, date, and point of arrival (including flight numbers). Any changes to the itinerary should be reported to the sponsor immediately.
- Provide the sponsor a unit mailing address and telephone number (commercial or DSN).
- Inform the sponsor of the expected departure date from the losing duty station.
- If desired, provide the sponsor with leave addresses and telephone numbers.

Orientation Program

Commanders and supervisors are responsible for conducting a thorough and timely orientation to start new arrivals off properly. These orientations should make the new soldier feel needed and wanted and instill in him or her the motivation to contribute to the unit's mission.

13

Promotion
and Reduction

Nearly all soldiers want to get promoted, but not all do. Many times this is through neglect on their part; sometimes it's through a leader's neglect. On the whole, soldiers control their own destiny.

Soldiers are recommended for promotion only after they develop the skills, knowledge, and behavior to perform the duties and assume the responsibility of the next higher grade. Generally, if soldiers do well in their present grades, they will work well in the next higher grades.

By using standard promotion scoring forms with predetermined promotion point factors, corporals, specialists, and sergeants can measure whether they qualify for promotion. They can set goals to increase their promotion potential. They can then judge their qualifications when compared with those of other soldiers in their MOS. The Army promotes soldiers who are qualified and who will accept Army-wide assignments.

Commanders at the grades indicated may promote soldiers, subject to authority and delegation of responsibility by higher commanders.

- *Specialist (SPC) and below.* Unit commanders may advance or promote assigned soldiers to private E-2, private first class, and SPC. When soldiers are fully eligible, promotions to PVT, PFC, and SPC are automatic unless the commander submits DA Form 4187 blocking the promotion no later than the twentieth of the preceding month.
- *Sergeant (SGT) and staff sergeant (SSG).* Field-grade commanders lieutenant colonel or higher may promote soldiers attached or assigned or on temporary duty (TDY) to their command or installation.
- *Sergeant first class (SFC) and above.* Headquarters, Department of the Army.
- *Hospitalized soldiers.* Commanders of medical facilities may promote hospitalized soldiers to SSG and below.
- *Students.* Commandants and commanders of training installations and activities.
- *Posthumous promotion.* Headquarters, Department of the Army.

PROMOTION OF PRIVATES TO PRIVATE FIRST CLASS

Active Army personnel are advanced to the rank of private E-2 when they have completed six months of active federal service, unless it is stopped by the commander. National Guard and Army Reserve personnel on initial active-duty training are advanced to private E-2 when they complete six months of service from the day of entry, unless it is stopped by the commander. To recognize outstanding performance, local commanders may advance to private E-2 a limited numbers of soldiers who have at least four but less than six months' active service.

Under normal conditions, unit commanders may advance soldiers to private first class who qualify with twelve months' time in service and four months' time in grade. To recognize outstanding performance, unit commanders may advance soldiers with a minimum of six months in service and two months' time in grade (which may be waived).

PROMOTION TO SPECIALIST OR CORPORAL

Normally, commanders may advance to specialist or corporal those soldiers who meet the following qualifications:

- Twenty-six months in service.
- Six months' time in grade, waiverable to three months.
- Security clearance appropriate for the MOS in which promoted; advancement may be based on granting an interim security clearance.

To recognize outstanding performance, commanders may advance soldiers on an accelerated basis, providing advancements do not cause more than 20 percent of the total number of assigned specialists and corporals to have less than twenty-four months' time in service, and providing that soldiers meet the following qualifications:

- Eighteen months in service.
- Three months' time in grade.
- Security clearance required for the MOS in which advanced; may be based on an interim clearance.

PROMOTION TO SERGEANT AND STAFF SERGEANT

Field-grade commanders and Department of the Army both have a hand in promotions to SGT and SSG. The normal sequence from recommendation to promotion to SGT and SSG follows.

1. *The soldier meets requirements.* The time-in-service requirement for attaining eligibility for promotion to SGT is thirty-six months active federal service for the primary zone and eighteen months for the secondary zone. The time-in-grade requirement for attaining eligibility for promotion to SGT is eight months as a corporal/specialist (CPL/SPC), waiverable to four months for those recommended in the secondary zone. Soldiers in the secondary zone may appear before a promotion board with sixteen months time-in-service and four months time-in-grade as of the first day of the board month.

The time-in-service requirement for attaining eligibility for promotion to SSG is eighty-four months active federal service for the primary zone and forty-eight months for the secondary zone. The time-in-grade requirement for attaining eligibility for promotion to SSG is ten months as a SGT, waiverable to five months for those recommended in the secondary zone. Soldiers in the secondary zone may be boarded with forty-six months time-in-service and five months time-in-grade as of the first day of the board month.

Once a soldier reaches primary zone eligibility, the commander must either recommend that he or she appear before a promotion board, or, if a soldier is fully eligible but not recommended, complete the DA Form 3355, *Promotion Worksheet*, with counseling documents and forward them to the promotion authority for final decision. After forty-eight months service and twelve months in the grade of E4, soldiers are automatically put on the promotion list unless denied by the commander. (See Directed Automatic Promotion List Integration below.)

Soldiers competing for promotion to SGT or SSG must possess a high school diploma, GED equivalency, or an associate or higher degree. Soldiers competing for promotion to SSG must be graduates of the Primary Leadership Development Course (PLDC) before being recommended for promotion.

2. *Soldier's chain of command recommends for promotion.* Soldiers may compete for promotion only in their career progression military occupational specialty (CPMOS), as outlined in AR 611-201. Eligible CPLs/SPCs and SGTs compete Army-wide by a three-character MOS, and their relative standing is determined by the points attained on an 800-point system. If a soldier is in the primary zone for promotion and is not selected for appearance before the board, he or she must be counseled in writing about why he or she was not selected to appear.

3. *Administrative points computed (600 points available).* See the table on pages 154–55.

4. *Battalion commander convenes promotion board.* Although AR 600-8-19, *Enlisted Promotions,* states that officers may serve as members of the promotion board with an officer as president, in most cases the board is composed of senior NCOs with the battalion command sergeant major sitting as president. If a command sergeant major is not available, a serving sergeant major may sit as president. Rules for conduct of the promotion board are found in AR 600-8-19.

5. *Board recommends soldier for promotion (150 points available).* See the table on pages 154–55. Based on the soldier's personal appearance, self-confidence, bearing, oral expression and conversational skill, knowledge of world affairs, awareness of military programs, and knowledge of basic soldiering and attitude, the board awards up to 150 promotion points.

6. *Total promotion points computed (800 total points available).* The minimum score for attaining recommended list status for promotion to SGT is 350

points. The minimum score for attaining recommended list status for promotion to SSG is 450. Upon being recommended for promotion, obtain copies of all source documents used for promotion points (if you're not sure, ask). Soldiers should turn one set in with their initial promotion point worksheet and maintain a second set with a copy of their promotion board proceedings and each DA Form 3355 (initial evaluation and reevaluations). Promotion points cannot be backdated. Soldiers must understand that the Enlisted Distribution and Assignment System (EDAS) generates the promotion points' year/month/date to accurately determine promotions by MOS and grade. EDAS uses the points that are on file at HQDA. Following input to the Total Army Personnel Database (TAPDB) via EDAS input, promotion points are effective for promotion eligibility purposes on the first day of the third month after input.

7. *Education requirements met.* Effective October 1, 1992, soldiers must be a graduate of the Basic NCO Course (BNCOC) in order to be unconditionally promoted to SSG. Soldiers competing for promotion to SSG must be graduates of the Primary Leadership Development Course (PLDC) prior to being recommended for promotion. Soldiers competing for promotion to SGT must be graduates of PLDC before being promoted. Conditional promotions may be made for soldiers who lack the education requirements through no fault of their own. Those soldiers who accept conditional promotions but are subsequently denied enrollment, declared no-shows, become academic failures, or otherwise do not meet graduation requirements will have their promotions revoked and be administratively removed from the promotion list.

8. *DA sets monthly promotion points.* Each month the Department of the Army establishes the total number of soldiers to be promoted based on budgetary and strength constraints. The number of promotions are allocated by primary military occupational specialty (PMOS) within these constraints. Department of the Army promotion cutoff scores are announced monthly. (See the section on cutoff scores in this chapter.)

9. *Soldiers' points meet or exceed DA established points.* After three months on the waiting list, soldiers who meet or exceed the announced cutoff score are promoted if otherwise eligible. Each soldier promoted to SSG must have a minimum of twelve months' active federal service remaining at the time of promotion. For promotion to SGT, there is no service obligation.

Congratulations!

Your Key to Success
Become familiar with AR 600-8-19, chapters 1 and 3, the Monthly Cutoff Score and Junior Enlisted Issues Memorandum, and applicable military personnel (MILPER) messages (which are available at the battalion adjutant (BNS1), the personnel services battalion/military personnel division (PSB/MPD) promotion section, and on HRC online at *198.97.189.85/HRC_edit/Active/index2.asp*).

WHERE THE POINTS COME FROM
(CHAPTER 3 AR 600-8-19)

Performance Evaluation and Military Training Points	Maximum Allowable	How Achieved	Individual Points
Duty Performance	150	Unit Commander	
a. Competence			30
b. Military Bearing			30
c. Leadership			30
d. Training			30
e. Responsibility and Accountability			30
Weapons Qualification	50	Score ranges from 50 to 14 dependent upon number of targets hit.	
Physical Readiness Test	50	Score ranges from 50 to 5 dependent upon APFT Score	

Administrative Points

Awards: MAXIMUM	100		
Soldier's Medal or higher award			35
Bronze Star Medal (BSM); Purple Heart			30
Defense Meritorious Service; Medal Meritorious Service Medal (MSM) 25			
Air Medal; Joint Service Commendation Medal; Army Commendation Medal (ARCOM)			20
Joint Service Achievement Medal; Army Achievement Medal (AAM)			15
Good Conduct Medal; Army Reserve Component Achievement Medal			10
Combat Infantry Badge; Combat Field Medical Badge			15
Expert Infantry Badge; Expert Field Medical Badge; Basic U.S. Army Recruiter Badge (additional badges 5 each); Ranger Tab; Special Forces Tab; Drill Sergeant Identification Badge			10
Parachutist Badge; Air Assault Badge; Parachute Rigger Badge; Divers Badge; Explosive Ordnance Disposal Badge; Pathfinder Badge; Aircraft Crewman Badge; Nuclear Reactor Operator Badge; Awards of higher skill badge count as subsequent awards and will receive points (senior parachutist, master diver, additional recruiting badges); Driver and Mechanic Badge (maximum 5 points); Tomb Guard Identification Badge			5
Soldiers receiving incentive pay for parachute duty:		Parachutist	20
		Senior	25
		Master	30
Campaign Service Star			5
Southwest Asia Medal (max 12 points)			3
Soldier/NCO of the Quarter—Brigade (BDE) Level			10
Soldier/NCO of the Quarter—Installation/Division			15
Soldier/NCO of the Year—Major Army Command (MACOM)			25
Distinguished Honor Graduate			15

WHERE THE POINTS COME FROM *continued*
(CHAPTER 3 AR 600-8-19)

Performance Evaluation and Military Training Points	Maximum Allowable	How Achieved	Individual Points
Distinguished Leadership Award			10
Commandants List			5
Certificate of Achievement awarded by commanders/deputy commanders serving in positions authorized in the grade of lieutenant colonel (LTC) or higher or any general officer, or command sergeant major (CSM) at the brigade or higher level. (max 20)			5
Military Education	**200**		
Active component (AC) PLDC			16
PLDC Equivalency (as approved by HRC-A) To be determined (TBD)			
AC BNCOC			40
Additional completed BNCOC (per week)			4
Ranger School			32
Special Forces Qualification Course			60
Battalion level or higher training certified by a DA Form 87, "Certificate of Training" signed by a LTC or above (per week)			4
Completion of military correspondence, extension, or nonresident subcourses (per five hours)			1
Other courses of at least one week duration (40 hours)			4
Civilian education	**100**		
For each semester hour earned of business/trade school/college			1.5
Any soldier completing a degree while on active duty			10
CLEP Tests (for each semester hour earned)			1.5
Promotion Board	**150**		
Personal Appearance			25
Oral Expression			25
Awareness of World Affairs			25
Knowledge of Military Programs			25
Basic Soldiering			25
Soldier's Attitude			25
Total Possible Points			800

Promotable soldiers must monthly review and initial the recommended list. This is the most important document you have to refer to after undergoing any type of promotion board or point adjustment action. If you disagree with the promotion points and/or promotion points date data reflected on the EDAS C10, bring it to the attention of your first sergeant and BNS1, and be prepared to document all promotion related requests.

Records Check

The total elimination of the Military Personnel Records Jacket (MPRJ) is fast approaching. Soldiers are responsible for maintaining individual personnel documents that have a direct impact on their career. These documents are essential to the promotion process establishing promotion points for SGT/SSG and for establishing the Official Military Personnel File. Ultimately, the soldier, along with the chain of command are responsible for accuracy of promotion paperwork and follow up of action requests.

You may now review your OPMF online by logging on to the Human Resources Command Enlisted Records and Evaluation Center Web site, *www.hrc.army.mil/site/erec/index.htm*, using your Army Knowledge Online (AKO) user ID and password.

Recommended List

After completion of all promotion actions during the month, a recommended list is published. It lists all soldiers of the organization who have been selected but not yet promoted. Names are listed by grade and zone in ascending MOS and descending promotion point score order.

Soldiers are promoted from the current recommended list by MOS. Promotions are made on the first calendar day of the month in which they are authorized. Promotion orders may be published with future effective dates.

Soldiers are eligible for promotion on the first day of the second month following date of selection; for example, a soldier recommended in January 2003 becomes eligible for promotion on March 1, 2003.

A soldier's name on the secondary zone list for promotion to sergeant is transferred to the primary zone list on the first day of the month in which he or she completes thirty-three months of active service. The soldier becomes eligible for promotion in the primary zone on the first day of the month in which he or she completes thirty-six months' active service.

A soldier's name on the secondary zone list for promotion to staff sergeant is transferred to the primary zone on the first day of the month in which he or she completes 81 months of active service. The soldier becomes eligible for promotion in the primary zone on the first day of the month in which he or she completes 84 months of active service.

Cutoff Scores

When a soldier's number of promotion points is known, many wonder why he or she cannot be promoted immediately if the cutoff is low enough. In the first place, soldiers may be selected for promotion three months before they have the required time-in-service.

Second, reports from the field reflecting the number of soldiers on promotion lists, their number of points, and their zones and MOSs arrive at HQDA about the middle of the month following the month in which the soldier appeared before the promotion board.

At this point, MOS and grade vacancies are computed. The total number of promotions for a particular grade (regardless of MOS) is determined by comparing the number of personnel projected to be in that grade against the number allowed in the Army budget for the month in which promotions are to be made. This projection includes losses, those promoted in and out of the grade, and reductions. Available promotions are distributed to MOSs based on the percentage of fill.

Promotions go to those MOSs with the greatest need first. Secondary zone (waiver) promotions are limited, so they go to MOSs with the greatest need after the primary zone (no waiver) promotions are distributed. At this time—which is one to two months after the soldier appeared before the promotion board—the soldier's number of promotion points comes into the process. For example, if vacancies and budget permit the promotion of 100 soldiers from the primary zone of a particular MOS, a promotion cutoff score is established by going down the scores until the 100 limit is reached. That is, if the top 100 sergeants in an MOS have 716 or more points, the cutoff score would be 716. If the top 100 have 796 or more, the cutoff would be 796.

Directed Automatic Promotion List Integration
This policy is designed to assist the Army in filling vacant sergeant authorizations. Each month, soldiers meeting the established criteria for list integration will be added to the recommended list with a minimum of 350 promotion points, unless previously denied. Commanders may block automatic integration by informing their supporting PSB/MPD which soldiers not to integrate

Soldiers in the rank of corporal/specialist (CPL/SPC) not earlier recommended for promotion will be automatically integrated onto the SGT recommended list upon meeting the following criteria:

- Forty-eight months time in service.
- Twelve months time in grade.
- Not denied integration by the commander.
- Otherwise not ineligible (AR 600-8-19).

The existing rules provide for an SPC to be fully eligible for promotion recommendation upon the attainment of thirty-four months service and six months in grade—with promotion eligibility at three years in service. This allows the chain of command one full year past the fully eligible point to recommend a soldier under the existing means—that is, by board appearance.

The only avenue for soldiers who are automatically integrated onto the list to increase their promotion points is to appear before the promotion board. Soldiers are only promoted from the automatic list integration (ALI) to SGT when their score meets the announced cutoff score and they have seniority over others within their primary military occupational specialty (PMOS) listed on the ALI.

Reevaluation
You may request an administrative reevaluation using a memorandum or total reevaluation by using the DA Form 3355. Dropping off source documents at the

unit or BNS1 does not constitute a request for reevaluation. You must be proactive and follow up on all action requests.

Total Reevaluation

A soldier on the current recommended list for six months may request a total reevaluation then and each six months thereafter if he or she is still promotable. A soldier reevaluated is not immediately eligible for promotion based on the new score. The soldier continues to be eligible for promotion based on the promotion point score he or she held immediately before reevaluation. Eligibility under the old score continues until the reevaluated score becomes effective. The new score becomes effective two months from the date of reevaluation because of the two-month reporting time.

After the request for reevaluation is approved, the soldier appears before the organization's next regularly scheduled promotion board. The soldier's promotion list status is then based on the number of points he or she attains. If a soldier remains on the list, his or her original selection date is adjusted to the date on which the promotion authority approves the board report. This gives the soldier a chance to improve his or her total score. The soldier, however, also runs the risk of lowering his or her standing by making a poor showing before the board.

Loss of recommended list status through reevaluation does not, however, preclude promotion consideration by future boards. Such consideration is not a vested right. Those being considered to regain recommended list status are subject to the provisions of chapter 3, AR 600-8-19, and the recommendations of their commanders.

Administrative Reevaluations

Soldiers believing they have twenty or more points to add to their promotion score may request an administrative reevaluation of their points by submitting DA Form 4187, *Personnel Action*. With the commander's approval, the promotions clerk will recalculate the promotion point worksheet and increase or decrease, as applicable, the duty performance points and erroneous points. The personnel service branch (PSB) will evaluate the new promotion points and those of the recomputed worksheet. If there is a promotion point increase of twenty points or more, the PSB will enter the new score into the appropriate database.

Removals

Soldiers may be removed from promotions lists for the following reasons:

- Failure to qualify, for cause, for the security clearance required for the MOS in which the soldier is recommended. Those who fail to qualify for a security clearance through no adverse reason are reclassified and remain on the list in the new MOS.
- Failure to reenlist or extend to meet a service-remaining obligation.
- Being barred to reenlist.
- Reclassification from an MOS because of inefficiency or misconduct.

- Erroneous listing due to not meeting the criteria for promotion.
- Enrollment in the weight-control program.
- Failure to pass reclassification training.
- Reduction in grade after being placed on the recommended list.

A removal board is convened when required to determine whether a soldier should be removed from a recommended list. The board will be constituted as for promotion boards. The soldier being considered for removal has certain rights. The soldier may choose to do the following:

- Appear before the board.
- Challenge any member of the board for cause.
- Request an available witness whose testimony is pertinent to his case.
- Elect to remain silent, to make an unsworn statement, to make a sworn statement, or to be verbally examined by the board.
- Question any witness appearing before the board.
- Present written affidavits and depositions of witnesses.

Failure on the part of a soldier to exercise these rights is not a bar to the board proceedings or its findings and recommendations. The promotion authority is the final approval or disapproval authority on the board's recommendations. This action is final.

A soldier removed from a list and later exonerated is reinstated to the current local recommended list as soon as possible but not more than ten days after being completely exonerated.

REDUCTIONS IN GRADE

Commanders at the grades indicated may administratively reduce the grade of assigned soldiers:

- Specialist or corporal and below—company, troop, battery, and separate detachment commanders.
- Sergeant and staff sergeant—field-grade commanders of any organization that is authorized a lieutenant colonel or higher-grade commander. For separate detachments, companies, or battalions, reduction authority is the next senior headquarters within the chain of command authorized a lieutenant colonel or higher-grade commander.

Erroneous Enlistment Grades

Soldiers in higher grades than authorized upon enlistment or reenlistment in the Regular Army or Army Reserve will be reduced to the one to which they are entitled. Authorized grades are prescribed in AR 601-210, AR 140-11, or AR 140-158.

Misconduct

For reductions imposed by court-martial, see the *Manual for Courts-Martial*. Sergeants first class and above cannot be reduced under the provision of Article 15, UCMJ.

Inefficiency

Inefficiency is defined as "demonstration of characteristics which show that the person cannot perform the duties and responsibilities of the grade and MOS (AR 600-8-19, chapter 7)." It may include any act or conduct that shows a lack of abilities and qualities required and expected of a person of that grade and experience. Commanders may consider misconduct, including conviction by civil court, as bearing on efficiency.

A soldier may be reduced under the authority of chapter 7, AR 600-8-19, for long-standing unpaid personal debts that he or she has not made a reasonable attempt to pay.

An assigned soldier who has served in the same unit for at least ninety days may be reduced one grade for inefficiency. The commander starting the reduction action documents the soldier's inefficiency. The documents should establish a pattern of inefficiency rather than identify a specific incident.

The commander reducing a soldier informs him or her, in writing, of the action contemplated and the reasons. The soldier must acknowledge receipt of the letter, by endorsement, and may submit any pertinent matters in rebuttal. Sergeants and above may request to appear before a reduction board. If appearance is declined, it must be done in writing and is considered acceptance of the reduction action. A reduction board, when required, must be convened within thirty days after the individual is notified in writing.

Reduction Boards

When required, reduction boards are convened to determine whether an enlisted soldier's grade should be reduced. This convening authority must ensure that the following conditions exist:

- The board consists of officers and enlisted personnel of mature judgment and senior in grade to the person being considered for reduction.
- For inefficiency cases, at least one member must be thoroughly familiar with the soldier's specialty.
- The board must consist of at least three voting members and will comprise both officer and enlisted voting members.
- The board has an officer or senior enlisted member (or both) of the same sex as the soldier being considered for reduction.
- The composition of the board represents the ethnic population of soldiers under its jurisdiction.
- No soldier with direct knowledge of the case is appointed to the board.

A soldier who is to appear before the board will be given at least fifteen working days' written notice before the date of the hearing so that the soldier or his or her counsel has time to prepare the case.

The convening authority may approve or disapprove any portion of the recommendation of the board, but his action cannot increase the severity of the board's recommendation. If the convening authority approves a recommended reduction, he or she may direct it. When the board recommends a reduction and the convening

authority approves it, the soldier will be reduced without regard to any action taken to appeal the reduction.

The soldier has the right to:

- Decline, in writing, to appear before the board.
- Have a military counsel of his or her own choosing, if reasonably available, or may employ a civilian counsel at his or her own expense, or both.
- Appear in person, with or without counsel, at all open proceedings of the board.
- If the soldier appears before the board without counsel, have the president counsel him or her on the action being contemplated, the effect of such action on his or her future in the Army, and the right to request counsel.
- Challenge (dismiss) any member of the board for cause.
- Request any reasonably available witness whose testimony the soldier believes to be pertinent to the case. When requested, the soldier must tell the nature of the information the witness will provide.
- Submit to the board written affidavits and depositions of witnesses who are unable to appear before the board.
- Employ the provisions of article 31, UCMJ (prohibition against compulsory self-incrimination), or submit to an examination by the board.
- Have his or her counsel question any witness appearing before the board. Failure of the soldier to exercise his or her rights is not a bar to the board proceedings or its findings and recommendations.

Appeals

Appeals from reduction for misconduct are governed by article 15, UCMJ; paragraph 135, Manual for Courts-Martial (MCM); and AR 27-10.

Appeals based on reduction for failure to complete training will not be accepted.

Appeals from staff sergeants and below based on reduction for inefficiency or conviction by civil court are allowed. They must be submitted in writing within thirty workdays from the date of reduction. The officer having general court-martial jurisdiction or the next higher authority, may approve, disapprove, or change the reduction if he or she determines that the reduction was without sufficient basis, should be changed, or was proper. His or her action is final.

ADDITIONAL INFORMATION

The book *Career Progression Guide for Soldiers*, 2nd Edition, by Audie Lewis (Stackpole, 2003), offers greater detail on the promotion process and gives loads of advice on practical means to acquire the necessary promotion points.

To prepare for appearances before promotion boards, CSM (Ret.) Walter Jackson's *Soldier Study Guide*, 5th Edition (Stackpole, 2004), is recommended.

14

Pay and
Entitlements

The purpose of this chapter is to explain some basic facts about your Army pay and benefits and provide you a quick reference for questions that may come up in your day-to-day duties.

The soldier who enlists in the Army for the money is in the wrong business. Relatively substantial paychecks do not begin until a soldier reaches the senior noncommissioned ranks with twenty to twenty-six years of service, although service overseas in a combat zone does increase take home pay substantially. That said, if pay and benefits were the only inducement to a military career, then we would have no Army. Unlike first-term soldiers, soldiers who reenlist understand the "score" and accept the challenges and rewards, intangible though they may be, of being a soldier.

PAY AND ALLOWANCES
Military pay consists of basic pay, special and incentive pay, and allowances. Pay is computed on the basis of a thirty-day month, and soldiers may elect to be paid once a month (at the end of the month) or twice a month (on the fifteenth and the thirtieth of each month).

To change your pay option, contact your local finance and accounting office to execute DA Form 3685, *JUMPS—Army Pay Elections*. Which option you select depends upon how you budget your money. Some soldiers find that they can get along quite well with one lump-sum payment at the end of the month; others prefer to get paid twice a month. Read the pay elections form carefully before filling it out. Submit your options to the finance officer as early in the month as possible to give the finance center enough time to process your request so that your new option will be reflected during the next pay period.

Report discrepancies in your pay immediately. To do so, you must know what you are authorized.

Leave and Earnings Statement
The leave and earnings statement (LES) is a computerized monthly statement of account for each soldier paid. The LES shows all entitlements earned, collections

DEFENSE FINANCE AND ACCOUNTING SERVICE MILITARY LEAVE AND EARNINGS STATEMENT

ID	NAME (LAST, FIRST, MI) 1	SOC. SEC. NO. 2	GRADE 3	PAY DATE 4	YRS SVC 5	ETS 6	BRANCH 7	ADSN/DSSN 8	PERIOD COVERED 9

ENTITLEMENTS		DEDUCTIONS		ALLOTMENTS		SUMMARY	
TYPE	AMOUNT	TYPE	AMOUNT	TYPE	AMOUNT	+ AMT FWD	13
10		11		12		+ TOT ENT	14
						− TOT DED	15
						− TOT ALMT	16
						= NET AMT	17
						− CR FWD	18
						= EOM PAY	19

| TOTAL 20 | | 21 | | 22 | | DIEMS 23 | RET PLAN 24 |

LEAVE

BF BAL 25	ERND 26	USED 27	CR BAL 28	ETS BAL 29	LV LOST 30	LV PAID 31	USE/LOSE 32

FED TAXES

WAGE PERIOD 33	WAGE YTD 34	M/S 35	EX 36	ADD'L TAX 37	TAX YTD 38

FICA TAXES / STATE TAXES

WAGE PERIOD 39	SOC WAGE YTD 40	SOC TAX YTD 41	MED WAGE YTD 42	MED TAX YTD 43	ST 44	WAGE PERIOD 45	WAGE YTD 46	M/S 47	EX 48	TAX YTD 49

PAY DATA

BAQ TYPE 50	BAQ DEPN 51	VHA ZIP 52	RENT AMT 53	SHARE 54	STAT 55	JFTR 56	DEPNS 57	2D JFTR 58	BAS TYPE 59	CHARITY YTD 60	TPC 61	PACIDN 62

BASE PAY RATE 63	BASE PAY CURRENT 64	SPEC PAY RATE 65	SPEC PAY CURRENT 66	INC PAY RATE 67	INC PAY CURRENT 68	BONUS PAY RATE 69	BONUS PAY CURRENT 70
CURRENTLY NOT USED 71							

Thrift Savings Plan (TSP)

TSP YTD DEDUCTIONS 72	DEFERRED 73	EXEMPT 74	CURRENTLY NOT USED 75

REMARKS 76

YTD ENTITLE 77	YTD DEDUCT 78

www.dfas.mil

DFAS Form 702, Jan 02

affected, and payments made during the period covered by the statement. In addition, this statement provides the soldier a complete record of transactions that affect his or her leave account for the period of the statement. It also serves as the official leave record. You may also access your LES at the MyPay Web site at *mypay.dfas.mil/mypay.aspx.*

Content of the Leave and Earnings Statement

The LES reflects a soldier's involvement in the Thrift Savings Plan (TSP). These blocks are located directly above the "Remarks" area of the LES. The four entitlement categories are Base Pay (blocks 63 and 64 on sample), Special Pay (blocks 65 and 66), Incentive Pay (blocks 67 and 68), and Bonus Pay (blocks 69 and 70). There are two new blocks for each of four entitlement categories. The blocks containing the word "Rate" reflect the percentage rate of the monthly entitlement that the servicemember elects to contribute to TSP. The blocks that contain the word "Current" reflect the dollar amount designated by the servicemember. The "TSP YTD [year-to-date] Deductions" block (72) is simply what a soldier has contributed to date. The "Deferred" block (73) will contain the amount of TSP YTD contributions that are tax deferred. There is a yearly maximum for tax-deferred contributions, and once a soldier reaches the yearly maximum, the system generates a stop transaction and creates a remark with a stop date. The "Exempt" block (74) contains the amount of YTD tax-exempt TSP contributions. Deductions for TSP contributions and loan payments appear in the "Deductions" block (11) of the LES. If a soldier receives a TSP loan payment and any TSP contribution refund, the "Entitlements" block (10) of the LES will denote the amount.

Additionally, two blocks advise the soldier on his or her retirement status. These blocks are located on the far right side of the document, under the "EOM Pay" block. The "DIEMS" block (date initially entered military service) (23) reflects the date used to establish the soldier's retirement plan. The "RET Plan" block (24) indicates the retirement plan a soldier is under, based on the DIEMS date shown in the preceding block.

Study your LES very carefully. Should you discover any item you believe to be in error or should there be an entry recorded thereon that you do not understand, consult with your local finance office immediately. If, during a routine audit of your pay record, it should be discovered that you have been overpaid at some time in the past, the government will collect what is due.

Duty in a Combat Zone

As an enlisted member, if you serve in a combat zone for any part of a month, all of your military pay for that month is excluded from your income for income tax reporting purposes. You also can exclude military pay earned while you are hospitalized as a result of wounds, disease, or injury incurred in the combat zone. The exclusion of your military pay while you are in hospital extends to two years past the termination of hostilities in the designated combat zone. You hospitalization does not have to be in the combat zone.

MONTHLY BASIC PAY (Effective 1 January 2006)

Years of Service

Grade	<2	2	3	4	6	8	10	12	14	16	18	20	22	24	26
Commissioned officers															
O-10	0.00	0.00	0.00	0.00	0.00	0.00	0.00	0.00	0.00	0.00	0.00	13,365.00	13,430.40	13,709.70	14,196.30
O-9	0.00	0.00	0.00	0.00	0.00	0.00	0.00	0.00	0.00	0.00	0.00	11,689.50	11,857.50	12,101.10	12,525.60
O-8	8,271.00	8,541.90	8,721.60	8,772.00	8,996.10	9,371.10	9,458.10	9,814.20	9,916.20	10,222.80	10,666.20	11,075.40	11,348.70	11,348.70	11,348.70
O-7	6,872.70	7,191.90	7,339.80	7,457.10	7,669.80	7,879.50	8,122.50	8,364.90	8,607.90	9,371.10	10,015.80	10,015.80	10,015.80	10,015.80	10,066.50
O-6	5,094.00	5,596.20	5,963.40	5,963.40	5,985.90	6,242.70	6,276.60	6,276.60	6,633.30	7,263.90	7,634.10	8,004.00	8,214.60	8,427.60	8,841.30
O-5	4,246.50	4,783.50	5,115.00	5,177.10	5,383.50	5,507.40	5,779.20	5,978.70	6,236.10	6,630.60	6,818.10	7,003.80	7,214.40	7,214.40	7,214.40
O-4	3,663.90	4,241.40	4,524.30	4,587.60	4,850.10	5,131.80	5,482.20	5,755.80	5,945.40	6,054.30	6,117.60	6,117.60	6,117.60	6,117.60	6,117.60
O-3	3,221.40	3,651.90	3,941.70	4,297.50	4,503.00	4,728.90	4,875.30	5,115.90	5,240.70	5,240.70	5,240.70	5,240.70	5,240.70	5,240.70	5,240.70
O-2	2,783.10	3,170.10	3,651.00	3,774.30	3,852.00	3,852.00	3,852.00	3,852.00	3,852.00	3,852.00	3,852.00	3,852.00	3,852.00	3,852.00	3,852.00
O-1	2,416.20	2,514.60	3,039.60	3,039.60	3,039.60	3,039.60	3,039.60	3,039.60	3,039.60	3,039.60	3,039.60	3,039.60	3,039.60	3,039.60	3,039.60
Officers with more than 4 years' active duty as enlisted or warrant officer															
O-3E	0.00	0.00	0.00	4,297.50	4,503.00	4,728.90	4,875.30	5,115.90	5,318.40	5,434.50	5,592.90	5,592.90	5,592.90	5,592.90	5,592.90
O-2E	0.00	0.00	0.00	3,774.30	3,852.00	3,974.70	4,181.40	4,341.60	4,460.70	4,460.70	4,460.70	4,460.70	4,460.70	4,460.70	4,460.70
O-1E	0.00	0.00	0.00	3,039.60	3,246.30	3,366.00	3,488.70	3,609.30	3,774.30	3,774.30	3,774.30	3,774.30	3,774.30	3,774.30	3,774.30
Warrant officers															
W-5	0.00	0.00	0.00	0.00	0.00	0.00	0.00	0.00	0.00	0.00	0.00	5,720.10	5,916.30	6,113.10	6,311.10
W-4	3,328.80	3,581.10	3,684.00	3,785.10	3,959.40	4,131.30	4,305.90	4,475.70	4,651.50	4,927.20	5,103.60	5,276.10	5,454.90	5,631.00	5,811.00
W-3	3,039.90	3,166.80	3,296.40	3,339.30	3,475.50	3,631.50	3,837.30	4,040.40	4,256.40	4,418.40	4,579.80	4,649.10	4,720.80	4,876.80	5,032.50
W-2	2,673.90	2,826.60	2,960.40	3,057.30	3,140.70	3,369.60	3,544.50	3,674.40	3,801.30	3,888.30	3,961.50	4,100.70	4,239.00	4,379.10	4,379.10
W-1	2,361.30	2,554.50	2,683.80	2,767.50	2,990.40	3,124.80	3,243.90	3,376.80	3,465.00	3,544.80	3,674.70	3,773.10	3,773.10	3,773.10	3,773.10
Enlisted members															
E-9	0.00	0.00	0.00	0.00	0.00	0.00	4,022.10	4,113.30	4,228.20	4,363.50	4,499.40	4,717.80	4,902.30	5,097.00	5,394.00
E-8	0.00	0.00	0.00	0.00	0.00	3,292.50	3,438.30	3,528.30	3,636.30	3,753.30	3,964.50	4,071.60	4,253.70	4,354.80	4,603.50
E-7	2,288.70	2,498.10	2,593.80	2,720.70	2,819.40	2,989.50	3,084.90	3,180.30	3,350.40	3,435.60	3,516.30	3,565.80	3,732.60	3,840.60	4,113.60
E-6	1,979.70	2,178.00	2,274.30	2,367.60	2,465.10	2,685.00	2,770.50	2,865.30	2,948.70	2,978.10	2,998.50	2,998.50	2,998.50	2,998.50	2,998.50
E-5	1,814.10	1,935.30	2,028.60	2,124.60	2,273.70	2,402.10	2,496.60	2,526.60	2,526.60	2,526.60	2,526.60	2,526.60	2,526.60	2,526.60	2,526.60
E-4	1,662.90	1,748.10	1,842.60	1,935.90	2,018.40	2,018.40	2,018.40	2,018.40	2,018.40	2,018.40	2,018.40	2,018.40	2,018.40	2,018.40	2,018.40
E-3	1,501.20	1,595.70	1,692.00	1,692.00	1,692.00	1,692.00	1,692.00	1,692.00	1,692.00	1,692.00	1,692.00	1,692.00	1,692.00	1,692.00	1,692.00
E-2	1,427.40	1,427.40	1,427.40	1,427.40	1,427.40	1,427.40	1,427.40	1,427.40	1,427.40	1,427.40	1,427.40	1,427.40	1,427.40	1,427.40	1,427.40
E-1	1,273.50	1,273.50	1,273.50	1,273.50	1,273.50	1,273.50	1,273.50	1,273.50	1,273.50	1,273.50	1,273.50	1,273.50	1,273.50	1,273.50	1,273.50
E-1<four months: 1,178.10															

RESERVE DRILL PAY (Four Drills) (Effective 1 January 2006)

Grade	<2	2	3	4	6	8	10	12	14	16	18	20	22	24	26
Commissioned officers															
O-7	916.36	958.92	978.64	994.28	1,022.64	1,050.60	1,083.00	1,115.32	1,147.72	1,249.48	1,335.44	1,335.44	1,335.44	1,335.44	1,342.20
O-6	679.20	746.16	795.12	795.12	798.12	832.36	836.88	836.88	884.44	968.52	1,017.88	1,067.20	1,095.28	1,123.68	1,178.84
O-5	566.20	637.80	682.00	690.28	717.80	734.32	770.56	797.16	831.48	884.08	909.08	933.84	961.92	961.92	961.92
O-4	488.52	565.52	603.24	611.68	646.68	684.24	730.96	767.44	792.72	807.24	815.68	815.68	815.68	815.68	815.68
O-3	429.52	486.92	525.56	573.00	600.40	630.52	650.04	682.12	698.76	698.76	698.76	698.76	698.76	698.76	698.76
O-2	371.08	422.68	486.80	503.24	513.60	513.60	513.60	513.60	513.60	513.60	513.60	513.60	513.60	513.60	513.60
O-1	322.16	335.28	405.28	405.28	405.28	405.28	405.28	405.28	405.28	405.28	405.28	405.28	405.28	405.28	405.28
Commissioned officers with more than 4 years' active duty as enlisted or warrant officer															
O-3E	0.00	0.00	0.00	573.00	600.40	630.52	650.04	682.12	709.12	724.60	745.72	745.72	745.72	745.72	745.72
O-2E	0.00	0.00	0.00	503.24	513.60	529.96	557.52	578.88	594.76	594.76	594.76	594.76	594.76	594.76	594.76
O-1E	0.00	0.00	0.00	405.28	432.84	448.80	465.16	481.24	503.24	503.24	503.24	503.24	503.24	503.24	503.24
Warrant officers															
W-5	0.00	0.00	0.00	0.00	0.00	0.00	0.00	0.00	0.00	0.00	0.00	762.68	788.84	815.08	841.48
W-4	443.84	477.48	491.20	504.68	527.92	550.84	574.12	596.76	620.20	656.96	680.48	703.48	727.32	750.80	774.80
W-3	405.32	422.24	439.52	445.24	463.40	484.20	511.64	538.72	567.52	589.12	610.64	619.88	629.44	650.24	671.00
W-2	356.52	376.88	394.72	407.64	418.76	449.28	472.60	489.92	506.84	518.44	528.20	546.76	565.20	583.88	583.88
W-1	314.84	340.60	357.84	369.00	398.72	416.64	432.52	450.24	462.00	472.64	489.96	503.08	503.08	503.08	503.08
Enlisted members															
E-9	0.00	0.00	0.00	0.00	0.00	0.00	536.28	548.44	563.76	581.80	599.92	629.04	653.64	679.60	719.20
E-8	0.00	0.00	0.00	0.00	0.00	0.00	458.44	470.44	484.84	500.44	528.60	542.88	567.16	580.64	613.80
E-7	305.16	333.08	345.84	362.76	375.92	398.60	411.32	424.04	446.72	458.08	468.84	475.44	497.68	512.08	548.48
E-6	263.96	290.40	303.24	315.68	328.68	358.00	369.40	382.04	393.16	397.08	399.80	399.80	399.80	399.80	399.80
E-5	241.88	258.04	270.48	283.28	303.16	320.28	332.88	336.88	336.88	336.88	336.88	336.88	336.88	336.88	336.88
E-4	221.72	233.08	245.68	258.12	269.12	269.12	269.12	269.12	269.12	269.12	269.12	269.12	269.12	269.12	269.12
E-3	200.16	212.76	225.60	225.60	225.60	225.60	225.60	225.60	225.60	225.60	225.60	225.60	225.60	225.60	225.60
E-2	190.32	190.32	190.32	190.32	190.32	190.32	190.32	190.32	190.32	190.32	190.32	190.32	190.32	190.32	190.32
E-1	169.80	169.80	169.80	169.80	169.80	169.80	169.80	169.80	169.80	169.80	169.80	169.80	169.80	169.80	169.80

Years of Service

Online Finance

The Defense Finance and Accounting Service (DFAS) MyPay Web site at *mypay.dfas.mil/mypay.aspx* allows soldiers to access their pay record and update certain payroll information directly, without having to fill out any paper forms. The Employee/Member Self Service (E/MSS) allows you access to your financial records at either your home or office through the Internet using a personal computer or through an Interactive Voice Response Telephone System (IVRS) using a touch-tone telephone. MyPay allows you to review or make changes to your federal and state tax information, financial allotments, home or correspondence address, savings bonds, and direct deposit or electronic funds transfer (EFT) information without the problems involved with paperwork. When you make a change, the system saves the transaction and sends it to the payroll system the next day for update. This system also allows you to view and print your Leave and Earnings Statement online.

Collections of Erroneous Payments

Overpayments for two months in a row are collected from the next month's pay. If these payments are two or more months old, collection is delayed to allow time for unit commanders to arrange for prorated collection, if necessary, before computer collection action is initiated.

Normally, the amount deducted for any period will not exceed an amount equal to two-thirds of a soldier's pay. Monthly installments may be increased or decreased to reflect changes in pay.

Soldiers may appeal the validity of a debt, the amount, or the rate of payment. If an enlisted soldier's appeal is denied, the chief of personnel operations, Department of the Army, may consider his or her case for remission or cancellation of the indebtedness.

Advance Payments

An advance of pay is authorized upon permanent change of station to provide a soldier funds for expenses, such as transportation, temporary storage of household goods, packing and shipping costs, and securing new living quarters. Advance payments are limited to no more than one month's advance pay of basic pay less deductions or, if warranted, not more than three months' basic pay less deductions at the old station, en route, or within sixty days after reporting to a new station.

Requests for advance pay from enlisted personnel in pay grades E-1 through E-4 must be approved by their commander, and this approval must be indicated in the *Pay Inquiry Form* (DA Form 2142), together with a statement that the circumstances in the individual's case warrant advancing the amount requested and that advancing a lesser amount would result in hardship to the soldier or his or her family.

The commander's approval for an advance of pay is not required for enlisted personnel in pay grades E-5 through E-9, but advances are not made to senior-grade personnel when it is apparent that the tour of duty (obligated service) will terminate before completion of the scheduled repayment of the advance.

Lump-Sum Payments

A lump-sum payment is made to pay bonuses and accrued leave paid on immediate reenlistments. These payments are made by cash or check through the use of a local payment. Lump-sum payments are always made in even dollar amounts. The maximum amount that may be paid is the gross amount of the enlistment minus the estimate of federal and, when applicable, state taxes. When the computation results in a new amount due in dollars and cents, the amount to be paid may either be the lesser full dollar amount or be rounded to the next higher dollar.

Basic Pay

Basic pay is established by law and is that pay a soldier receives, based on grade and length of service, exclusive of any special or incentive pay or allowances.

Reserve Drill Pay

Reserve drill pay, like basic pay, is established by law. And like basic pay, reserve drill pay is pay a soldier receives based on grade and length of service. Unlike monthly basic pay, however, reserve drill pay is computed and paid for the number of days' service rendered. It is comparable to basic pay.

Other Pay

Assignment Incentive Pay

Assignment Incentive Pay is used to voluntarily fill hard to fill assignments and is taxable unless in a combat zone. In Iraq and Afghanistan soldiers can receive $300

Soldiers Qualify for Additional Pay While in a Combat Zone

per month for a three-month extension, $600 per month for a six-month extension, and $900 per month for a twelve-month extension. In South Korea, soldiers extending their twelve-month tours for an additional year receive $300 in assignment-incentive pay.

Reserve component soldiers assigned in Iraq or Afghanistan who have completed twenty-two-months mobilization and volunteer (for Army National Guard [ARNG] with the consent of the governor) to extend on active duty beyond twenty-four-months cumulative mobilization will be offered the opportunity to contract for Assignment Incentive Pay (AIP). Soldiers will be offered $1,000 per month upon completion of their twenty-second month of mobilization. The AIP terminates when the Soldier leaves the Central Command Area of Operations.

Experimental Stress Pay

Experimental stress duty pay is authorized for all Army personnel who, on or after July 1, 1965, performed as human experimental subjects in duties utilizing acceleration/deceleration experimental devices, in thermal stress experiments, and in low-pressure or high-pressure chamber duty.

Foreign Duty Pay

All enlisted personnel assigned to an area outside the contiguous forty-eight states and the District of Columbia where an "accompanied by dependents" tour of duty is not authorized have entitlement to foreign duty or "overseas pay." Chapter 6, part 1, *DOD Pay Manual*, lists the places where foreign duty pay is authorized.

Hardship Duty Pay

Hardship duty pay (HDP) is payable to members entitled to basic pay, at a monthly rate not to exceed $300, while such members are performing specified hardship duty. HDP is paid to members (a) for performing specific missions or (b) when assigned to designated locations. Except for certain restrictions, HDP is payable in addition to all other pay and allowances. Hardship duty pay for mission assignment (HDP-M) is payable to members, both officer and enlisted, for performing designated hardship mission. HDP-M is payable at the full monthly rate, without prorating or reduction, for each month during any part of which the member performs a specified mission. Hardship duty pay for location assignment (HDP-L) is payable only to enlisted members when they are assigned to duty in designated locations.

Hostile Fire Pay

Hostile fire pay is paid to soldiers permanently assigned to units performing duty in designated hostile fire areas or to soldiers assigned to temporary duty in such areas. Hostile fire pay is authorized on a monthly basis or one-time basis, depending upon the soldier's period of exposure to enemy fire. While drawing hostile fire pay, soldiers are exempt from federal and state taxes.

Diving Pay
To qualify for special pay for diving duty, a soldier must be a rated diver in accordance with AR 611-75 and be assigned to a table of organization and equipment (TOE) or a table of distribution and allowances (TDA) position of MOS 00B, or to a position that has been designated diving duty by the assistant chief of staff for force development, Department of the Army.

Demolition Pay
A soldier is entitled to receive incentive pay for demolition duty for any month or portion of a month in which he or she was assigned and performed duty in a primary duty assignment.

Flight Pay
Flight pay is authorized for enlisted crew members.

Parachute Pay
Soldiers who have received a designation as a parachutist or parachute rigger or are undergoing training for such designations, and who are required to engage in parachute jumping from an aircraft in aerial flight and actually perform the specified minimum jump of once per three months are authorized parachute duty pay. In imminent danger areas, however, the commanding officer may determine a soldier cannot meet the minimum requirements due to the absence of jump equipment, aircraft, or military operations. In this situation the soldier may perform the required four jumps anytime in the twelve-month period. An additional amount is authorized for parachutists who are assigned to positions requiring high-altitude, low-opening (HALO) jump status.

Special Duty Assignment Pay
Special duty pay is authorized on a graduated scale for enlisted members in designated specialties who are required to perform extremely demanding duties or duties demanding an unusual degree of responsibility. Qualifying jobs include career counselor, recruiter, and drill sergeant.

ALLOWANCES

Basic Allowance for Subsistence (BAS)
Upon entitlement to BAS (separate rations) a soldier's unit commander forwards to the finance officer DA Form 4187, *Personnel Action Request* (see chapter 8, DA Pamphlet 600-8), in duplicate, showing the effective date and hour of entitlement to BAS. When a soldier ceases to be entitled to BAS, the unit commander forwards to the finance officer a DA Form 4187 showing date and hour of termination.

BAS rates for enlisted personnel is $267.18 as of January 1, 2005.

Entitlement to BAS terminates automatically upon permanent change of station (PCS). Care should be taken during in-processing at a new duty station that entitlement is revalidated for personnel authorized separate rations.

Basic Allowance for Housing (BAH)

The basic allowance for housing combines the two older allowances (basic allowance for quarters [BAQ] and variable housing allowance [VHA]) into one single payment based on rank, with or without dependents. The new rates are based on housing costs for civilians with comparable income levels in the same area. Under this system, the annual growth in the housing allowance will be indexed in the national average monthly housing cost.

BAH terminates for married personnel when they occupy government quarters or when dependency terminates. Dependency is verified by the local finance and accounting officer. The documentary evidence that must be submitted to substantiate dependence includes the original or certified copy of a marriage certificate, the individual's signed statement (when called to active duty or active duty for training for ninety days or less), birth certificate, or a public church record of marriage issued over the signature of the custodian of the church or public records, and, if applicable, a divorce decree. Entitlements must be recertified upon permanent change of station.

RC mobilized soldiers are entitled to BAH based on their primary residence; however, they are not be authorized to change the BAH from which they were ordered to active duty, regardless of whether or not their primary residence changes

Family Separation Allowance (FSA)

A family separation allowance is paid to soldier who has dependents and is serving in an overseas location where dependents are not permitted. It is in the amount of $250 per month.

Soldiers in a temporary change of station status may be authorized FSA Type II (T) at the rate of $250 per month when a soldier is away from his or her permanent duty station (PDS)—for mobilized reserve component (RC) personnel this is their home of residence—continuously for a period of thirty days, and the soldier's dependents are not residing at or near the TCS station. Army/service married couples who were living together prior to and immediately before the deployment and single soldiers with authorized primary dependents may be paid family separation allowance for temporary duty (FSA-T). Relocation of dependents at government expense is not authorized.

Station Allowances

A list of areas where station allowances are authorized is in chapter 4, part 3, *DOD Pay Manual*, and chapter 4, part G, volume 1, *Joint Travel Regulations*. These allowances are paid to offset the high cost of living in certain geographical areas (overseas and in the United States). They consist of housing (HOUS) and cost of

living allowances (COLAs). A temporary lodging allowance (TLA) and interim housing allowance (IHA) may also be paid in certain cases.

Reserve component (RC) mobilized soldiers may receive COLA based on the location of their residence when ordered to active duty. CONUS COLA is normally determined by the zip code provided by the soldier of the location for their residence. Regular active duty soldiers located in CONUS or OCONUS areas, who are authorized COLA, will continue to draw COLA as determined by the area to which they are assigned.

Clothing Maintenance Allowance

Clothing maintenance allowance is paid at two different rates:

- Basic, which covers replacement of unique military items that would normally require replacement during the first three years of service.
- Standard, which covers the replacement of unique military items after the first three years of service.

Female personnel are also authorized an initial cash allowance established by AR 700-84 for the purchase of undergarments, dress shoes, and stockings.

A soldier receives the clothing maintenance allowance annually, on the last day of the month in which the soldier's anniversary date of enlistment falls.

Civilian Clothing Allowance

When duty assignments require soldiers to wear civilian clothing, they receive lump-sum payments under the following circumstances:

- Permanent duty requiring civilian clothing.
- Temporary Duty in graduations of fifteen to thirty days and over thirty days.

Temporary Lodging Allowance (TLA)

TLA is the allowance received when arriving at an overseas base that offsets some of the expense of temporary housing and meals. The amount of the TLA depends on variables that include family size, the cost and cooking/dining facilities of quarters, and other allowances the family is receiving.

Temporary Lodging Expense (TLE)

TLE is the allowance received when arriving at a CONUS base that offsets some of the expense of temporary housing and meals. The TLE is up to $110 per day and can last up to ten days. It applies to stateside base arrivals from both CONUS and OCONUS bases.

BONUSES

The enlistment bonus is an enlistment incentive offered to those enlisting in the Regular Army for duty in a specific MOS. The objective of the bonus is to increase the number of enlistments in MOSs that are critical and have inadequate first-term manning levels. Section A, chapter 9, part 1, of the *DOD Pay Manual* gives basic

conditions of entitlement, amount of the bonus, time of payment, and reduction and termination of the award.

Selective Reenlistment Bonus

The selective reenlistment bonus (SRB) is a retention incentive paid to soldiers in certain selected MOSs who reenlist or voluntarily extend their enlistment for additional obligated service. The objective of the SRB is to increase the number of reenlistments or extensions in critical MOSs that do not have adequate retention levels to man the career force.

The SRB is established in three zones: zone A consists of those reenlistments falling between twenty-one months and six years of active service; zones B and C consist of those reenlistments or extensions of enlistments falling between six and fourteen years of service.

Payments are based on multiples, not to exceed six, of a soldier's monthly basic pay at the time of discharge or release from active duty or the day before the beginning of extension, multiplied by years of additional obligated service.

The SRB is paid by installments. Up to 50 percent of the total bonus may be paid as the first installment, with the remaining portion paid in equal annual amounts over the remainder of the enlistment period.

A list of the MOSs designated for award of SRB and enlistment bonuses is in the DA Circular 611 series, *Announcement of Proficiency Pay/Selective Reenlistment Bonus/Enlistment Bonus/Comparable MOS for Bonus Recipients.* Periodic program changes are announced by Headquarters, Department of the Army.

ALLOTMENTS

An allotment is a specified amount of money withheld from military pay, normally upon the soldier's authorization, for a specific purpose. Payment is made by government check and mailed to the payee.

Allotments are made by filling out DD Form 2558, *Authorization to Start, Stop, or Change an Allotment for Active Duty or Retired Personnel.* These forms are prepared by the individual's military personnel office, unit personnel office, or finance office, and by Army Emergency Relief and the American Red Cross. Preparation of allotment documents in the finance office, rather than in the personnel office, is intended to eliminate delays of one or more days. When there is a delay near the end of the processing month, the effective date of an allotment may be delayed a full month. Commanders may have DD Form 2558 prepared in the unit personnel office, if it will conserve time and assure that there will be no delays in transmission to the finance office.

Repayment of Army Emergency Relief (AER) Loans. These allotments are authorized in multiples. AER allotments are established for a definite term of not less than three months (although this provision may be waived in certain cases).

Combined Federal Campaign (CFC) Contributions. This allotment is authorized to be in effect one at a time only. CFC allotments are made for a period

of twelve months, beginning in January and ending in December. Military personnel who execute the *Payroll Withholding Authorization for Voluntary Charitable Contributions* (a Civil Service form) may do so in lieu of DA Form 1341.

Payment to a Dependent (SPT-V). This kind of allotment is authorized in multiples. This voluntary allotment is paid to a soldier's dependent without regard to whether the soldier is already receiving BAH. In addition, involuntary SPT-V allotments can be administratively established. Normally, the amount of these allotments is not permitted to exceed 80 percent of a soldier's pay. Not more than one SPT-V allotment may be made to the same person.

Payment to a Financial Institution for Credit to a Member's Account (FININ). Only two of these allotments are authorized to be in effect at any one time. FININ allotments are for payment to a financial organization for credit to the allotter's savings, checking, or trust accounts. The FININ allotment may be established for an indefinite term and for any amount the soldier designates, provided he or she has sufficient pay to satisfy the deduction of the allotment.

Payment for Indebtedness to the United States (FED). FED allotments are for the purpose of payment of delinquent federal, state, and local taxes and/or indebtedness to the United States. A separate allotment is required for each debt or overpayment to be repaid.

Payment of Home Loans (HOME). Only one HOME allotment is authorized to be in effect at any one time. This allotment is authorized for repayment of loans for the purchase of a house, mobile home, or house trailer. A HOME allotment is established for an indefinite term and for any amount designated provided the soldier's pay credit is sufficient to satisfy the deduction of the allotment.

Payment of Commercial Life Insurance Premiums (INS). These allotments are authorized in multiples. INS allotments must be made payable to a commercial life insurance firm. INS allotments are not authorized for payment of insurance on the life of a soldier's spouse or children except under a family group contract or for health, accident, or hospitalization insurance. INS allotments are established for an indefinite period and in the amount of the monthly premium, as indicated by the number on DA Form 1341.

Repayment of American Red Cross Loans (REDCR). REDCR allotments are authorized in multiples.

Educational Savings Allotment (EDSAV). This allotment is authorized to allow soldiers entering service after December 13, 1976 (except those who enlisted under the Delayed Entry Program before January 1, 1977), to participate in the Veterans Educational Assistance Program (VEAP). Only one such allotment is authorized. The EDSAV allotment is established with no discontinuance date. The soldier may stop it at any time after one year of participation.

Class X Allotments. A Class X allotment is paid locally and is authorized in emergency circumstances when other classes of allotments are impracticable. This instance applies overseas only. Class X allotments may be ordered by a commander as a standby allotment when adequate provision for the financial support of a soldier's dependents has not been made.

PCS WEIGHT ALLOWANCE (POUNDS)

Pay Grade	With Dependents	Without Dependents
E-9	14,500	12,000
E-8	13,500	11,000
E-7	12,500	10,500
E-6	11,000	8,000
E-5	9,000	7,000
E-4 (over 2 years' service)	8,000	7,000
E-4 (2 years' service or less)	7,000	3,500
E-3	5,000	2,000
E-2, E-1	5,000	1,500

BENEFITS

Transportation of Household Goods
Transportation of household goods at government expense is authorized for soldiers in accordance with the table on the previous page. For information on authorized weight limitations for other grades, see Joint Federal Travel Regulations (JFTR).

Government Quarters
Bachelor accommodations for enlisted personnel range from the fairly austere communal living conditions offered junior enlisted personnel in troop units to the small but private and well-appointed quarters offered senior NCOs in bachelor enlisted quarters (BEQ). During the course of an Army career, you will see them all if you do not marry at a young age.

Modern troop billets are dormitory-style facilities with central air conditioning and heating; two-, three-, or four-person rooms; recreational facilities; and convenience facilities. Less than a generation ago, the bulk of the Army's bachelor enlisted personnel were living in one- and two-story wooden World War II barracks that were hot in the summer, cold in the winter, a real effort to keep clean, and generally overcrowded. Older soldiers remember very well living in large troop bays, double-bunked, with only a small wooden footlocker and a metal wall locker to use for the storage of their uniforms and personal clothing.

Family housing—where it is available—ranges in style from detached single-family housing to high-rise apartment-style buildings accommodating scores of families. In some cases, the quarters you are assigned will be in excellent condition and will require little maintenance to keep them that way; others will cause you constant maintenance headaches.

When reporting to some new duty stations, you will find pleasant family housing waiting for you; at other stations, you will have to wait weeks or even months to

get any kind of quarters. In some areas, the waiting list for government housing is so long that you might find it necessary to buy or rent off the post. Your family housing officer will be of great assistance to you if you should decide to occupy off-post quarters. Each installation and each major overseas command has a different family housing situation.

Because of your rank, you may very well find yourself responsible to a more senior occupant of a multiple dwelling or of a stairwell of such a dwelling. These assignments are necessary, and you should consider them a necessary part of living in close proximity to one another. Assist in keeping your communal living areas in good order and be considerate of your neighbors, and the time you spend in government housing will be some of your most memorable moments.

Occupancy of family quarters carries the responsibility for doing "handyman work." The facilities engineer performs all maintenance and repairs other than those that are within the capabilities of the occupants. Emergency work or work beyond your individual capabilities can be obtained by making a service call or submitting a job order request to the installation repair and utilities office. Do not, however, expect the engineers to drop everything and run to your quarters, no matter how severe the emergency.

If you are fortunate enough to be assigned to a single-family dwelling, you will be expected to perform that type of self-help maintenance that is done by any prudent homeowner to conserve funds and preserve the premises, such as minor carpentry, maintenance of hardware (door hinges, and so forth), touch-up and partial interior painting, caulking around doors and windows, repair of screens, repair of simple plumbing malfunctions (minor leaking, defective washers, simple drainage stoppages), and so forth. Accumulate a set of tools that you can use around the house or apartment for this minor maintenance work.

No matter where you live—family quarters or the barracks—you are expected to exercise individual initiative to preserve energy and utilities. Soldiers are among the most flagrant violators of good energy conservation, wasting water and electricity and fuel as if there were no tomorrow. Remind yourself and others to be conservation conscious.

Your quarters will be inspected by someone from the housing office before you are cleared to vacate your quarters. This inspection can be very rigorous. The specific details will be furnished to you by the housing officer. Some people prefer to hire a civilian contractor to do the work for them. You can avoid this unnecessary expense if you and your family take proper care of your quarters while you are living in them. For example, use rugs on the floors, keep the walls clean and in good repair, and keep your appliances clean.

Commissary and Post Exchange Services

The price you pay for a grocery item in the commissary is the same price the government pays for it: If an item is sold to the government for eighty-five cents, then that is its cost to you. Even the commissary surcharge and tipping do not add as

much to the cost of an item as do the standard markups found on similar items in civilian retail outlets.

The commissary surcharge pays for operating supplies, equipment, utilities, facility alterations, and new construction.

The Post Exchange Service was designated the Army and Air Force Exchange Service (AAFES) in 1948. What originally began as an outlet "to supply troops at reasonable prices with articles of ordinary use . . . not supplied by the Government . . . to afford them the means of rational recreation and amusement" has since become a multibillion-dollar enterprise that spans the globe. Many post exchange stores are actually department stores designed for family shoppers, although single soldiers can buy all the necessities of barracks life. Some stores even permit personnel in uniform to be waited on first during certain hours of the day, such as the lunch hour.

Several hundred military exchanges are operated throughout the world by the Department of Defense. AAFES, headquartered in Dallas, Texas and headed by a general officer, operates outlets worldwide. At a minimum, AAFES customers save the state sales tax, which is not charged.

IDENTIFICATION CARDS
Your DD Form 2A, *U.S. Armed Forces Identification Card* (green, active duty, and reserve duty), is possibly the most important military document you possess. DD Form 1173, *Uniformed Services Identification and Privilege Card*, is equally important to military dependents. These cards identify the bearers as persons who are entitled to the wide range of entitlements, privileges, and benefits authorized for military personnel and their dependents.

DD Form 2A (green) is issued to the following:
- All military personnel on active duty for more than thirty days.
- Members of the Army National Guard and the U.S. Army Reserve.
- Cadets of the U.S. Military Academy.

DD Form 2A (red) is issued to inactive reserves who are not yet entitled to receive retired pay at age sixty and to ROTC college program students in their last two years of training or in receipt of a full service scholarship.

DD Form 2A (retired—blue) is issued to retired personnel of the uniformed services who are entitled to retirement pay. The DD Form 2A (retired) is also issued to persons who retired from ARNG or USAR at age sixty after completing federal service under Section 1331, Title 10, U.S. Code, and personnel permanently retired for physical disability.

All ID cards are the property of the U.S. government. They are not transferable. The individual (or sponsor) to whom the card is issued must turn in cards in the following circumstances:
- Expiration of the card.
- Change in eligibility status (such as change in grade or rank and changes caused by disciplinary action, discharge, death, retirement, reenlistment, age, marriage, or release to inactive duty of the sponsor).

- Replacement by another card.
- Request from competent authority.
- Demand of the installation commander, verifying activity, or issuing activity.
- Recovery of a lost card after a replacement has been issued.
- Request by the installation commander for temporary safekeeping while an individual is taking part in recreation and gymnastic activities.
- Official placement of a sponsor in a deserter status.
- Change in the status of a sponsor if it terminates or modifies the right to any benefit for which the card may be used.

A lost ID card must be reported promptly to military law enforcement authorities or to ID card issuing authorities. DD Form 1172, *Application for Uniformed Services Identification and Privilege Card*, is used for this purpose. The form also becomes the application for a new card, provided the individual continues to be eligible to receive it. DD Form 1172 must contain a statement of the circumstances of the loss, what was done to recover the card, and the card number, if known.

Any NCO who is performing his or her official duties may confiscate an ID card that is expired, mutilated, used fraudulently, or presented by a person not entitled to use it. Managers and employees of benefit and privilege activities may confiscate any expired or obviously altered ID card or document.

Commissary Cards

In 2004, Congress authorized unlimited commissary access for members of the Ready Reserve, (which includes members of the Selected Reserve, Individual Ready Reserve, and Inactive National Guard) and members of the Retired Reserve who possess a Uniformed Services Identification Card. Former members eligible for retired pay at age sixty but who have not yet attained the age of sixty and who possess a Department of Defense Civilian Identification Card are also eligible. Dependents of the members described above who have a Uniformed Services Identification Card or who have a distinct identification card used as an authorization card for benefits and privileges administered by the Uniformed Services also have access.

Dependent ID Cards

DD Form 1173 is used throughout the Department of Defense to identify persons, other than active-duty or retired military personnel, who are eligible for benefits and privileges offered by the armed forces.

Dependent ID cards are authorized for issue to lawful spouses; unremarried former spouses married to the member or former member for a period of at least twenty years, during which period the member or former member performed at least twenty years of service; children (adopted, legitimized, stepchildren, wards); parents (in special cases); and surviving spouses of active-duty or retired members. See AR 640-3 for specific details.

Generally, DD Forms 1173 are replaced for the same reasons that govern replacement of military ID cards.

To verify initial eligibility for issue of a dependent ID card and entry into the Defense Enrollment Eligibility Reporting System (DEERS), sponsors must be prepared to show marriage certificates, birth certificates, death certificates (in the case of unremarried widows or widowers), or any other documentation prescribed by AR 640-3 required to establish dependency.

Abuse of Privileges

All DD Forms 2, DD Form 1173, and other authorized identification documents issued to Army members and their dependents may be confiscated and overstamped for abuse of privileges in Army facilities. Medical benefits, however, cannot be suspended for these reasons.

Abuse of privileges includes the following:

- Unauthorized resale of commodities bought in Army activities to unauthorized persons, whether or not to make a profit (customary personal gifts are permissible).
- Shoplifting.
- Unauthorized access to activities.
- Misuse of a privilege (such as allowing an unauthorized person to use an otherwise valid ID card to gain access to a facility).
- Issuing dishonored checks in Army facilities.

Penalties for abuse of privileges in an appropriated or nonappropriated fund facility are a warning letter, temporary suspension of privileges, and indefinite suspension of privileges.

Thrift Savings Plan

The purpose of the Thrift Savings Plan (TSP) is to provide retirement income. It offers soldiers the same type of savings and tax benefits that many private corporations offer their employees under so-called 401(k) plans. Under the plan, soldiers save a portion of their pay in a special retirement account administered by the Federal Retirement Thrift Investment Board. The total amount contributed generally cannot exceed 9 percent of your basic pay plus up to 100 percent of any bonus or incentive pay you may receive up to the limits established by the Internal Revenue Service. Contributions from pay earned in a combat zone do not count against the ceiling.

Participation in the TSP is neither optional nor automatic. You must sign up through your finance office to participate. Soldiers have two "open seasons" per year in which to enroll. (Open seasons are currently May 15 through July 31 and November 15 through January 31.) You contribute to the TSP from your own pay on a pretax basis, and the amount you contribute and the earnings attributable to your contributions belong to you. They are yours to keep even if you do not serve the twenty years ordinarily necessary to receive military retired pay.

While you are a member of the uniformed services, any tax-deferred money withdrawn before the age of fifty-nine and a half as a result of financial hardship is

subject to the IRS 10 percent early withdrawal penalty, as well as regular income tax. With respect to postseparation withdrawals, if you separate from the service during or after the year in which you turn age fifty-five, your withdrawals are not subject to the early withdrawal penalty. If you separate before the year you reach age fifty-five, you can transfer your TSP account to an IRA or other eligible retirement plan (e.g., 401(k) plan, your civilian TSP account) or begin receiving annuity payments without penalty.

LEAVES AND PASSES

Military Leave

AR 600-8-10 governs leaves and passes. All members of the Army serving on active duty are entitled to leave with pay and allowances at the rate of two and one-half calendar days each month of active duty or active duty for training, including the following:

- Members of the Army serving in active military service, including members of the Army National Guard and the Army Reserve serving on active duty for a period of thirty days or more.
- Members of the Army National Guard and reserve who are serving on initial active duty for training or active duty for training for a period of thirty days or more and for which they are entitled to pay.
- Members of the Army National Guard who are serving on full-time training duty for a period of thirty days or more and for which they are entitled to pay.

The following circumstances do not qualify as periods of earned leave:

- AWOL.
- Confinement as a result of a sentence of court-martial; confinement for more than one day while awaiting court-martial (providing the court-martial results in a conviction).
- When in excess leave.
- Unauthorized absence as a result of detention by civil authorities.
- Absence due to misconduct.

The total accumulation of accrued leave (earned leave) at the end of a fiscal year (September 30) cannot exceed 60 days. Leave accumulated after that date is forfeited. The single exception to this policy applies to personnel who were prohibited from taking leave during the latter part of the fiscal year due to assignment or deployment to hostile fire or imminent danger pay areas. Eligible members can accumulate up to 30 additional days in excess of 60 but cannot carry over more than 120 days into the next fiscal year. Leave that begins in one fiscal year and is completed in another is apportioned to the fiscal year in which each portion falls. Upon discharge and immediate reenlistment, separation at expiration of term of service (ETS), or retirement, soldiers are authorized to settle their leave accounts for a lump-sum cash payment at the rate of one day of basic pay for each day of earned leave, up to 60 days. Public Law 94-212, February 9, 1976, limited settlement for accrued leave during a military career to a maximum of 60 days.

The following types of leave are authorized:

- *Advance leave.* Leave granted before its actual accrual, based on a reasonable expectation that it will be earned by the soldier during the remaining period of active duty.
- *Annual leave.* Leave granted in execution of a command's leave program, chargeable to the soldier's leave account. Also called "ordinary leave," as distinguished from emergency leave and special leave.
- *Convalescent leave.* A period of authorized absence granted to soldiers under medical treatment that is prescribed for recuperation and convalescence for sickness or wounds. Also called "sick leave," convalescent leave is not chargeable. Soldiers who sustain illness or injury while eligible for Hostile Fire Pay are entitled to funded transportation per Joint Federal Travel Regulations (JFTR), paragraph U7210. Reference AR 600-8-10, para. 5-5.
- *Emergency leave.* Leave granted for a bona fide personal or family emergency requiring the soldier's presence. Emergency leave is chargeable.
- *Environmental and morale leave.* Leave granted in conjunction with an environmental and morale leave program established at overseas installations where adverse environmental conditions exist that offset the full benefit of annual leave programs. This leave is chargeable.
- *Excess leave.* This leave is in excess of accrued and/or advance leave, granted without pay and allowances.
- *Graduation leave.* A period of authorized absence granted, as a delay in reporting to the first permanent duty station, to graduates of the U.S. Military Academy who are appointed as commissioned officers. Not chargeable, providing it is taken within three months of graduation.
- *Leave awaiting orders.* This is an authorized absence—chargeable to accrued leave and in excess of maximum leave accrual—taken while awaiting further orders and disposition in connection with disability separation proceedings under the provisions of AR 635-40.
- *Reenlistment leave.* This leave is granted to enlisted personnel as a result of reenlistment. May be either advance leave or leave accrued or a combination thereof; chargeable against the soldier's leave account.
- *Rest and recuperation (R&R)—extensions of overseas tours.* This is a nonchargeable increment of R&R leave authorized for enlisted soldiers in certain specialties who voluntarily extend their overseas tours. It is authorized in lieu of $50 per month special pay. The tour extension must be for a period of at least twelve months. Options under this program include nonchargeable leaves of fifteen or thirty days.
- *Rest and recuperation leave.* Leave is granted in conjunction with rest and recuperation programs established in those areas designated for hostile fire pay, when operational military considerations preclude the full execution of ordinary annual leave programs. R&R leave is chargeable to the normal leave account; however, the Army pays for transportation to and from the leave destination. Currently, soldiers, Active or Reserve, assigned to a

twelve-month tour of duty within the U.S. Central Command's Area of Responsibility (USCENTCOM AOR) in support of the Global War on Terror (GWOT) may take up to fifteen days of leave during their deployment with leave beginning the day the soldier arrives at the leave destination and ends the day before travel begins to return to the theater of operations. The commander determines priority for personnel who are eligible for R&R leave based on the criteria above, as well as operational, safety, and security requirements.

- *Special leave.* This is leave accrual that is authorized in excess of sixty days at the end of a fiscal year for soldiers assigned to hostile fire/imminent danger areas or certain deployable ships, mobile units, or other duty.
- *Terminal leave.* This leave is granted in connection with separation, including retirement, upon the request of the individual.

When possible, soldiers should be encouraged to take at least one annual leave period of about fourteen consecutive days or longer (paragraph 203b, AR 630-5). Personnel who refuse to take leave when the opportunity is afforded them should be counseled and informed that such refusal may result in the loss of earned leave at a later date.

Leave is requested on part I, DA Form 31, *Request and Authority for Leave.* Requests for leave must be processed through the individual's immediate supervisor, although this step may be waived where supervisory approval or disapproval is inappropriate. This approval authority (generally, the soldier's commanding officer) ascertains that the individual has sufficient leave accrued to cover the entire period of absence requested.

Personnel should be physically present when DA Form 31 is authenticated and when commencing and terminating leave. Commanders may, at their discretion, authorize telephonic confirmation of departure and return.

Passes

A pass is an authorized absence not chargeable as leave, granted for short periods to provide respite from the working environment or for other specific reasons, at the end of which the soldier is actually at his or her place of duty or in the location from which he or she regularly commutes to work. This provision includes both regular and special passes.

Regular passes are granted to deserving military personnel for those periods when they are not required to be physically present with their unit for the performance of assigned duties. Normally, regular passes are valid only during specified off-duty hours, not more than seventy-two hours, except for public holiday weekends and holiday periods which, by discretion of the president, are extended to the commencement of working hours on the next working day.

Special passes are granted for periods of three or four days (seventy-two to ninety-six hours) to deserving personnel on special occasions or in special circumstances for the following reasons: as special recognition for exceptional performance of duty, such as soldier of the month or year; to attend spiritual retreats or to

observe other major religious events; to alleviate personal problems incident to military service; to vote; or as compensatory time off for long or arduous duty away from the home station or for duty in an isolated location where a normal pass is inadequate.

Passes may not be issued to soldiers so that two or more are effective in succession or used in a series, through reissue immediately after return to duty.

Extension of a pass is authorized provided the total absence does not exceed seventy-two hours for a regular pass, seventy-two hours for a special three-day pass, and ninety-six hours for a special four-day pass. Special passes will not be extended by combination with public holiday periods or other off-duty hours in cases in which the combined total will exceed the maximum limits of a three-day or four-day pass. Passes may not be taken in conjunction with leave, and extensions beyond the authorized maximum are chargeable to leave (AR 600-8-10).

15

Uniforms, Insignia,
and Personal Appearance

WEARING THE UNIFORM

Your Army uniform is the outward evidence of your profession and your standing
in that profession and a prime indicator of the degree of respect with which you
regard your service to the United States of America and the Army. The condition of
your uniform and the way you wear it are also a reflection of your own self-respect.

Occasions When the Uniform Is Required to Be Worn

The Army uniform is worn by all personnel when on duty unless Headquarters,
Department of the Army (HQDA), has authorized the wearing of civilian clothes.
The following general rules apply:
- Installation commanders may prescribe the uniforms to be worn in formations; duty uniforms are generally prescribed by local commanders or heads
  of agencies, activities, or installations.
- The wearing of combinations of uniform items not prescribed in AR 670-1 is
  prohibited.
- Uniform items changed in design or material may continue to be worn until
  wear-out date unless specifically prohibited by Headquarters, Department of
  the Army.

Occasions When the Uniform May Not Be Worn

The wearing of the Army uniform is prohibited for all Army personnel under the
following circumstances:
- In connection with the promotion of any political interests or when engaged
  in off-duty civilian employment.
- Except as authorized by competent authority, when participating in public
  speeches, interviews, picket lines, marches, rallies, or public demonstrations.
- When wearing the uniform would bring discredit upon the Army.
- When specifically prohibited by Army regulations.

Wearing of Headgear

The Army uniform is not complete unless the proper form of hat, cap, or beret is worn with it. Headgear is worn when outdoors and indoors when under arms.

Soldiers are exempt from wearing headgear to evening social events (after retreat). The appropriate headgear is, however, worn when wearing these uniforms on all other occasions.

Headgear is not required to be worn only when it would interfere with the safe operation of military vehicles. Military headgear is not required to be worn in privately owned or commercial vehicles.

Berets

The black beret is now the Army standard headgear and is worn by those soldiers not currently wearing the green, maroon, or tan beret. Soldiers will wear the beret with the utility and service uniforms in garrison environments only and will wear the patrol cap (formerly called the battle dress uniform [BDU] cap) in the field when authorized to remove their Kevlar helmet. Commanders may authorize the wear of the patrol cap on work details or in other situations when wear of the beret is impractical.

New soldiers receive the black beret at their first permanent duty assignment after the completion of initial entry training or officer/warrant officer basic courses. Soldiers who are not issued or who do not wear the black beret will wear the patrol cap with utility uniforms and the garrison cap with service uniforms.

For enlisted soldiers, the crest of the unit to which the soldier is assigned is worn centered on the blue Army flash on the black beret. Soldiers wear the beret so that the headband is straight on the head, one inch above the eyebrows, with the flash over the left eye and the excess material draped over to the right, down to at least the top of the ear, but no lower than the middle of the ear. A dip is formed in the wool, just behind the flash stiffener, and a slight fold is formed to the right front of the beret, next to the flash. Soldiers will tie off the adjusting ribbon into a nonslip knot, cut off the excess adjusting ribbon as close to the knot as possible, and tuck the knot into the edge binding at the back of the beret. The beret is formfitting to the head when worn properly; therefore, soldiers may not wear hairstyles that distort the beret.

The blue and white service caps remain the prescribed headgear for the blue and white dress and mess dress uniforms.

Uniform Appearance

The word "uniform" as used in this context means "conforming to the same standard or rule." Although absolute uniformity of appearance by all soldiers at all times cannot reasonably be expected as long as armies are composed of so many various individuals, uniformed soldiers should project a military image that leaves no doubt that they live by a common standard.

One important rule of uniformity is that, when worn, items of the uniform should be kept buttoned, zippered, and snapped; metallic devices (such as collar brass insignia) should be kept in proper luster; and shoes should be cleaned and shined. In instances where boots are worn with uniforms, soldiers will not blouse boots any lower than the third eyelet from the top.

Lapels and sleeves of coats and jackets for both male and female personnel should be roll pressed (without creasing). Trousers, slacks, and sleeves of shirts and blouses should be creased.

Care and Maintenance of the Uniform

All solid brass items (belt buckles, belt-buckle tips, collar brass insignia) should be maintained in a high state of luster at all times. These items come coated with a lacquer, and if their surfaces are kept protected and gently rubbed clean with a soft clean cloth, they will keep their shine for a long time. But when the lacquer coating becomes scratched, dirt begins to accumulate in the scratches, and the item can be kept shined only by completely removing the lacquer surface. The safest and most reliable method for removing the coating from brass items is to use Brasso polish applied with thumb and forefinger or a cloth.

Spit-shining does make shoes, boots, and equipment look sharp, but it dries out the leather.

Replace heels on shoes and boots after wear of seven-sixteenths of an inch or more. To check your soldiers' footgear, attempt to role a pencil under the heel.

Pay attention to the removal of stains from your clothing.

Never press dirty clothing, and be careful when you do press clothing that the iron is not too hot. Use a damp cloth between the iron and the fabric when pressing wool items, dampen the surface of cotton clothing before applying the iron, and observe the various fabric settings on the iron when pressing synthetic fabric.

Frequent cleaning of uniform items will increase their longevity and maintain the neat soldierly appearance that the uniform is designed to project. Rotating items of clothing, such as shoes and boots, will contribute to their longer life.

Fitting of Uniforms

Uniform items purchased in the Clothing Sales Store are fitted (or should be fitted) before they are taken off the premises. Personnel who purchase uniform items through the post exchange or from commercial sources should pay close attention to the proper fit of the items before wearing them.

An NCO should be able to tell at a glance whether a soldier (male or female) is wearing a properly fitted uniform. Fitting instructions and alterations of uniforms are made in accordance with AR 700-84 and TM 10-227, *Fitting of Army Uniforms and Footwear.*

The Clothing Allowance System

Clothing allowances are provided so that each soldier may maintain the initial clothing issue. Monthly clothing allowances provide for the cost of replacement and pur-

chase of new items or the purchase of additional clothing items, not cleaning, laundering, and pressing. The basic allowance begins on the soldier's 181st day of active duty and is paid each month for the remainder of the first three-year period. The standard allowance begins the day after the soldier completes thirty-six months on active duty. The clothing allowance accrues monthly and is paid annually during the month of the soldier's basic active service date.

CLASSIFICATION OF SERVICE AND UTILITY FIELD UNIFORMS

Class A Service Uniform

For men: consists of the Army green AG 489 coat and trousers, a short-sleeved or long-sleeved AG 415 shirt with pleated pockets, a black four-in-hand tie (tied in a slip knot with the ends left hanging), and other accessories.

For women: consists of the appropriate Army green coat and skirt or slacks of the Army green classic uniform; a short-sleeved or long-sleeved AG 415 shirt; a black neck tab; and authorized accessories. The Army green maternity uniform (slacks or skirt) is also a Class A service uniform when the tunic is worn.

Class B Service Uniform

For men: consists of the same as for the Class A except that the service coat is not worn. The black tie is required when wearing the long-sleeved AG 415 shirt and is optional with the short-sleeved shirt.

For women: consists of the same as for the Class A except that the service coat and the maternity tunic are not worn. The black neck tab is required when wearing the long-sleeved AG 415 shirt and the long-sleeved maternity shirt. It is optional with the short-sleeved version of both shirts.

Class C Uniforms

These are utility, field, and other organizational uniforms, such as the battle dress (BDU), hospital duty, and food service uniforms.

Optional Dress Uniforms

The Army blue uniform, white uniform, blue mess uniform, and white mess uniform are available for optional purchase by enlisted soldiers. The Army blue uniform is issued to soldiers when required as a duty uniform, such as when assigned to the Old Guard at Arlington Cemetery.

MEN'S ARMY GREEN UNIFORM

The Army green uniform, Class A and Class B variations, may be worn by male personnel when on duty, off duty, or during travel. These uniforms are also acceptable for informal social functions after retreat, unless other uniforms are prescribed by the host.

Men's Class A Uniform

The Army green uniform (Class A) consists of the Army green (AG) shade 489 coat and trousers, worn with either the new long-sleeved or short-sleeved 415 pleated pocket shirt and a black four-in-hand necktie.

The coat should fit with a slight drape in both the front and the back. No pronounced tightness at the waist or flare below the waist is authorized. The length of the coat should extend to below the crotch.

Matching Army green uniform trousers are straight-legged and reach the top of the instep and are cut on a diagonal line to reach a point approximately midway between the top of the heel and the top of the standard shoe in the back. The trousers may have a slight break in the front.

Accessories (Class A)

The U.S. insignia disk is worn on the right lapel collar approximately one inch above the notch. The branch insignia disk is worn on the left lapel collar approximately one inch above the notch. Both are centered on the lapel collar so as to be parallel with the inside of the lapel.

Distinctive unit insignia (unit crests) of the currently assigned unit are worn centered on both shoulder loops (epaulets) of the coat between the outside edge of the shoulder loop button and the seam of the loop.

The current organization shoulder sleeve insignia (patch) is sewn on the left sleeve one-half inch down from the shoulder seam and centered. When the Ranger, Special Forces, Sappers, or President's Hundred Tab is worn, the tab will be placed one-half inch below the shoulder seam, other tabs one-eighth inch below it, and the current organization shoulder patch worn one-quarter inch below the bottom of the lowest tab. A shoulder patch for a former wartime organization may be worn on the right sleeve one-half inch below the shoulder seam.

With the Class A Army green uniform, rank insignia is sewn on the sleeve halfway between the elbow and the shoulder seam of the coat.

When awarded, sew-on service stripes (hash marks) are placed four inches above the bottom of the left sleeve and centered on the sleeve. Overseas bars are placed four inches above the bottom of the right sleeve.

The nameplate is worn on the right breast pocket of the coat, centered between the top of the button and the top of the pocket. Unit awards, such as the Presidential Unit Citation, Joint Meritorious Unit Award, and so forth, are worn one-eighth inch above the right breast pocket.

Individual decorations and service ribbons are worn one-eighth inch above the left breast pocket of the coat. When combat and special skill badges are worn, they are centered one-quarter inch above the ribbons. When more than one badge is worn above the ribbons, badges will be stacked one-half inch apart and may be aligned to the left to present a better appearance.

Marksmanship badges are worn on the left breast pocket flap one-eighth inch below the top seam of the pocket. If more than one badge is worn, they are spaced

Class A Uniform for Men

one inch apart and centered in relation to the bottom edge of the ribbons and the pocket button. When special skill badges, e.g. driver's badge, are worn on the pocket flap, they are placed to the right of the marksmanship badges.

The Army black beret, organizational berets, and drill sergeant hats are authorized for wear with the Class A and Class B uniforms.

Men's Army Green Dress Uniform
The men's Army green dress uniform consists of the Army green coat and trousers, with a commercially purchased long-sleeved white shirt and black bow tie. The dress uniform is restricted to formal social functions, private or official, and transit to and from such functions. It cannot be worn for duty or travel. Boots, berets, or organizational items, such as brassards or military police (MP) accessories, are not used with the green dress uniform.

Class B Uniform for Men

Men's Class B Uniform

The men's Class B uniform merely omits the coat. It consists of the long-sleeved or short-sleeved AG 415 shirt and AG 489 trousers with black web belt and brass buckle. The black four-in-hand necktie must be worn with the long-sleeved shirt and is optional for the short-sleeved shirt. Soldiers are required to have one long-sleeved and two short-sleeved AG 415 pleated pocket shirts.

Individual awards and decorations are authorized to be worn on the Class B uniform shirts. Their placement is as on the coat. Check AR 670-1 for additional details.

Shoulder mark rank insignia is worn on the Class B uniform shirt for all NCOs and on the shirt collars for non-NCO enlisted grades.

Class A Uniform for Women

WOMEN'S CLASS A UNIFORM

The women's Class A uniform consists of the Army green classic coat and either the Army green classic skirt or slacks, a new AG 415 short-sleeved or long-sleeved tuck-in shirt, and a black neck tab. The short-sleeved and long-sleeved tuck-in shirts replace the long-sleeved and short-sleeved AG 415 overblouse, which are now an optional purchase item.

The women's coat is a hip-length, single-breasted coat with four buttons and button-down shoulder loops. The Army green classic skirt has a waistband and side zipper closure. The skirt length will not be more than one inch above or two inches below the crease in the back of the knee. Women now wear the new AG 489 green slacks, which have belt loops and are worn with a one-inch black web belt and matching brass buckle.

Accessories (Class A)

Specifications for wear of the organizational shoulder sleeve insignia (patch), unit crests, rank insignia, service stripes, overseas bars, and regimental crests are the same for the women's Class A uniform as they are for the men's Class A uniform and are described above. There are, however, some differences.

The U.S. insignia disk is centered on the right collar of the coat approximately five-eighths inch up from the notch, with the center line of the insignia parallel to the inside edge of the lapel. The branch insignia disk is centered in the same manner on the left collar.

The key to the alignment of accessories on the women's Class A uniform is the placement of the plastic nameplate. The nameplate can be adjusted to conform to individual figure differences. The nameplate is centered horizontally on the right side between one and two inches above the top button of the coat. Individual and service ribbons are aligned on the left side parallel to the bottom edge of the nameplate. Other badges are aligned on the nameplate or the ribbons in the same manner as on the men's Class A uniform.

The Army black beret, organizational berets, and drill sergeant hats are authorized for wear with the Class A and Class B uniforms. No hair should show on the forehead below the front bottom edge of the beret or hat, which should be situated approximately one inch above the eyebrows.

Women's Army Green Dress Uniform
The women's Army green dress uniform consists of the Army green coat and skirt or slacks, with a commercially purchased long-sleeved white shirt. The Army black neck tab is worn. The dress uniform is restricted to formal social functions, private or official, and transit to and from such functions. It cannot be worn for duty or travel. Boots, berets, or organizational items, such as brassards or MP accessories, are not used with the women's green dress uniform.

Women's Class B Uniforms
The women's Class B uniform merely omits the coat. It consists of the long-sleeved or short-sleeved AG 415 shirt, which is worn with either the new AG 489 slacks,

**Polished Pin-on Insignia
of Grade on Collars**

Sew-on Insignia of Grade

Class B Uniform for Women

black web belt, and brass buckle or the AG 489 classic skirt. The black neck tab must be worn with the long-sleeved shirt and is optional for the short-sleeved shirt.

Soldiers are required to have one long-sleeved and two short-sleeved AG 415 shirts with tuck-in shirts. Female soldiers must also possess two pairs of AG 489 slacks with belt loops. Individual awards and decorations are authorized to be worn on the Class B uniform shirts. Their placement is as on the coat. Check AR 670-1 for additional details.

Shoulder mark rank insignia is worn on the Class B uniform shirt for all NCOs and on the shirt collars for non-NCO enlisted grades.

Green Maternity Uniform

The pregnant soldier has been provided with a special uniform. Accessories, insignia, awards, badges, and accoutrements for the maternity uniforms follow the same regulations as those for the women's Class A, Class B, and green dress uniforms.

WORK AND DUTY UNIFORMS

Army Combat Uniform

The Army combat uniform (ACU) has been developed and fielding to the total Army should be complete by December 2007. There are currently twenty changes to the uniform, including removing the color black and adapting the digital print from

ACU Worn With the Patrol Cap

the Marine Corps uniform. The bottom pockets on the jacket were removed and placed on the shoulder sleeves so soldiers can have access to them while wearing body armor. The pockets were also tilted forward so that they are easily accessible. Buttons were replaced with zippers that open from the top and bottom to provide comfort while wearing armor. Patches and tabs are affixed to the uniform with Velcro to give the wearer more flexibility. The ACU consists of a jacket, trousers, moisture wicking T-shirt, and the brown combat boots. It will replace both versions of the battle dress uniform (BDU) and the desert camouflage uniform. The black beret will be the normal headgear for the ACU, but there is a matching patrol cap to be worn at the commander's discretion.

Temperate and Enhanced Hot Weather Battle Dress Uniforms (EHWBDU)
The temperate, hot-weather (HW), and enhanced hot-weather (EHW) battle dress uniforms (BDUs) are authorized for year-round wear by all personnel when prescribed by the commander, until replaced by the ACU.

Temperate and Enhanced Hot Weather BDU

Desert BDU   **Night Desert Coverall**

Desert Battle Dress Uniform (DBDU)

These uniforms are issued as organizational utility, field, training, or combat uniforms, and they are not intended for wear as all-purpose uniforms when other uniforms are more appropriate. Personnel wear the DBDU on duty when prescribed by the commander. Soldiers may wear the DBDU off post, unless prohibited by the commander, but may not wear DBDUs for commercial travel, unless authorized. Personnel may not wear DBDUs in establishments that primarily sell alcohol. If the establishment sells alcohol and food, soldiers may not wear utility uniforms if their activities in the establishment center on drinking alcohol only.

Cold Weather Uniform

The OG 108 cold weather uniform is designed for year-round wear by all personnel when issued as organizational clothing and prescribed by the commander. It is not

Hospital Duty Uniforms

authorized for travel or wear off military installations except in transit. Components of this uniform may be worn with utility and other organization uniforms as part of a cold weather ensemble when issued and prescribed by the commander.

Hospital Duty Uniform (Male)

This year-round duty uniform for all male soldiers in the Army Medical Specialist Corps and those in medical, dental, or veterinary MOSs is worn in medical health-care facilities as prescribed by the medical commander. The commander may authorize the wear of this uniform in a civilian community when in support of civilian activities.

Flight Uniform and Combat Vehicle Crewman Uniform

Hospital Duty and Maternity Uniform
This authorized year-round uniform is worn by Army Medical Specialist Corps personnel and enlisted women with medical, dental, or veterinary MOSs.

Flight Uniform
This uniform is authorized for year-round wear when on duty in a flying or standby-awaiting-flight status. Commanders may direct exceptions to wear policy.

Combat Vehicle Crewman (CVC) Uniform

The CVC is a year-round duty uniform for combat vehicle crewmen when on duty or as directed by the commander. This uniform is not for travel.

Maternity Work Uniform

This uniform is authorized for year-round on-duty wear by pregnant soldiers. It is not intended as a travel uniform, but it may be worn in transit between the individual's quarters and duty station.

OPTIONAL UNIFORMS

Army Blue Uniform (Male and Female)

This uniform is authorized for optional wear by enlisted personnel. Although primarily a uniform for social functions of a general or official nature before or after retreat, it may be worn on duty if prescribed by the commander. In certain honor guard assignments, the Army blue uniform is an issue item.

Army Blue Uniform

Other Authorized Uniforms
- Army white uniform.
- Army blue mess uniform.
- Army white mess uniform.

OUTERWEAR

A unisex cardigan sweater (optional) replaces the individual male and female black army cardigan and may be worn buttoned or unbuttoned indoors, but must be buttoned outdoors. The old style cardigan sweaters may no longer be worn.

A black double-breasted and belted all-weather coat replaced the unbelted black all-weather coat.

A unisex black, waist-length jacket with liner for wear with the Class B uniform is also authorized for optional purchase in clothing sales stores.

DISTINCTIVE UNIFORM ITEMS

The following uniform items are distinctive and should not be sold to or worn by unauthorized personnel: all Army headgear, badges, decorations, service medals, awards, tabs, service ribbons, appurtenances, and insignia of any design or color that have been adopted by the Department of the Army.

Headgear

The following items of headgear are authorized for Army personnel:

Item	Female Version*
Beret, black (Army)	Beret, black (Army)
Beret, green (Special Forces)	
Beret, maroon (Airborne)	
Beret, tan (Ranger)	
Cap, cold weather (AG 344)	
Cap, cold weather, utility	
Cap, food handler's, white, paper	
Cap, garrison, green (AG 489)	Cap, garrison (AG 489)
Cap, hot weather	
Cap, service, blue	Hat, service, blue
Cap, service, white	Hat, service, white
Hat, camouflage, desert	
Hat, drill sergeant	Hat, drill sergeant

*These are distinctively female items. Other items of headgear listed may be worn by female soldiers, as prescribed in AR 670-1.

Leader's Identification Insignia

The leader's identification (LI) insignia is a green cloth loop, one and five-eighths inches wide, worn in the middle of both shoulder loops of the Army green and cold weather coats. Personnel cease to wear them when reassigned from a command position. Leaders in all units (Active Army, Army National Guard, and Army Reserves), regardless of unit category (modification table of organization and equipment [MTOE] or table of distribution and allowance [TDA]), will wear the LI insignia. The specific leaders in units authorized to wear the Leader's Identification insignia are these: commanders, deputy commanders, platoon leaders, command sergeants major, first sergeants, platoon sergeants, section leaders (when designated in TOE), squad leaders and tank commanders, and rifle squad fire team leaders.

Distinctive Unit Insignia and Heraldic Items

Distinctive unit insignia (DUI) are made of metal or metal and enamel and are usually based on elements of the design of the coat of arms or historic badge approved for a specific unit. Sometimes erroneously referred to as "unit crests," DUI are subject to the approval of the Institute of Heraldry, U.S. Army, and, like shoulder sleeve insignia, are authorized for wear on the uniform as a means of promoting esprit de corps.

When authorized, these insignia are worn by all assigned personnel of an organization, except general officers. A complete set of insignia consists of three pieces: one for each shoulder loop and one for headgear (garrison, utility, cold weather caps, or berets).

Regimental Insignia

Regimental DUI are worn by all personnel affiliated with a regiment. The "unit crest" of the affiliated regiment is worn centered and one-eighth inch above the pocket seam or one-half inch above unit and foreign awards, if worn, on the Army green, white, and blue uniforms. The DUI worn on the shoulder loops of the Army green, white, and blue (enlisted men only) coats and jackets is always the unit of assignment. If assigned and affiliated to the same regiment, then all three crests are the same.

Distinctive Items for Infantry

Infantry personnel are authorized to wear the following distinctive items:

- A shoulder cord of infantry blue formed by a series of interlocking square knots around a center cord. The cord is worn on the right shoulder of the Army green, blue, and white uniform coats and shirts, passed under the arm and through the shoulder loop, and secured to the button on the shoulder loop.
- A plastic infantry blue disk, one and one-quarter inches in diameter, is worn by enlisted personnel of the infantry, secured beneath the branch of the service and the U.S. insignia, with a one-eighth-inch border around the insignia. It is authorized to be worn on the Army green, blue, and white uniforms.

Enlisted Insignia of Branch

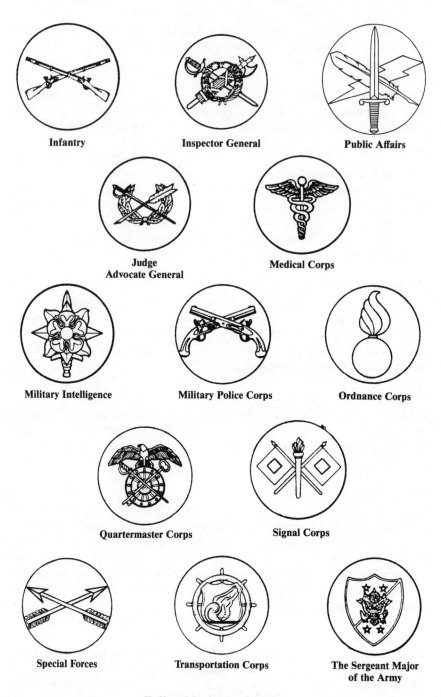

Infantry

Inspector General

Public Affairs

Judge
Advocate General

Medical Corps

Military Intelligence

Military Police Corps

Ordnance Corps

Quartermaster Corps

Signal Corps

Special Forces

Transportation Corps

The Sergeant Major
of the Army

Enlisted Insignia of Branch

- An insignia disk of infantry blue plastic, one and three-quarter inches in diameter, is worn secured beneath the insignia on the service cap. Criteria for wear are the same as those for the infantry blue insignia disk.

Organizational Flash
This shield-shaped embroidered patch with a semicircular bottom approximately two and one-quarter inches long and one and seven-eighths inches wide is worn centered on the stiffener of the beret by personnel authorized to wear one of the organizational berets (Ranger, Special Forces, and Airborne).

Airborne Background Trimming
Background trimming is authorized for wear with the parachutist or air assault badge. When authorized, such background will be worn by personnel of an airborne-designated organization who have been awarded one of the parachute badges or by personnel in an organization designated air assault who have been awarded the air assault badge.

PERSONAL APPEARANCE
A vital ingredient of the Army's strength and military effectiveness is the pride and discipline that soldiers bring to their service. It is the responsibility of noncommissioned officers to ensure that the military personnel under their supervision present a neat and soldierly appearance. It is the duty of each individual soldier to always take pride in his or her appearance.

Standards for All
Tattoos or brands anywhere on the head, face, and neck above the class A uniform collar are prohibited. Tattoos regardless of location on the body that are extremist, indecent, sexist, or racist are prohibited as they are prejudicial to good order and discipline within units.

Standards for Men
Many hairstyles are acceptable in the Army. The hair must be neatly groomed, and the length and bulk of the hair cannot be excessive or present a ragged, unkempt, or extreme appearance. Hair should present a tapered appearance and, when combed, should not fall over the ears or eyebrows or touch the collar. Block cuts are permitted in moderate degree, but in all cases the bulk and length of hair cannot interfere with the normal wear of headgear or protective mask. Men may shave their heads bald; they may not wear nail polish.

A soldier's face should be clean shaven, except that Army regulations do permit mustaches. No portion of a mustache is permitted to cover the upper lip line or extend beyond the crease of the upper and lower lips. Handlebar mustaches, goatees, and beards are not authorized. Where beard growth is prescribed by appropriate medical authority, as is sometimes necessary in the treatment of different types of skin disorders, the length required for medical treatment should be specified: "A

neatly trimmed beard is authorized. The length will not exceed one-quarter inch," for example. If you have such a medical condition, be sure to keep your exemption slip handy at all times when in uniform.

Standards for Women

The principle that soldiers should always maintain a neat and well-groomed personal appearance applies equally to men and to women, though the specific grooming standard for each reflects the traditional differences in appearance between the sexes.

Hair must be neatly groomed. The length and bulk of the hair should not be excessive or present a ragged, unkempt, or extreme appearance. Women may wear braids and cornrows. Hair should not fall over the eyebrows or extend below the bottom edge of the collar. Hairstyles cannot interfere with the proper wearing of military headgear or protective masks.

Cosmetics should be applied conservatively and in good taste. Two-tone or multitone manicures and nail designs are prohibited. Prohibited nail polish colors include bright fire engine red, khaki or camouflage, purple, gold, blue, and black.

Wearing of Civilian Jewelry

The wearing of a personal wristwatch, identification wrist bracelet, and no more than two rings is authorized with the Army uniform as long as they are not prohibited for safety reasons and the style is conservative and in good taste. The wearing of a purely religious medal on a chain around the neck is authorized, provided that neither the medal nor the chain is exposed.

No jewelry, watch chains, or similar civilian items, including pens or pencils, should be allowed to appear exposed on the uniform. Exceptions are that a conservative tie tack or tie clasp may be worn with the black four-in-hand necktie, and a pen or pencil may appear exposed on the hospital duty and food service uniforms.

Soldiers in and out of uniform are prohibited from displaying pierced body parts while on military installations worldwide—except for women with pierced ears. Women may wear screw-on or post-type earrings with the service, dress, or mess uniforms. Earrings may not be worn with Class C utility uniforms (utility, field, or organization, including hospital duty and food service uniforms). Earrings must be small in diameter, six millimeters or one-quarter inch; gold, silver, or white pearl; unadorned; and spherical. They must fit snugly against the ear and must be worn as a matched pair with only one in each earlobe.

One electronic device is authorized for wear on the uniform in official duties. It must be black in color and measure not more than four inches by two inches by one inch. Items that do not comply must be carried elsewhere.

Wearing of Civilian Clothing

Civilian clothing is authorized for wear off duty unless the wear is prohibited by the installation commander within CONUS or the major command overseas. When on duty in civilian clothes, soldiers must conform to the appearance standards of AR 670-1, unless specifically authorized for mission requirements.

Security Badges
Security identification badges are worn in restricted areas as prescribed by local commanders. They are usually laminated plastic identification badges worn suspended from clips. They should never be worn outside the secure area for which they authorize an individual access. To prevent the possibility of losing them, some personnel suspend them from a chain worn around the neck and, when in public, under their outer garments.

REFERENCES
> AR 600-8-22, *Military Awards.*
> AR 670-1, *Uniform and Insignia.*
> AR 700-84, *Issue and Sale Of Personal Clothing.*
> FM 3-21-15 [21-15], *Care and Use of Individual Clothing and Equipment.*

16

Awards
and Decorations

The Army's awards and decorations program provides tangible recognition for acts of valor, exceptional service or achievement, special skills or qualifications, and acts of heroism not involving actual combat. It is the responsibility of any soldier having personal knowledge of an act, an achievement, or a service believed to warrant the award of a decoration to submit a formal recommendation for consideration.

Under this criterion, it is possible that a private may recommend a captain for a decoration, but usually the system works the other way. As an NCO, you must be alert for service or acts that warrant special recognition. The only consideration that should be used is this one: Does the person's act or service warrant an award?

CRITERIA
Award recommendations must be factual and specific, and they must clearly demonstrate that the person being recommended deserves recognition. If your narrative does not support award of a decoration—if you use clichés in place of straightforward and factual prose narrative writing—your recommendation likely will be disapproved.

TIME LIMITATION
Awards for meritorious service should be anticipated, and your recommendation should be submitted far enough in advance to ensure that the award is ready in time to be presented to the individual before his or her departure.

Another reason for acting quickly is that the closer you are to the act or service for which an individual is being recommended, the fresher the details will be in your memory. In any event, each recommendation for an award of a military decoration must be entered into military channels within two years of the act, achievement, or service to be honored. No recommendation except the Purple Heart is awarded more than three years after the act or period of service to be honored (with the exception of lost recommendations or those circumstances covered in paragraph 1-14c, AR 600-8-22). If a soldier under your supervision deserves an award, let him or her know that you've submitted a recommendation. If the recommendation is not approved, at least the soldier will know you tried and will respect you for it.

PRECEDENCE

Decorations, the Good Conduct Medal, and service medals are ranked in the following order of precedence when worn or displayed:

U.S. military decorations.
U.S. unit awards.
U.S. nonmilitary decorations.
U.S. service (campaign) medals and service and training ribbons.
U.S. Merchant Marine awards.
U.S. nonmilitary unit awards.
Foreign military decorations.
Foreign unit awards.
Non-U.S. service awards.
State awards for Army National Guard (ARNG) soldiers.

U.S. military decorations are ranked in the following order of precedence when worn or displayed:

Medal of Honor (Army, Navy, Air Force).
Distinguished Service Cross.
Navy Cross.
Air Force Cross.
Defense Distinguished Service Medal.
Distinguished Service Medal (Army, Navy, Air Force, Coast Guard).
Silver Star.
Defense Superior Service Medal.
Legion of Merit.
Distinguished Flying Cross.
Soldier's Medal.
Navy and Marine Corps Medal.
Airman's Medal.
Coast Guard Medal.
Bronze Star Medal.
Purple Heart.
Defense Meritorious Service Medal.
Meritorious Service Medal.
Air Medal.
Aerial Achievement Medal.
Joint Service Commendation Medal.
Army Commendation Medal.
Navy Commendation Medal.
Air Force Commendation Medal.
Coast Guard Commendation Medal.
Joint Service Achievement Medal.
Army Achievement Medal.

Navy Achievement Medal.
Air Force Achievement Medal.
Coast Guard Achievement Medal.
Combat Action Ribbon.

U.S. service (campaign) medals, and service and training ribbons authorized for wear on the uniform are listed below, in their order of precedence. Personnel may wear service medals and service and training ribbons awarded by other U.S. Services on the Army uniform, except for the Air Force Longevity Service Award ribbon and Air Force, Navy, and Coast Guard marksmanship medals and ribbons. Personnel will wear service and training medals and ribbons awarded by other U.S. Services after U.S. Army service and training ribbons and before foreign awards.

Prisoner of War Medal.
Good Conduct Medal. (Good Conduct Medals from the other Services in order of precedence.)
Army Reserve Components Achievement Medal. (This medal and equivalents awarded by other Service reserve components follow the Army Good Conduct Medal and Good Conduct Medals from the other Services.)
Army of Occupation Medal.
Medal for Humane Action.
National Defense Service Medal.
Korean Service Medal.
Antarctica Service Medal.
Armed Forces Expeditionary Medal.
Vietnam Service Medal.
Southwest Asia Service Medal.
Kosovo Campaign Medal.
Afghanistan Campaign Medal.
Iraq Campaign Medal.
Global War on Terrorism Expeditionary Medal.
Global War on Terrorism Service Medal.
Korean Defense Service Medal.
Armed Forces Service Medal.
Humanitarian Service Medal.
Military Outstanding Volunteer Service Medal.
Armed Forces Reserve Medal.
NCO Professional Development Ribbon.
Army Service Ribbon.
Overseas Service Ribbon.
Army Reserve Components Overseas Training Ribbon.
Coast Guard Special Operations Service Ribbon.
Air Force Combat Readiness Medal.
Navy Sea Service Deployment Ribbon.

UNIT AWARDS

U.S. unit awards are given to an operating unit and are worn by members of that unit who participated in the cited action. Personnel who did not participate in the cited action, but who are assigned in the cited unit, are authorized temporary wear of some unit awards. U.S. unit awards authorized for wear on Army uniforms are listed below in their order of precedence:

Presidential Unit Citation (Army, Air Force).
Presidential Unit Citation (Navy).
Joint Meritorious Unit Award.
Valorous Unit Award.
Meritorious Unit Commendation (Army).
Navy Unit Commendation.
Air Force Outstanding Unit Award.
Coast Guard Unit Commendation.
Army Superior Unit Award.
Meritorious Unit Commendation (Navy).
Navy "E" Ribbon.
Air Force Organizational Excellence Award.
Coast Guard Meritorious Unit Commendation.

WEARING OF MEDALS AND RIBBONS

All individual U.S. decorations and service medals (full-size medals, miniature medals, and ribbons) are worn above the left breast pocket or centered on the left side of the coat or jacket of the prescribed uniform (with the exception of the Medal of Honor [MOH], which may be worn suspended around the neck). Decorations are worn with the highest displayed above and to the wearer's right of the others.

Ribbons Representing
Decorations and Service Medals

1		2	
3	4		5
6	7		8
9	10		11

1. Medal of Honor	7. Soldier's Medal
2. Distinguished Service Cross	8. Bronze Star Medal
3. Distinguished Service Medal	9. Purple Heart
4. Silver Star	10. Meritorious Service Medal
5. Legion of Merit	11. Air Medal
6. Distinguished Flying Cross	

Full-size decorations and service medals may be worn on the Army blue, white, and green uniforms when worn for social functions or when directed. They are worn in order of precedence from the wearer's right to left, in one or more lines, without overlapping within a line, with one-eighth-inch space between lines. No line will contain fewer medals than the one above it. The Medal of Honor is worn with the neck band ribbon around the neck, outside the shirt collar and inside the coat collar, with the medal hanging over the necktie.

Miniature decorations and service medals are authorized for wear on the mess and evening mess uniforms only. They may be worn side by side or overlapped, but the overlap will not exceed 50 percent and will be equal for all. There are no miniature medals authorized for the Medal of Honor.

Service ribbons are worn in the order of precedence from the wearer's right to left in one or more lines either without a space between rows or with a one-eighth-inch space. No row should contain more than four service ribbons. Male and female personnel are authorized to wear them on the Army green, white, and blue uniforms.

Retired personnel and former soldiers may wear either full-size or miniature medals on appropriate civilian clothing on Veterans Day, Memorial Day, and Armed Forces Day, and at formal occasions of ceremony and social functions of a military nature.

Unauthorized Wearing of Decorations and Badges

Federal law prescribes stiff penalties for the unauthorized wearing of U.S. decorations, badges, appurtenances, and unit awards:

> Whoever knowingly wears . . . any decoration or medal authorized by Congress for the Armed Forces of the United States or any of the service medals or badges awarded to the members of such forces, or the ribbon, button, or rosette of any such badge, decoration or medal, or any colorable imitation thereof, except when authorized under regulations made pursuant to law, shall be fined not more than $250 or imprisoned not more than six months, or both.
>
> —62 Stat. 732, June 25, 1948, as amended 18 U.S.C. 704

The U.S. Code (18 U.S.C. 703) further prescribes:

> Whoever, within the jurisdiction of the United States, with intent to deceive or mislead, wears any naval, military, police, or other official uniform, decoration, or regalia of any foreign state, nation, or government with which the United States is at peace, or anything so nearly resembling the same as to be calculated to deceive, shall be fined not more than $250 or imprisoned not more than six months or both.

U.S. Military Decorations

The Medal of Honor

The Army and Air Force version of the Medal of Honor (MOH) is the highest award for the risk of life "above and beyond the call of duty" involving actual conflict with an enemy; the Navy version can and has been awarded to noncombatants in peacetime, and Congress has similarly awarded special medals to honor individual exploits during peacetime.

The Medal of Honor is designed in the form of a five-pointed star, made of silver and heavily electroplated in gold. In the center of the star appears the head of Minerva—the Roman goddess whose name is associated with wisdom and righteousness in war—surrounded by the words "United States of America." An open laurel wreath, enameled in green, encircles the star, and the oak leaves at the bases of the prongs of the star are likewise enameled. The medal is suspended by a blue silk ribbon, spangled with thirteen white stars (representing the thirteen original states), and attached to an eagle supported by a horizontal bar upon which is engraved the word "Valor."

The reverse of the medal is plain so that the name of the recipient may be engraved thereon; the reverse of the bar is stamped "The Congress to . . . ."

On December 21, 1861, Pres. Abraham Lincoln approved the Medal of Honor for enlisted men of the Navy and Marine Corps; a similar medal was established for the Army on July 12, 1862, further amended by legislation enacted on March 3, 1863, to include officers and making the provisions retroactive to the beginning of the Civil War. The first Army Medals were awarded on March 25, 1863. The Medal of Honor is awarded only to U.S. citizens. The Army Medal may be awarded only to military personnel on active federal service (paragraph 3.6, AR 600-8-22).

Distinguished Service Cross

Established by legislation on July 9, 1918 (as amended July 25, 1963), the Distinguished Service Cross (DSC) evolved from the Certificate of Merit of 1847. The DSC is the second highest decoration for valor in war and is bestowed to recognize extraordinary heroism in connection with military operations in time of war. Unlike the Medal of Honor, however, the DSC may be awarded for heroism involving several acts over a short period of time that need not have been performed in actual conflict with an enemy but must have involved extraordinary risk of life. Successive awards are denoted by oak-leaf clusters (paragraph 3.7, AR 600-8-22).

Defense Distinguished Service Medal

Established by Executive Order 11545, July 9, 1970, the Defense Distinguished Service Medal (DDSM) is awarded to any military officer who, while assigned to joint staffs and other joint activities of the Department of Defense, distinguishes himself or herself by exceptionally meritorious service in a position of unique and great responsibility. It is not awarded for a period of service for which a Distin-

guished Service Medal or similar decoration is awarded. Subsequent awards are denoted by oak-leaf clusters (paragraph 2.3, AR 600-8-22).

Distinguished Service Medal

Established by an act of Congress of July 9, 1918, the Distinguished Service Medal (DSM) is awarded to any person who, while serving in any capacity with the U.S. Army, has distinguished himself or herself by exceptionally meritorious service in a duty of great responsibility. Awards may be made to persons other than members of the armed forces of the United States for wartime services only, and then only under exceptional circumstances with the approval of the president. Successive awards are denoted by oak-leaf clusters (paragraph 3.8, AR 600-8-22).

Silver Star

Established by an act of Congress of July 9, 1918 (as amended by an act of July 25, 1963), the Silver Star (SS) is the third-ranking U.S. decoration for heroism in wartime.

When first established, the SS was worn in the form of a small silver star, three-sixteenths inch in diameter, upon the respective service medal and ribbon to indicate each separate citation for gallantry in action earned during the campaign for which the service medal was authorized. These stars were known as "citation stars."

The current version of the SS is gilt bronze in the shape of a star one and one-quarter inches across. On the obverse is a laurel wreath, within which is a silver star three-sixteenths inch in diameter; on the reverse are inscribed the words "For Gallantry in Action." The SS may be awarded by any commander who has the authority to award the DSC, and the SS, like the DSC, may be awarded for acts of heroism that take place over a period of time. Successive awards are denoted by oak-leaf clusters (paragraph 3.9, AR 600-8-22).

Defense Superior Service Medal

Established by Executive Order 11904, February 6, 1976, the Defense Superior Service Medal (DSSM) may be awarded to U.S. personnel who give superior meritorious service in a position of significant responsibility. It is not awarded to any individual for a period of service for which a Legion of Merit or similar decoration is awarded. Successive awards are denoted by oak-leaf clusters (paragraph 2.4, AR 600-8-22).

Legion of Merit

Established by an act of Congress of July 20, 1942, the Legion of Merit (LM) is awarded to any member of the armed forces of the United States or a friendly foreign country who distinguishes himself or herself by outstanding meritorious conduct in the performance of outstanding services. Successive awards are denoted by oak-leaf clusters (paragraph 3.10, AR 600-8-22).

Distinguished Flying Cross

Established by an act of Congress of July 2, 1926, the Distinguished Flying Cross (DFC) may be awarded, in war or peace, to U.S. military personnel who distinguish themselves by heroism or extraordinary achievement while participating in aerial flight. Such awards are made only to recognize single acts of heroism or extraordinary achievement that are not sustained operational activities against an armed enemy. An act of heroism must be evidenced by voluntary action above and beyond the call of duty. Achievement awards must have resulted in an accomplishment so exceptional and outstanding as to clearly set the individual apart from other persons in similar circumstances. Awards to foreign personnel serving with the U.S. armed forces may be made only in connection with actual wartime operations. Successive awards are denoted by oak-leaf clusters (paragraph 3.11, AR 600-8-22).

Soldier's Medal

Established by an act of Congress of July 2, 1926, the Soldier's Medal (SM) is awarded to U.S. and foreign military personnel in recognition of heroism not involving actual conflict with an enemy. The performance must have involved personal hazard or danger and voluntary risk of life of approximately the same degree as that required for award of the Distinguished Flying Cross, but awards of the SM are not made solely on the basis of having saved a life. Subsequent awards of this decoration are denoted by oak-leaf clusters (paragraph 3.12, AR 600-8-22).

Bronze Star Medal

Originally established by Executive Order 9419 of February 4, 1944 (superseded by Executive Order 11046 of August 26, 1962), the Bronze Star Medal (BSM) can be awarded to U.S. and foreign personnel, both military and civilian, for acts that display heroism, meritorious achievement, or service performed in connection with military operations against an armed force. A bronze V device is worn to denote awards for heroism, and successive awards are denoted by oak-leaf clusters (paragraph 3.13, AR 600-8-22).

Purple Heart

Originally established by Gen. George Washington on August 7, 1782, the Purple Heart (PH) is the oldest U.S. military decoration. The PH is awarded in the name of the president to any member of the armed forces or any civilian of the United States who, while serving under competent authority in any capacity with one of the U.S. armed services after April 5, 1917, has been wounded or killed or who has died or may die after being wounded.

A "wound" is defined as any injury (not necessarily one that breaks the skin) caused by an outside force or agent. Multiple injuries suffered at the same moment from the same agent are considered as one wound. Specific examples of injuries that would be authorized the award of the PH are those incurred while making a parachute landing from an aircraft that had been brought down by enemy fire,

or injuries received as the result of a vehicle accident caused by enemy fire. Subsequent awards of the PH are denoted by oak-leaf clusters. (paragraph 2-8, AR 600-8-22).

Defense Meritorious Service Medal

Established by Executive Order 12019 of November 3, 1977, the Defense Meritorious Service Medal (DMSM) is awarded in the name of the secretary of defense to any member of the armed forces who, while serving in any joint activity of the Department of Defense on or after November 3, 1977, for a period of sixty days or more, demonstrates incontestably exceptional service or achievement of a magnitude that clearly places him or her above his or her peers. Subsequent awards of the DMSM are denoted by oak-leaf clusters (paragraph 2-5, AR 600-8-22).

Meritorious Service Medal

Established by Executive Order 1144.8 on January 16, 1969, the Meritorious Service Medal (MSM) is awarded to any member of the armed forces of the United States who, while serving in a noncombat area after January 16, 1969, has distinguished himself or herself by outstanding meritorious achievement or service. The achievement or service must have been comparable to that required for the Legion of Merit but in a position of lesser, though considerable, responsibility. This decoration is the equivalent of the Bronze Star Medal for recognition of outstanding meritorious noncombat achievement or service and takes precedence with, but after, the BSM when both are worn on the uniform. This decoration is not awarded to foreign personnel. Subsequent awards are denoted by oak-leaf clusters (paragraph 3-14, AR 600-8-22).

Air Medal

Established by Executive Order 9242-A, September 11, 1942, the Air Medal (AM) is awarded to any person who, while serving in any capacity in or with the Army, shall have distinguished himself by meritorious achievement while participating in aerial flight. Awards may be made in recognition of single acts of merit or heroism or for meritorious service. A system of denoting successive awards of the medal was devised using bronze arabic numerals instead of oak-leaf clusters. Therefore, an individual holding fifteen awards of the AM wears the numeral "14" on the suspension ribbon and service ribbon (paragraph 3-15, AR 600-8-22).

Joint Service Commendation Medal

The Joint Service Commendation Medal (JSCM) is awarded to any member of the armed forces who distinguishes himself or herself by meritorious achievement or service while serving in any joint assignment. Awards made for acts or services involving direct participation in combat operations on or after June 25, 1963, may be denoted by the bronze V device. Subsequent awards of the JSCM are denoted by oak-leaf clusters (paragraph 2-6, AR 600-8-22).

Army Commendation Medal

The Army Commendation Medal (ARCOM) is awarded to any member of the armed forces who distinguishes himself or herself by heroism, meritorious achievement, or meritorious service. The ARCOM may also be awarded to a member of the armed forces of a friendly foreign nation who distinguishes himself or herself by an act of heroism, extraordinary achievement, or meritorious service that has been of mutual benefit to a friendly nation and the United States. Awards of the ARCOM may be made for acts of valor performed under circumstances described above that are of lesser degree than those required for award of the Bronze Star Medal and may include acts that involve aerial flight. Awards may also be made for noncombat acts of heroism that do not meet the requirements for award of the Soldier's Medal. This decoration is primarily awarded to company-grade officers, warrant officers, and enlisted personnel (paragraph 3.16, AR 600-8-22).

Joint Service Achievement Medal

The Joint Service Achievement Medal (JSAM) is awarded to any member of the armed forces of the United States, below the grade of full colonel, who distinguishes himself or herself by meritorious achievement or service while serving in any joint activity after August 3, 1983. Military personnel on temporary duty to a joint activity for at least sixty days are also eligible.

The required achievement or service, while of lesser degree than that required for award of the Joint Service Commendation Medal, must have been accomplished with distinction. Subsequent awards are designated by oak-leaf clusters (paragraph 2.7, AR 600-8-22).

Army Achievement Medal

The Army Achievement Medal (AAM) is awarded to any member of the armed forces of the United States, or to any member of the armed forces of a friendly foreign nation, who, while serving in any capacity with the Army in a noncombat area on or after August 1, 1981, distinguishes himself or herself by meritorious service or achievement of a lesser degree than that required for award of the Army Commendation Medal. Subsequent awards are designated by oak-leaf clusters (paragraph 3.7, AR 600-8-22).

Prisoner of War Medal

The Prisoner of War Medal (POWM) is authorized for all U.S. military personnel who were taken prisoner of war after April 6, 1917, during an armed conflict and who served honorably during the period of captivity (paragraph 2.9, AR 600-8-22).

Good Conduct Medal

The Good Conduct Medal (GCM) is awarded to enlisted personnel for exemplary behavior, efficiency, and fidelity to active federal military service. Generally, the qualifying period is three years of continuous active service completed on or after

August 26, 1940. Exceptions are for those who are separated from the service by reason of physical disability incurred in the line of duty, who died or were killed before completing one year of service, or who separated after more than one year but less than three years (draftees). Those exceptions apply only to the first award.

Isolated examples of nonjudicial punishment are not necessarily automatically disqualifying but must be considered on the basis of the soldier's whole record; consideration as to the nature of the infraction, the circumstances under which it occurred, and when it occurred must be duly weighed by the individual's commander. Conviction by court-martial terminates a period of qualifying service; a new period begins following the completion of the sentence imposed by court-martial.

Successive awards of the GCM are identified by clasps, or bars, one-eighth inch by one and three-eighths inches, of bronze, silver, or gold, with loops (also called knots) that indicate each period of service for which the medal is authorized. The first award is the actual medal itself. Successive awards are indicated with clasps with loops (chapter 4, section 1, AR 600-8-22).

Army Reserve Components Achievement Medal

The Army Reserve Components Achievement Medal (ARCAM) may be awarded upon recommendation of the unit commander for four years of honest and faithful service on or after March 3, 1972. Service must have been consecutive, in the grade of colonel or below, and in accordance with the standards of conduct, courage, and duty required by law and customs of the service of an active-duty member of the same grade. The reverse of this medal is struck in two designs for award to personnel whose service has been primarily in the Army Reserve or primarily in the National Guard (chapter 4, section 111, AR 600-8-22).

Unit Awards

Unit awards are authorized in recognition of group heroism or meritorious service, usually during a war, as a means of promoting esprit de corps. They are of the following categories: unit decorations, infantry and medical streamers, campaign streamers, war service streamers, and campaign silver bands.

U.S. unit decorations, in order of precedence listed in this section, have been established to recognize outstanding heroism or exceptionally meritorious conduct in the performance of outstanding services. These awards may be worn permanently by those who served with the unit during the cited period. The Presidential Unit Citation (Army), the Valorous Unit Award, the Meritorious Unit Commendation, and the Army Superior Unit Award may be worn temporarily by those serving with the unit subsequent to the cited period.

Presidential Unit Citation

The Presidential Unit Citation is awarded to units of the armed forces of the United States and cobelligerent nations for extraordinary heroism in action against an armed enemy occurring on or after December 7, 1941. The unit must display such

gallantry, determination, and esprit de corps in accomplishing its mission under extremely difficult and hazardous conditions as to set it apart from and above other units participating in the same campaign. The degree of heroism required is the same as that which would warrant award of a Distinguished Service Cross to an individual. The Presidential Unit Emblem (Army) is a blue ribbon set in a gold-colored metal frame of laurel leaves (paragraph 7.13, AR 600-8-22).

Joint Meritorious Unit Award
The Joint Meritorious Unit Award is awarded to joint activities of the Department of Defense for meritorious achievement or service, superior to that normally expected, during combat with an armed enemy of the United States, during a declared national emergency, or under extraordinary circumstances that involve the national interest (paragraph 7.15, AR 600-8-22).

Valorous Unit Award
Criteria for the Valorous Unit Award are the same as those for the Presidential Unit Citation except that the degree of valor required is that which would merit award of the Silver Star to an individual. The emblem is a scarlet ribbon with the Silver Star color design superimposed in the center, set in a gold-colored metal frame with laurel leaves (paragraph 7.14, AR 600-8-22).

Meritorious Unit Commendation
The Meritorious Unit Commendation is awarded for at least six months of exceptionally meritorious conduct in support of military operations to service and support units of the armed forces of the United States and cobelligerent nations. The degree of achievement is that which would merit the award of the Legion of Merit to an individual. The emblem is a scarlet ribbon set in a gold-colored metal frame with laurel leaves (paragraph 7.15, AR 600-8-22).

Army Superior Unit Award
The Army Superior Unit Award is given for outstanding meritorious performance of a difficult and challenging mission under extraordinary circumstances by a unit during peacetime. The emblem is a scarlet ribbon with a vertical green stripe in the center, on each side of which is a narrow yellow stripe, set in a gold-colored metal frame with laurel leaves (paragraph 7.16, AR 600-8-22).

U.S. Service Medals
Service or campaign medals denote honorable performance of military duty within specified limited dates in specified geographical areas. With the exception of the Humanitarian Service Medal, the Armed Forces Reserve Medal, the Army Reserve Component Achievement Medal, the Army Service Ribbon, and the NCO Professional Development Ribbon, they are awarded only for active federal military service.

Service medals are worn in order by the date when the person became eligible for the award, not by the date of entry in the records or the date upon which the award was established. Foreign military service medals are worn following authorized U.S. decorations. Not more than one service medal is awarded for service involving identical or overlapping periods of time, except that each of the following groups of service medals may be awarded to an individual provided he or she meets the criteria prescribed by chapter 5, AR 600-8-22. For information concerning the criteria for the award of any service medal not listed below, see chapter 5, AR 600-8-22.

Army of Occupation Medal

Established by the War Department General Orders 32, 1946, this medal is awarded for service for thirty consecutive days at a normal post of duty with the Army of Occupation of Berlin during the period 1945–1990. This medal was previously authorized for post–World War II occupation duty in Germany, Austria, Italy, Japan, and Korea (see paragraph 5.1, AR 600-8-21). Berlin service does not authorize the wearing of a clasp on either the service medal or the service ribbon.

National Defense Service Medal

This medal is awarded for honorable active service for any period between the periods June 27, 1950, to July 27, 1954; January 1, 1961, to August 14, 1974; August 2, 1990, to November 30, 1995; and September 11, 2001, to a date to be later determined. Subsequent award of the NDSM is denoted by a bronze service star (paragraph 2.10, AR 600-8-22).

Antarctica Service Medal

Any member of the armed forces of the United States who participates in or has participated in scientific, direct support, or exploratory operations in Antarctica under sponsorship and approval of the U.S. government. This included flights as a member of the crew of an aircraft flying to or from the Antarctic continent or as a member of a U.S. ship operating south of latitude sixty degrees south in support of U.S. programs in Antarctica (paragraph 2.11, AR 600-8-22).

Armed Forces Expeditionary Medal

The Armed Forces Expeditionary Medal is authorized for U.S. military operations, U.S. operations in direct support of the United Nations, and U.S. operations of assistance for friendly foreign nations. Operations are defined as military actions or the carrying out of strategic, tactical, service, training, or administrative military missions and the process of carrying on combat, including movement, supply, attack, defense, and maneuvers needed to gain the objectives of any battle or campaign.

Designated areas and dates of service for eligibility are in AR 600-8-22. Subsequent awards of this medal are denoted by bronze service stars (paragraph 2.12, AR 600-8-22).

Vietnam Service Medal

The Vietnam Service Medal is awarded to all members of the armed forces who served in Vietnam and contiguous waters or airspace there after July 3, 1965, and through March 28, 1973. Members of the armed forces in Thailand, Laos, or Cambodia or the airspace thereover who during the same period served in direct support of operations in Vietnam are also eligible. See AR 600-8-22, appendix B, for authorized campaigns and dates. One bronze service star (or a combination of bronze and silver stars, as applicable) may be worn on the suspension ribbon and bar representing this medal (paragraph 2.13, AR 600-8-22).

Southwest Asia Service Medal

The Southwest Asia Service Medal (SWASM) is awarded to U.S. military personnel who have served in the Persian Gulf area since August 2, 1990. Subsequent awards of the SWASM are denoted by service stars affixed to the medal (paragraph 2.14, AR 600-8-22).

Kosovo Campaign Medal

The Kosovo Campaign Medal is to recognize the accomplishments of military servicemembers who participated in, or were in direct support of, the conflict in Kosovo. Members authorized the Kosovo Campaign Medal must have participated in or served in direct support of the Kosovo operation after March 24, 1999. Servicemembers must be bona fide members of a unit participating in, or engaged in direct support of, the operation for thirty consecutive days in the area of eligibility, or for sixty nonconsecutive days provided this support involves entering the area of eligibility. One bronze service star is worn on the suspension and service ribbon of the Kosovo Campaign Medal for qualified participation during the campaign period. Meeting the qualification in each of the two campaigns would warrant the medal and two bronze service stars.

Afghanistan Campaign Medal

The Afghanistan Campaign Medal is awarded to soldiers who deploy to Afghanistan in direct support of Operation Enduring Freedom (OEF) on or after October 24, 2001, to a date to be determined or the cessation of OEF. The area of eligibility encompasses all land area of the country of Afghanistan and all air spaces above the land.

Iraq Campaign Medal

The Iraq medal is awarded to soldiers who deploy to Iraq in direct support of Operation Iraqi Freedom (OIF) on or after March 19, 2003, to a date to be determined or the cessation of OIF. The area of eligibility encompasses all land area of the country of Iraq and the contiguous water area out to twelve nautical miles, and all air spaces above the land area of Iraq and above the contiguous water area out to twelve nautical miles.

Global War on Terrorism Expeditionary Medal

The Global War on Terrorism Expeditionary Medal (GWOTEM) is awarded to ser-vice members who serve in military expeditions to combat terrorism on or after September 11, 2001. Beginning April 30, 2005, the Global War on Terrorism Expeditionary Medal is no longer authorized to be awarded for service in Afghanistan and/or Iraq. The GWOTEM is still authorized for service in the other geographical areas of eligibility.

The Global War on Terrorism Service Medal

The Global War on Terrorism Service Medal (GWOTSM) is awarded to service-members who have participated in or served in support of Global War on Terrorism Operations outside the designated areas of eligibility (AOE) for the Global War on Terrorism Expeditionary Medal, on or after September 11, 2001, to a date to be determined. All soldiers serving on active duty between September 11, 2001, and March 2004 are all authorized the GWOTSM. After March 2004, battalion com-manders—the award approval authority—must determine if a soldier serving on active duty has qualified for the GWOTSM.

Soldiers will not receive more than one of the following medals for the same act, time period, or service: Afghanistan Campaign Medal, Iraq Campaign Medal, Global War on Terrorism Expeditionary Medal, or Armed Forces Expeditionary Medal.

Korea Defense Service Medal

The Korea Defense Service Medal (KDSM) is authorized to members of the armed forces who have served on active duty in support of the defense of the Republic of Korea from July 28, 1954, to a date to be determined. The area of eligibility encom-passes all the land area of the Republic of Korea, and the contiguous water out to twelve nautical miles, and all air spaces above the land and water areas. Effective February 3, 2004, the Overseas Service Ribbon (OSR) is no longer authorized for overseas tours in the Republic of Korea.

Armed Forces Service Medal

Awarded to members of the armed forces, who as of June 1, 1992, are participating or have participated as members of U.S. military units in a U.S. military operation, which is deemed to be a significant activity, and are encountering or have encoun-tered no foreign armed opposition or imminent threat of hostile action.

Servicemembers must be bona fide members of a unit participating for one or more days in the operation or engaged in direct support in the area of eligibility, or for sixty nonconsecutive days—provided this support involves entering the area of eligibility or participating as a regularly assigned aircrew member of an aircraft fly-ing into, out of, within, or over the area of eligibility in support of the operation. Second and subsequent awards will be denoted by bronze service stars (MILPER msg 96-098, March 11, 1996).

Humanitarian Service Medal

The Humanitarian Service Medal is authorized to be awarded to any armed forces personnel who directly participated in a Department of Defense–approved humanitarian act or operation, except when a by-name eligibility list is published. No more than one award of this medal may be made for the same act or operation. Subsequent awards are designated by bronze numerals. Operations for which award of the Humanitarian Service Medal have thus far been approved are listed in appendix C, AR 600-8-22 (paragraph 2.15, AR 600-8-22).

Military Outstanding Volunteer Service Medal

Received by members of the armed forces of the United States who subsequent to December 31, 1992, perform outstanding volunteer community service of a sustained, direct, and consequential nature. To be eligible, an individual's service must (1) be to the civilian community, including the military family community; (2) be significant in nature and produce tangible results; (3) reflect favorably on the military service and the Department of Defense; and (4) be of a sustained and direct nature. The Military Outstanding Volunteer Service Medal (MOVSM) is intended to recognize exceptional community support over time and not a single act or achievement. Further, it is intended to honor direct support of community activities (paragraph 2.16, AR 600-8-72).

Armed Forces Reserve Medal

Awarded for honorable and satisfactory service as a member of one or more of the reserve components of the armed forces of the United States for a period of ten years within a twelve-year period. Subsequent ten-year awards are denoted by a bronze hourglass. A gold hourglass is awarded on completion of the fourth ten-year period.

Awarded for mobilization on or after August 1, 1990, to members called to active duty volunteered and served on active duty in support of U.S. Military operations or contingencies designated by the secretary of defense. The "M" device is worn to indicate mobilization. Subsequent mobilizations are denoted by the wearing of a number to indicate the number of times mobilized. No hourglass is worn unless authorized under the above paragraph (paragraph 5.7, AR 600-8-22, and MILPER msg 96-196).

NCO Professional Development Ribbon

Established by the secretary of the Army on April 10, 1981, and effective August 1, 1981, the NCO Professional Development Ribbon is awarded to members of the U.S. Army, Army National Guard, and Army Reserve for successful completion of designated NCO professional development courses. The ribbon is awarded for four levels of professional development: Primary (1); Basic (2); Advanced (3); and the Sergeants Major Academy (4) (paragraph 5.6, AR 600-8-22).

Army Service Ribbon
Established by the secretary of the Army on April 10, 1981, and effective August 1, 1981, the Army Service Ribbon is awarded to members of the U.S. Army, Army National Guard, and Army Reserve who have successfully completed initial entry training. Enlisted persons are eligible upon completion of initial MOS-producing courses. For those enlisted persons assigned an MOS based on civilian or other-service acquired skills, it is awarded after four months of honorable active service (paragraph 5.5, AR 600-8-22).

Overseas Service Ribbon
Established by the secretary of the Army on April 10, 1981, and effective August 1, 1981, the Overseas Service Ribbon is awarded to all members of the U.S. Army, Army National Guard, and Army Reserve credited with a normal overseas tour completed in accordance with AR 614-30. A soldier who has overseas service credited by another armed service is also eligible for this ribbon. The ribbon is not authorized for completion of an overseas tour of duty for which a service medal has been authorized (paragraph 5.4, AR 600-8-22).

Army Reserve Components Overseas Training Ribbon
Established by the secretary of the Army on July 11, 1984, the ribbon is awarded to members of the U.S. Army Reserve components for successful completion of annual training or active-duty training for a period of not less than ten days on foreign soil (paragraph 5.3, AR 600-8-22).

Non-U.S. Service Medals

United Nations Medal
This medal may be awarded to personnel who have been in the service of the United Nations for a period of not less than six months with one of the units designated in paragraph 9.17, AR 688-8-2. The United Nations has, to date, cast medals for eleven different operations. Effective October 13, 1995, soldiers awarded any of these medals may wear the first medal and ribbon for which they qualify. Not more than one U.N. Medal may be worn. Award of a medal in a different U.N. mission is denoted by a bronze service star on the one U.N. Medal.

NATO Medal
Qualifying periods of service for the NATO medal are either thirty days (continuous or accumulated) in the territory and airspace of the former Republic of Yugoslavia and the Adriatic Sea, or ninety days (continuous or accumulated) in the area of operations outside the former Republic of Yugoslavia and the Adriatic Sea between July 1, 1992, and date to be determined.

Multinational Force and Observers Medal
To qualify for this medal, a soldier must have served with the Multinational Force and Observers at least ninety days after August 3, 1981. Subsequent awards for each completed six-month tour are indicated by an appropriate numeral, starting with numeral "1" (paragraph 9.18, AR 600-8-22).

Republic of Vietnam Campaign Medal
Authorized for acceptance by Department of Defense instructions 1348.17, January 31, 1974, this medal is worn by members of the armed forces who have served in the Republic of Vietnam for six months during the period March 1, 1961, to March 28, 1973, inclusive, or have served outside the geographical limits of the Republic of Vietnam and contributed direct combat support to the Republic of Vietnam Armed Forces for six months. Such persons must meet the criteria established for the Armed Forces Expeditionary Medal (Vietnam) or the Vietnam Service Medal during the period of service required to qualify for the Republic of Vietnam Campaign Medal. Soldiers serving under the above conditions for less than six months but who were wounded by hostile forces, captured, or killed in action or otherwise in the line of duty are also authorized this medal (paragraph 9.19, AR 600-8-22).

Kuwait Liberation Medal (Kingdom of Saudi Arabia)
Awarded by the Kingdom of Saudi Arabia to members of the armed forces of the United States who served within the designated war zone of Operation Desert Storm during the period January 17, 1991, through February 28, 1991.

Kuwait Liberation Medal (Government of Kuwait)
Awarded by the Government of Kuwait to U.S. military personnel who were assigned to one of several designated areas in and around Kuwait from August 2, 1990, to August 31, 1993. To be eligible, personnel must have been attached to or regularly served for one day or more with an organization participating in ground and/or shore operations; with a naval vessel directly supporting military operations; or as a crew member in one or more aerial flights that directly supported military operations in the designated areas. Temporary duty for thirty or sixty nonconsecutive days supporting such operations during the designated period also qualifies for award of the medal. The time requirement may be waived for temporary duty (TDY) soldiers who actually participated in combat operations (paragraph 9.20, AR 600-8-22).

Foreign Individual Awards
Decorations received from a foreign government in recognition of active field service in connection with combat operations or for outstanding or unusually meritorious performance may be accepted and worn upon approval of the Department of the Army. Without this approval, they become the property of the United States and must be deposited with the Department of the Army for use or disposal.

Qualification and special skill badges may be accepted if awarded in recognition of meeting the criteria, as established by the awarding foreign government, for the specific award.

Foreign badges are authorized for wear only on service and dress uniforms. The German marksmanship award (Schutzenschnur) may be worn only by enlisted personnel, on the right side of the uniform with the upper portion attached under the center of the shoulder loop and the bottom portion attached under the lapel.

U.S. Army Badges and Tabs

Badges and tabs are appurtenances of the uniform. In the eyes of their wearers, several badges have a significance equal to or greater than all but the highest decorations. There is no established precedence with badges as there is with decorations and service medals or ribbons. The badges are of three types: combat and special skill badges, marksmanship badges and tabs, and identification badges. Badges are awarded in recognition of attaining a high standard of proficiency in certain military skills. Subdued combat and special skill badges and the Ranger and Special Forces tabs are authorized on field uniforms.

Combat and Special Skill Badges

The following badges are awarded to denote excellence in performance of duties under hazardous conditions and circumstances of extraordinary hardship as well as for special qualifications and successful completion of prescribed courses of training. (See chapter 8, AR 600-8-22, for details.)

Combat Infantryman Badge (CIB). Awarded to infantry personnel in the grade of colonel or below who, after December 6, 1941, satisfactorily perform duty while assigned or attached as a member of an infantry brigade, regiment, or smaller unit during any period that such unit is engaged in active ground combat. Members of attached Ranger companies are also eligible (paragraph 8.6, AR 600-8-22).

Combat Medical Badge (CMB). Awarded to medical personnel assigned or attached by appropriate orders to an infantry unit of brigade, regimental, or smaller size—or to a medical unit of company or smaller size organic to an infantry unit of brigade or smaller size—during any period the infantry unit is engaged in actual ground combat. Such medical personnel are eligible for award of the badge, provided they are personally present and under fire during such ground combat.

In the Global War on Terror, medical personnel assigned or attached to or under operational control of any ground combat arms units (not to include members assigned or attached to aviation units) of brigade or smaller size are eligible for the Combat Medical Badge if they have satisfactorily performed medical duties while the unit is engaged in active ground combat, provided they are personally present and under fire. Retroactive awards are not authorized for service prior to September 18, 2001.

Combat Action Badge. Awarded to any soldier performing assigned duties in an area where hostile fire pay or imminent danger pay is authorized, who is person-

ally present and actively engaging or being engaged by the enemy, and performing satisfactorily in accordance with the prescribed rules of engagement. The soldier must not be assigned/attached to a unit that would qualify the soldier for the CIB/CMB.

Stars for Combat Infantryman, Combat Medical Badge, and Combat Action Badge. The second and succeeding awards of the CIB and the CMB, made to recognize participation and qualification in additional declared wars, are indicated by the addition of stars to the basic badges.

Expert Infantryman Badge. Awarded to infantry personnel of the active Army, ARNG, and USAR who satisfactorily complete prescribed proficiency tests (paragraph 8.8, AR 600-8-22).

Other Combat Medical Badges. Awarded to members of the Army Medical Department, the Naval Medical Department, or the Air Force Medical Service in the grade of colonel (Navy captain) or below who have satisfactorily performed medical duties while assigned or attached to a medical detachment of an infantry unit meeting the requirements for the combat infantryman badge (paragraph 8.7, AR 600-8-22).

Expert Field Medical Badge. Awarded to Army Medical Service personnel who satisfactorily complete prescribed proficiency tests (paragraph 8.9, AR 600-8-22).

Army Astronaut Badges. The Army Astronaut Badge has been added to the authorized special skill badges, but the requirements for award of this badge are not stated in the regulations. These badges are awarded in three degrees: basic, senior, and master.

Army Aviation Badges. There are nine badges relating to Army aviation—three each for Army aviators, flight surgeons, and aircraft crewmen—in the degrees of basic, senior, and master.

Master Army Aviator Badge, Senior Army Aviator Badge, and Army Aviator Badge. Awarded upon satisfactory completion of prescribed training and proficiency tests as outlined in AR 600-105.

Master Aircraft Crewman Badge, Senior Aircraft Crewman Badge, and Aircraft Crewman Badge. Authorized for award to enlisted personnel who meet the prescribed requirements (paragraph 8.24, AR 688-8-22).

Glider Badge. This badge is no longer awarded but is still authorized for wear by individuals who were previously awarded the badge (paragraph 8.29, AR 600-8-22).

Parachutist Badges. To be awarded the Master Parachutist Badge, an individual must meet the following criteria: have participated in sixty-five jumps, twenty-five with combat equipment, four at night, and five mass tactical jumps; have graduated as jumpmaster or served as jumpmaster on one or more combat jumps or on thirty-three noncombat jumps; have been rated excellent in character and efficiency; and have served on jump status for not less than thirty-six months (paragraph 8.13, AR 600-8-22).

For the Senior Parachutist Badge, an individual must meet the following criteria: have been rated excellent in character and efficiency with participation in thirty jumps, including fifteen jumps made with combat equipment, two night jumps, and two mass tactical jumps; have graduated from a jumpmaster course or served as jumpmaster on one or more combat jumps or fifteen noncombat jumps; and have served on jump status for not less than twenty-four months (paragraph 8.12, AR 600-8-22).

The Parachutist Badge is awarded for satisfactory completion of the course given by the airborne department of the Infantry School or while assigned or attached to an airborne unit or for participation in at least one combat jump (paragraph 8.11, AR 600-8-22).

Combat Parachutist Badges. Participation in a combat parachute jump entitles the individual to wear a bronze star, or stars, affixed to the Parachutist Badge.

Pathfinder Badge. Awarded upon successful completion of the Pathfinder course conducted at the Infantry School (paragraph 8.22, AR 600-8-22).

Air Assault Badge. Awarded to personnel who have satisfactorily completed either the Training and Doctrine Command (TRADOC) prescribed training course or the standard air assault course while assigned or attached to the 101st Air Assault Division since April 1, 1974 (paragraph 8.23, AR 600-8-23).

Diver Badges. Awarded after satisfactory completion of prescribed proficiency tests (AR 611-75). Five badges are authorized for enlisted personnel (paragraph 8.17, AR 600-8-22).

Driver and Mechanic Badge. Awarded only to enlisted personnel to denote a high degree of skill in the operation and maintenance of motor vehicles (paragraph 8.28, AR 600-8-22).

Explosive Ordnance Disposal Badges. There are three badges under this heading, any of which may be awarded to soldiers: Master Explosive Ordnance Disposal Badge, Senior Explosive Ordnance Disposal Badge, and Explosive Ordnance Disposal Badge. They are awarded to individuals assigned to duties involving the removal and disposition of explosive ammunition under hazardous conditions (paragraph 8.18, AR 600-8-22). This is now a Group 3 badge.

Nuclear Reactor Operator Badges. The Shift Supervisor Badge, the Operator First Class Badge, and the Operator Basic Badge were awarded upon completing the Nuclear Power Plant Operators Course or equivalent training and after operating nuclear power plants for specific periods. These badges are no longer awarded but are still authorized for wear by individuals to whom they were previously awarded (paragraph 8.30, AR 600-8-22).

Parachute Rigger Badge. Awarded to any individual who successfully completes the Parachute Rigger Course conducted by the U.S. Army Quartermaster School and who holds a Parachute Rigger MOS or skill identifier (paragraph 8.14, AR 600-8-22).

Physical Fitness Training Badge. This badge is awarded to soldiers who obtain a minimum score of 270 on the Army Physical Fitness Test (APFT) and

who meet the weight-control requirements of AR 600-9 (paragraph 8.48, AR 600-8-22).

Special Forces Tab
The Commander, U.S. Army John F. Kennedy Special Warfare Center (USAJFK-SWC), Fort Bragg, NC 28307-5000, may award the Special Forces Tab to any individual who has successfully completed the Special Forces Qualification Course or the Special Forces Officer Course. The Special Forces Tab may be awarded to any person on active duty, active status in the reserve components, in retired status, or honorably discharged who meets the appropriate criteria listed in AR 600-8-22.

Ranger Tab. Awarded to any person who successfully completes a Ranger course conducted by the Infantry School or who was awarded the Combat Infantryman Badge (CIB) while serving during World War II as a member of the 1st through 6th Ranger Battalions or the 5307th Composite Group (paragraph 8.46, AR 600-8-22).

Special Forces Tab. Awarded to any person who successfully completes the Special Forces Qualification Course conducted by the Special Forces School of the Special Warfare Center. This tab also may be awarded for former wartime service (paragraph 8.47, AR 600-8-22).

Sapper Tab. Successful completion of a Sapper leaders course conducted by the U.S. Army Engineer School or retroactively the Sapper tab may be awarded to any person successfully completing the Sapper Leaders Course on or after June 14, 1985.

Marksmanship Badges and Tabs
These badges and tabs include basic marksmanship qualification badges, excellence in competition badges, distinguished designation badges, the U.S. Distinguished International Shooter Badge, and the President's Hundred Tab.

Only members of the armed forces of the United States and civilian citizens of the United States are eligible for these qualification badges. Qualification badges for marksmanship are of three types: basic qualification, excellence in competition, and distinguished designation. Basic qualification badges (including Expert, Sharpshooter, and Marksman Badges) are awarded to those individuals who attain the qualification score prescribed in the appropriate field manual for the weapon concerned. Excellence in Competition Badges are awarded to individuals in recognition of an eminent degree of achievement in firing the rifle or pistol. Distinguished Designation Badges are awarded to individuals in recognition of a preeminent degree of achievement in target practice firing with the military service rifle or pistol (paragraph 8.44, AR 600-8-22).

Distinguished International Shooter Badge. Awarded to military or civilian personnel in recognition of an outstanding degree of achievement in international competition (paragraph 8.50, AR 600-8-22).

President's Hundred Tab. Awarded each person who qualifies among the top one hundred contestants in the President's Match held annually at the National Rifle Matches (paragraph 8.51, AR 600-8-22).

Identification Badges

Identification badges are worn to signify special duties.

Presidential Service Identification Badge. The Presidential Service Certificate and the Presidential Service Badge were established by Executive Order 11174, September 1, 1964. They are awarded in the name of the president of the United States as public evidence of deserved honor and distinction to members of the armed forces who have been assigned duty in the White House for at least one year after January 20, 1961. Once the badge is awarded, it may be worn as a permanent part of the uniform (paragraph 8.32, AR 600-8-22).

Vice-Presidential Service Identification Badge. The Vice-Presidential Service Badge was established by Executive Order 11544, July 8, 1970. It may be awarded upon recommendation of the military assistant to the vice president and may be worn as a permanent part of the uniform (paragraph 8.33, AR 600-8-22).

Secretary of Defense Identification Badge. Military personnel who have been assigned to duty and have served not less than one year after January 13, 1961, in the office of the secretary of defense are eligible for this badge. Once awarded, it may be worn as a permanent part of the uniform. It also is authorized for temporary wear by personnel assigned to specified offices of the secretary of defense (paragraph 8.34, AR 600-8-22).

Joint Chiefs of Staff Identification Badge. This badge may be awarded to military personnel who have been assigned to duty and who have served not less than one year after January 16, 1961, in a position of responsibility under the direct cognizance of the Joint Chiefs of Staff. Once awarded, the badge may be worn as a permanent part of the uniform (paragraph 8.35, AR 600-8-22).

Army Staff Identification Badge. This badge has been awarded by the Army since 1920 and is the oldest of the five types of identification badges now authorized for officers. It was instituted to give a permanent means of identification to those commissioned officers who had been selected for duty on the War Department General Staff, with recommendation for award based upon performance of duty. It has been continued under the present departmental organization.

Between September 30, 1979, and May 28, 1985, the badge could be awarded to the sergeant major (SGM) of the Army and to other senior NCOs (SGM E-9) assigned to duty with the same staff units. Effective May 28, 1985, qualifying service must be of at least one year while assigned to permanent duty on the Army General Staff or assigned to the Office of the secretary of the Army. Once awarded, this badge may be worn as a permanent part of the uniform (paragraph 8.36, AR 600-8-22).

Guard, Tomb of the Unknown Soldier Identification Badge. (Paragraph 8.37, AR 600-8-22).

Army ROTC Nurse Cadet Program Identification Badge. (Paragraph 8.38, AR 600-8-22).
Drill Sergeant Identification Badge. (Paragraph 8.39, AR 600-8-22).
U.S. Army Recruiter Identification Badge. (Paragraph 8.40, AR 600-8-22).
Army National Guard Recruiter Identification Badge. (Paragraph 8.42, AR 600-8-22).
U.S. Army Reserve Recruiter Identification Badge. (Paragraph 8.43, AR 600-8-22).
Career Counselor Badge. (Paragraph 8.41, AR 600-8-22).

Appurtenances
Appurtenances are devices affixed to service or suspension ribbons or worn in place of medals or ribbons. They are worn to denote additional awards, participation in a specific event, or other distinguished characteristics of the award.

Oak-Leaf Cluster
A bronze or silver twig of four oak leaves with three acorns on the stem, thirteen-thirty-seconds inch in length for the suspension ribbon and five-sixteenths inch in length for the service ribbon, is issued in lieu of a decoration for second or succeeding awards of decorations (other than the Air Medal) and service medals. A silver oak-leaf cluster is issued to be worn in lieu of five bronze clusters. Five one-sixteenth-inch oak-leaf clusters, joined together in series of two, three, and four clusters, are authorized for optional purchase and wear on service ribbons.

Numerals
Arabic numerals three-thirteenths inch high are issued in lieu of a medal or ribbon for second and succeeding awards of the Air Medal, the Humanitarian Service Medal, the Multinational Force and Observers Medal, the Army Reserve Components Overseas Training Ribbon, and the Overseas Service Ribbon. The numeral worn on the NCO Professional Development Ribbon denotes the highest completed level of NCO development. The numerals are worn centered on the suspension ribbon of the medal or the ribbon bar.

V Device
The V Device is a bronze letter V, one-quarter inch high with serifs at the top of the members (that is, the little strokes at the tops of the arms of the V that look like little rectangles). The V Device denotes awards of a medal for heroism and may be awarded with the Bronze Star Medal, the Air Medal, the Joint Service Commendation Medal (when the award is for acts or services involving direct participation in combat operations), and the Army Commendation Medal.

Clasps
Clasps are authorized to be worn on the Good Conduct Medal, the Army of Occupation Medal, and the Antarctic Service Medal.

Service Stars

The service star is a bronze or silver five-pointed star three-sixteenths inch in diameter. Three-sixteenths-inch service stars joined together in a series of two, three, and four stars are authorized for optional purchase and wear on service ribbons. Service stars, signifying participation in a combat campaign, are authorized for wear on the Armed Forces Expeditionary Medal and the Vietnam Service Medal. (Note: Bronze and silver stars are worn on U.S. Navy decorations in the same manner as oak-leaf clusters are worn on Army and Air Force decorations.)

Arrowhead

The arrowhead is a bronze replica of an Indian arrowhead, one-quarter inch high. It denotes participation in a combat parachute jump, combat glider landing, or amphibious assault landing, while assigned or attached as a member of an organized force carrying out an assigned tactical mission. It is worn on the service and suspension ribbons of the Vietnam Service Medal and the Armed Forces Expeditionary Medal.

Service Ribbons

Service ribbons are identical to the suspension ribbons of the medals they represent and are mounted on bars equipped with attaching devices; they are issued for wear in place of medals. The service ribbon for the Medal of Honor is the same color as the neck band, showing five stars in the form of a letter M.

Miniature Medals

Miniature replicas of all medals except the Medal of Honor are authorized for wear on specified uniforms, such as the blue and white mess uniforms, in lieu of the issued medals. Miniatures of decorations are issued only to foreign nationals. Awards issued by the secretary of defense include miniature medals.

Lapel Buttons

Lapel buttons are authorized for wear on the left lapel of civilian clothing only. They are available for service ribbons and other decorations and badges. Included in this category are the Army Lapel Button, which is awarded to any soldier (except retirees) who completed nine months' honorable active federal service after April 1, 1984, and the U.S. Army Retired Lapel Button.

CERTIFICATES AND LETTERS

Officers and senior NCOs may write and sign letters of appreciation and commendation for other enlisted personnel. Frequently, soldiers will ask for these accolades. Remember that a letter or certificate from an overseas commander or brigade or higher command sergeant major (CSM) is worth five promotion points.

Certificates and letters may be nothing more than pats on the back. Nevertheless, they go a long way toward boosting the morale of most recipients, and their judicious use is a good way to recognize faithful and competent service.

Certificate of Achievement

Commanders may recognize periods of faithful service, acts, or achievements that do meet the standards required for decorations by issuing to individual military personnel a Certificate of Achievement, DA Form 2442.

Certificates of Achievement are awarded under local criteria and may be used for awarding the Good Conduct Medal, for participation in the Department of the Army Suggestion Program, or to recognize meritorious acts or service.

Letters of Commendation and Appreciation

Acts or services that do not meet the criteria for decorations or a Certificate of Achievement may be recognized by written expressions of commendation or appreciation. These letters are typed on letterhead stationery and do not contain formalized printing, seals, or other distinguishing features that depart from normal letter form.

17

Military Justice

A fact of military life is that, despite the availability of information on the subject and the effort of commanders to keep their soldiers informed, many individuals simply do not know very much about the military justice system. Specific provisions pertaining to administration of the military justice system are in the *Manual for Courts-Martial* and AR 27-10, *Military Justice*.

NONJUDICIAL PUNISHMENT

Article 15 of the Uniform Code of Military Justice (UCMJ) provides commanding officers the authority and procedures to impose disciplinary punishments for minor offenses without a court-martial. Punishment without court-martial is called "nonjudicial" punishment. Such punishments may be in addition to or in lieu of admonition or reprimand. Unless the accused is embarked on a ship, Article 15 punishment may not be imposed if the accused demands trial by court-martial.

Punishments authorized under Article 15 are less severe than court-martial punishments. Unlike a special or general court-martial, Article 15 is not considered a federal conviction for a criminal offense. Article 15 is intended to provide a swift, efficient, and relatively easy method for punishing those committing minor offenses, for maintaining discipline, and for deterring future offenses. Under Article 15, commanders have wide latitude in punishments that may be imposed, ranging from oral reprimand to reduction in pay grades, fines, restriction, extra duty, or a combination of these.

It is a mistake to disregard the effect of an Article 15 on a soldier's career, although those received when in the junior enlisted grades can generally be overcome. The original copy of DA Form 2617, *Record of Proceedings under Article 15, UCMJ*, may be filed either in the official military personnel file performance portion of the permanent record or in the restricted portion. Records of Article 15 punishments can be used in a wide variety of personnel decisions and can lead to an involuntary administrative discharge.

Under Article 15 proceedings, legal rules of evidence do not apply, and providing defense counsel at the hearing is not mandatory. Nevertheless, the accused does have protection against arbitrary use of Article 15. In addition to the right to demand trial in lieu of Article 15 punishment, the accused has the right to consult

with counsel to decide whether to accept the punishment; if the accused accepts Article 15 and considers the punishment too harsh, he or she may appeal it. Other rights include the right to remain silent, to fully present his or her case in the presence of the imposing commander, to call witnesses, to present evidence, to be accompanied by a spokesperson, to request an open hearing, and to examine available evidence.

In order to find the soldier guilty, the commander must be convinced beyond a reasonable doubt that the soldier committed the offense. The maximum punishment depends on the rank of the commander imposing punishment and the rank of the soldier being punished.

Purposes of Nonjudicial Punishment

Nonjudicial punishment may be imposed in appropriate cases for the following purposes:

- To correct, educate, and reform offenders who have shown that they cannot benefit by less stringent measures.
- To preserve, in appropriate cases, an offender's record of service from unnecessary stigmatization by record of court-martial conviction.
- To further military efficiency by disposing of minor offenses in a manner requiring less time and personnel than trial by court-martial.

Generally, the term *minor offenses* includes misconduct not involving any greater degree of criminality than is involved in the average offense tried by summary court-martial.

Nonpunitive measures usually deal with misconduct resulting from simple neglect, forgetfulness, laziness, inattention to instructions, sloppy habits, immaturity, difficulty in adjusting to disciplined military life, and similar deficiencies. These measures are primarily tools for teaching proper standards of conduct and performance and do not constitute punishment. Included are denial of pass or other privileges, counseling, administrative reduction in grade, extra training, bar to reenlistment, and MOS reclassification. Certain commanders have the authority, apart from any under Article 15, to reduce enlisted persons administratively for inefficiency or other reasons. *Nonpunitive measures and nonjudicial punishment should not be confused.*

A written admonition or reprimand should contain a statement indicating that it has been imposed merely as an administrative measure and not as punishment under Article 15. Conversely, admonitions and reprimands that are imposed as punishment under Article 15 should be clearly stated to have been imposed as punishment under that article.

Commanding officers also have the authority to impose restraints or restrictions on a soldier for administrative purposes, such as to ensure the soldier's presence within the command. This authority exists apart from the authority to impose restriction as nonjudicial punishment. These nonpunitive measures may also include, subject to any applicable regulation, administrative withholding of privileges.

MAXIMUM PUNISHMENTS
FOR ENLISTED MEMBERS UNDER ARTICLE 15*

*Note: The maximum punishment imposable by any commander under summarized proceedings cannot exceed extra duty for fourteen days, restriction for fourteen days, oral reprimand, or any combination thereof.

Punishment	Imposed by Company Grade Officers	Imposed by Field Grade or General Officers
Admonition/Reprimand	Yes	Yes
and		
Extra Duties[1]	14 days	45 days
and		
Restriction	14 days	60 days
or		
Correctional Custody[2]		
(PV1, PV2, PFC)	7 days	30 days
or		
Restricted Diet Confinement		
(PV1, PV2, PFC attached or embarked on a vessel)	3 days	3 days
and		
Reduction		
(PV1, PV2, PFC, SPC, CPL)	One grade in peacetime[3]	One grade or more
(SGT, SSG)	One grade	
and		
Forfeiture[4]	7 days' pay	Half of 1 month's pay for 2 months

[1] Combinations of extra duties and restriction cannot exceed the maximum allowed for extra duty.

[2] Subject to limitations imposed by superior authority and presence of adequate facilities. If punishment includes reduction to private first class or below, reduction must be unsuspended.

[3] Only if imposed by a field grade commander of a unit authorized to have a commander who is a lieutenant colonel or higher.

[4] Amount of forfeiture is computed at the reduced grade, even if suspended, if reduction is part of punishment.

Extra training or instruction is one of the most effective nonpunitive measures available to a commander. It is used when a soldier's duty performance has been substandard or deficient. For example, a soldier who fails to maintain proper attire may be required to attend classes on the wearing of the uniform and stand inspection until the deficiency is corrected.

Summarized Proceedings

Summarized proceedings under Article 15 may be used if, after a preliminary inquiry, a commander determines that the punishment for an offense should not exceed extra duty or restriction for fourteen days; oral reprimand or admonition; or any combination of these punishments. The record of these proceedings is made on DA Form 2627-1. Generally, summarized proceedings are conducted like proceedings for more serious cases prosecuted under nonjudicial punishment, except that the individual normally is allowed twenty-four hours to decide whether to demand trial by court-martial and to gather matters in defense, extenuation, and/or mitigation. Because of the limited nature of the punishments imposed under these proceedings, the soldier has no right to consult with legally qualified counsel nor the right to a spokesperson.

Nature of Punishments

Nonjudicial punishments include the following actions:

Admonition and Reprimand. An admonition or reprimand may be imposed in lieu of or combined with Article 15 punishments.

Restriction. The severity of this type of restraint is dependent upon its duration and geographical limits specified when the punishment is imposed. A soldier undergoing restriction may be required to report to a designated place at specified times if it is considered reasonably necessary to ensure that the punishment is being properly executed.

Extra Duties. This involves the performance of duties in addition to those normally assigned to the person undergoing the punishment. Extra duties may include fatigue duties. In general, extra duties that would demean his or her position as a noncommissioned officer may not be assigned a corporal or above.

Reduction in Grade. This form involves the following considerations:

- Promotion authority. The grade from which a soldier is reduced must be within the promotion authority of the imposing commander or the officer to whom authority to punish under Article 15 has been delegated.
- Lateral appointments or reductions of corporal to specialist are not authorized. An NCO may be reduced to a lower pay grade, provided the lower grade is authorized in his or her primary MOS.
- Date of rank. When a soldier is reduced in grade as a result of unsuspended reduction, the date of rank in the grade to which reduced is the date the punishment of reduction was imposed.

- Entitlement to pay. When a soldier is restored to a higher pay grade because of a suspension or when a reduction is mitigated to a forfeiture, entitlement to pay at the higher grade is effective on the date of the suspension or mitigation.
- Senior noncommissioned officers. Sergeants first class and above may not be reduced under the authority of Article 15.

Forfeiture of Pay. Pay refers to basic pay of the individual plus any foreign duty pay. Forfeitures imposed by a company-grade commander may not be applied for more than one month, while those imposed by a field-grade commander may not be applied for more than two months. The maximum forfeiture of pay to which a soldier is subject during a given month—because of one or more actions under Article 15—is one-half of his or her pay per month. Article 15 forfeitures cannot deprive a soldier of more than two-thirds of his or her pay per month.

FORFEITURES OF PAY
AUTHORIZED UNDER ARTICLE 15

Maximum monthly authorized forfeitures of pay under Article 15, UCMJ, may be computed using the applicable formula below:

1. Upon enlisted persons:

$$\frac{\text{(monthly basic pay}^{1,2} + \text{foreign pay}^{1,3})}{2} = \text{maximum forfeiture per month if imposed by major or above}$$

$$\frac{\text{(monthly basic pay}^{1,2} + \text{foreign pay}^{1,3}) \times 7}{30} = \text{maximum forfeiture if imposed by captain or below}$$

2. Upon commissioned and warrant officers when imposed by an officer with general court-martial jurisdiction or by a general officer in command:

$$\frac{\text{(monthly basic pay}^{2})}{2} = \text{maximum authorized forfeiture per month}$$

---

[1]Amount of forfeiture is computed at the reduced grade, even if suspended, if reduction is part of the punishment imposed.
[2]At the time punishment is imposed.
[3]If applicable.

Combination and Apportionment

No two or more punishments involving deprivation of liberty may be combined in the same nonjudicial punishment to run either consecutively or concurrently, but other punishments may be combined. Restriction and extra duty may be combined in any manner to run for a period not in excess of the maximum duration imposable for extra duty by the imposing commander.

Suspension, Mitigation, Remission, and Setting Aside

Suspension. The purpose of suspending punishment is to grant a deserving soldier a probational period during which the individual may show that he or she deserves a remission of the suspended portion of his or her nonjudicial punishment. If—because of further misconduct within this period—it is determined that remission of the suspended punishment is not warranted, the suspension may be vacated and the suspended portion of the punishment executed.

Mitigation. Often there are factors other than the facts and circumstances of the offense that show that the accused should receive a light punishment. Examples include lack of past criminal record, good duty performance, and family hardship.

Remission. Remission can cancel any portion of the unexecuted punishment. Remission is appropriate under the same circumstances as mitigation.

Setting Aside and Restoration. Under this action, the punishment or any part or amount thereof, whether executed or unexecuted, is set aside, and any property, privileges, or rights affected by the portion of the punishment set aside are restored. The basis for this action is ordinarily a determination that under all the circumstances of the case, the punishment has resulted in a clear injustice.

Notification and Explanation of Rights

The imposing commander must ensure that the soldier is notified of the intention to dispose of the matter under Article 15. The imposing commander may delegate notification authority to another officer, warrant officer, or NCO (sergeant first class and above), providing that person outranks the person being notified. If an NCO is selected, that person should normally be the unit first sergeant or another NCO who is the senior enlisted person in the command in which the accused is serving.

The soldier must be given a "reasonable time" to consult with counsel, including time off from duty, if necessary, to decide whether to demand trial. The amount of time granted is normally forty-eight hours.

Before deciding to demand trial, the accused is not entitled to be informed of the type or amount of punishment he or she will receive if nonjudicial punishment is imposed. The imposing commander will inform the soldier of the maximum punishment allowable under Article 15 and the maximum allowable for the offense if the case proceeds to a trial by court-martial and conviction for the offense.

Right to Demand Trial

The demand for trial may be made at any time before imposition of punishment. The soldier will be told that if trial is demanded, it could be by summary, special, or

general court-martial. The soldier will also be told that he or she may object to trial by summary court-martial and that at a special or general court-martial he or she would be entitled to be represented by qualified military counsel or by civilian counsel obtained at the soldier's expense.

Appeals

Only one appeal is permitted under Article 15 proceedings. An appeal not made within a "reasonable time" may be rejected as untimely by the superior authority. The definition of what constitutes a "reasonable time" varies according to the situation. Generally, an appeal, including all documentary matters, submitted more than five calendar days (including weekends and holidays) after punishment is imposed will be presumed to be untimely. If, at the time of imposition of punishment, the soldier indicates a desire not to appeal, the superior authority may reject a subsequent election to appeal, even if it is made within the five-day period.

Appeals are made on DA Form 2627 or DA Form 2627-1 and forwarded through the imposing commander or successor-in-command to the superior authority. The superior must act on the appeal unless otherwise directed by competent authority. A soldier is not required to state the reasons for the appeal, but he or she may present evidence or arguments proving innocence or why the sentence should be mitigated or suspended. Unless an appeal is voluntarily withdrawn, it must be forwarded to the appropriate superior authority. A timely appeal does not terminate because a soldier is discharged from the service but must be processed to completion.

Announcement of Punishment

The punishment may be announced at the next unit formation after punishment is imposed or if appealed, after the decision. It also may be posted on the unit bulletin board. The purpose of announcing the results is to avert the perception of unfairness of punishment and to deter similar misconduct by others.

Records of Punishment

DA Forms 2627 are prepared in an original and five copies. What happens to those copies, especially the original, is of the utmost importance to soldiers who receive punishment under nonjudicial proceedings.

Original. For enlisted soldiers, the original copy is forwarded to the U.S. Army Enlisted Records and Evaluation Center, Indianapolis, Indiana. The decision on where in the punished soldier's Official Military Personnel File (OMPF) this copy will be placed is made by the imposing commander at the time punishment is imposed and is final. The imposing commander will decide whether it is to be filed in the performance fiche or the restricted fiche of the individual's OMPF.

Other Copies. For those Articles 15 filed in the performance fiche of the OMPF, copy one is placed in the permanent section of the Military Personnel Records Jacket (MPRJ) unless the original is transferred from the performance to the restricted fiche, at which time it is destroyed. Otherwise, it is kept in the unit personnel files and destroyed two years from the date of punishment or on the sol-

dier's transfer, whichever occurs first. Copies two through four are used variously as prescribed by AR 27-10, depending on whether forfeiture of pay is involved and whether the punished soldier appeals. Copy five is given to the individual.

COURTS-MARTIAL

Courts-martial are the agencies through which Army magistrates try personnel accused of violations of the punitive articles of the UCMJ. These are Articles 77 through 134 of the UCMJ and are designed to provide punishment of three broad groups of crimes and offenses:

- Crimes common to both the military and civilian law, such as murder, rape, sodomy, arson, burglary, larceny, and fraud against the United States.
- Crimes and offenses peculiar to the military services, such as desertion, disobedience, misbehavior before the enemy, and sleeping on post.
- General offenses that are prosecuted under Article 134, the General Article, which covers "all disorders and neglects to the prejudice of good order and discipline in the armed forces, all conduct of a nature to bring discredit upon the armed forces, and crimes and offenses not capital."

During peacetime, courts-martial may impose sentences ranging from simple forfeiture of pay to confinement and forfeiture of all pay and allowances to even death. (See appendix 12 of *Manual for Courts-Martial* for the Maximum Punishment Chart.) During time of war, a general court-martial may impose any penalty authorized by law, including death.

Who May Prefer Charges

Charges are initiated by anyone bringing to the attention of the military authorities information concerning an offense suspected to have been committed by a person subject to the UCMJ. This information may be received from anyone, whether subject to the UCMJ or not.

Action by Immediate Commander

Upon receipt of information that an offense has been committed, the commander exercising immediate jurisdiction over the accused under Article 15, UCMJ, must make a preliminary inquiry into the charges in order to permit an intelligent disposition of them.

Based on the outcome of the preliminary inquiry, a commander may decide that all or some of the charges do not warrant further action, and those charges may be dismissed. The commander may also decide, based on the preliminary investigation, that the offenses committed warrant punishment under Article 15, UCMJ, or he or she may refer more serious charges to higher authority for trial by court-martial.

Effective Dates of Sentences

Whenever a sentence includes a forfeiture of pay or allowances in addition to confinement, the forfeiture applies to pay or allowances becoming due on or after the date the sentence is approved by the convening authority.

Confinement included in a sentence begins to run from the date of sentencing by the court-martial. Reductions are effective on the date the sentence is approved. All other sentences of courts-martial are effective on the date they are ordered executed.

REFERENCES

AR 27-10, *Military Justice*, 1989.

FM 1-04.1 [27-1], *Legal Guide for Commanders*, 1987.

FM 1-04.14 [27-14], *Legal Guide for Soldiers*, 1986.

Manual for Courts-Martial, 1984.

Servicemember's Legal Guide, 5th Edition, by Lt. Col. Jonathan P. Tomes, U.S. Army, Ret. (Mechanicsburg, Pa.: Stackpole Books, 2005).

18

Personal Affairs

Soldiers often allow their personal needs to pile up under more pressing professional matters. Doing so can be costly to you, and especially to your loved ones.

Consider, for example, that neglecting to get life insurance and a last will and testament can cause surviving family members to be left out in the cold, financially and otherwise. Consider, too, that medical bills for unforeseen illnesses and injuries can devastate your financial future. What can you do about portions of major bills disallowed by TRICARE or Delta Dental? Do you really understand your family's medical and dental benefits, and how and under what circumstances TRICARE supplements are strongly recommended?

What happens, for example, when you deploy to a combat zone or elsewhere overseas and your spouse and children remain behind in local quarters? Do your family members have what they need to achieve a decent quality of life and standard of living in their new environment? Where can they turn for help when problems arise?

What if, for some reason beyond your control and ability to rectify, your end-of-month Leave and Earnings Statement reads "No Pay Due" and you must pay rent and meet other living expenses? Who can help fully or partially defray necessary payments to landlords, banks, and other creditors until your pay is sorted out?

Are your personal affairs in order? To what extent? Do you keep records? Where are they? Who else knows where your vital records are kept? Does your spouse or significant other know important account numbers and first and supplemental points of contact? You must make the effort to consider and take charge of your personal affairs. It is your responsibility to plan for your personal needs and those of your family. Remember that deployability includes personal readiness.

Keep your chain of command informed on personal issues. Your superiors don't want to involve themselves in your life; however, it is much easier for your leaders to assist you prior to the explosion, rather than trying to pick up the pieces afterward. Remember, helping you with your problems is one of the things they get paid to do. If they can't help, they will surely be able to point you in the right direction.

PERSONAL AFFAIRS RECORDS

The simplest way to keep your survivors informed about arrangements you have made for them is to prepare a record of your personal affairs. At the minimum, be sure that they know the location of the following:

- Your birth certificate and those of all members of your immediate family.
- Your marriage certificate.
- Divorce papers or previous spouse's death certificate, if applicable.
- Your life insurance policies.

If you put the original of your will and other key documents in a safe-deposit box, be sure that your spouse or executor has access to it. If you die and no one has access to the box, a court order must be obtained to open it.

A personal affairs record is a necessity for the married soldier because it serves as a vital source of information for his or her family.

A personal affairs record can be detailed, but make sure it includes at least the following:

- Insurance policy numbers and their amounts (include automobile and home-owner's policies).
- Previous years' tax records.
- Copies of titles and bills of sale.
- Information on bank accounts.
- A list of all pay allotments.
- Information regarding any veterans' benefits to which you may be entitled.

If you are married, be sure someone in your family knows how to pay your household bills, when they are due, and where to find them.

MILITARY RECORDS

Keep a file of all records about your military service. Keep copies of orders, discharge certificate, awards, citations, letters of appreciation and commendation, medical and dental records, Leave and Earnings Statements, and other information about your military history, even old NCOERs. Information is frequently needed throughout your active service career and afterward, when you apply for certain benefits.

Emergency Data

Your DD Form 93, *Record of Emergency Data*, must be accurate and up-to-date at all times. This record tells your military personnel office (MILPO) where your next of kin can be located immediately. It gives the name of the person you want to receive your pay if you are missing in action as well as other information of benefit to your dependents.

FAMILY CARE PLAN

The wrong time for you, either as dual military parents or a single parent, to begin planning who will take care of your children is when you find yourself on a short-

notice deployment. AR 600-20, *Army Command Policy*, stipulates that every single-parent soldier, dual military parents, and single and dual military pregnant soldiers must develop a Family Care Plan. The plan, DA Form 5305, as a minimum includes proof that a guardian has agreed to care for dependent children under the age of eighteen. Powers of attorney for medical care, guardianship, and the authorization to start or stop financial support should be in the packet, and the children should have military ID cards. Lastly, the regulation requires a letter of instruction to the guardian/escort. This letter should contain specific instructions needed for the guardian to ensure the care of the dependents.

Although not required for the packet, birth certificates, Social Security cards, shot records, other medical or insurance cards, medication dosages if necessary, and lists of family member addresses and phone numbers in case of emergency should be kept in a central location (an accordion-style organizer or file cabinet special drawer is suitable) and labeled to make it easy for the guardian to find documents fast. You might also want to contact financial institutions, children's doctors, schools, and day-care providers prior to deployment, so there will not be questions when your guardian comes to sign your child out of school to take him or her to the doctor.

Power of Attorney

A power of attorney is a legal document by which you give another person the power to act as your agent, either for some particular purpose or for the transaction of your business in general. In the wrong hands, a power of attorney can ruin you because the agent who holds such a power has, within the limits granted by it, full authority to deal with your property without consulting you. Grant it only to someone you can trust and then only when you must.

You may never need a power of attorney, or if you do need one, it may only be required to perform certain acts and no others—a limited or special power of attorney. Always consult a legal assistance officer or a lawyer before assigning a power of attorney and cancel it as soon as it is no longer required.

Bank Accounts

If you are married, you and your spouse should decide who manages the accounts. Make them joint accounts so that if anything happens to you, your family will have ready access to funds.

Current regulations require soldiers to have guaranteed direct deposit to a financial institution. With a guaranteed direct deposit from the U.S. Army Finance Center, you do not have to bother with anything but picking up your Leave and Earnings Statement on payday.

Your Will

The importance of having a will cannot be overemphasized. You may not consider that you "own" very much, but not having a will could cause many legal complications after your death. If you were to die without a will—intestate—your estate

FAMILY CARE PLAN

For use of this form, see AR 600-20; the proponent agency is DCSPER

PRIVACY ACT STATEMENT

AUTHORITY: 10 U.S.C. Section 3013, Secretary of the Army: Army Regulation 600-20, Army Command Policy and E.O. 9397 *(SSN)*

PRINCIPAL PURPOSE: To emphasize to soldiers the significance of their responsibilities to the military service and their family members while performing required military duties.

ROUTINE USES: None

DISCLOSURE: Mandatory; Failure to maintain a Family Care Plan could subject the soldier to separation, administrative action, or disciplinary action under the UCMJ.

PART I - SOLDIER'S FAMILY CARE

INITIALS

A. I was counseled on _____ *(date)*, and fully understand the policy on family member care responsibilities. I understand that I must arrange for care of my family members, remain available for deployment and training, and report for duty as required without interference of responsibility for family members. I assume responsibility for all obligations for such things as child care, food, adequate housing, transportation, and emergency needs of my family members regardless of age.

B. I have made and will maintain arrangements for the care of my family members during all the following:

1. Duty	6. Temporary Duty	11. Deployment
2. Exercises/field duty	7. Unit Training Assembly	12. Other Military Duty
3. Permanent Change of Station	8. Active Duty Training	13. Emergencies
4. Alerts	9. Unaccompanied Tours	14. Leave/non-duty Time
5. Annual Training	10. Mobilization	

C. I understand the importance of ensuring the proper care for my family members, and ensuring my own readiness and deployability as well. I further understand that in light of the critical nature of both these requirements:

1. Failure to make and maintain adequate family member care arrangements in accordance with the Army's policy is grounds for disciplinary action or separation.

2. Nonavailability for worldwide assignment and/or unit deployment may lead to my separation from the Army.

3. If arrangements for the care of my family members fail to work, I am not automatically excused from prescribed duties, unit deployment, or reassignment.

4. If I fail to maintain a Family Care Plan or provide false information regarding my plan, I am subject to separation, administrative action, or disciplinary action under UCMJ.

5. I must maintain an up-to-date Family Care Plan and revise my Plan when circumstances change. I understand that Family Care Plans may be tested at the discretion of the commander.

6. I will receive no special consideration in duty assignments or duty stations based on my responsibilities for my family members unless enrolled in the Exceptional Family Member Program *(EFMP)* in accordance with AR 600-75.

D. I have made all necessary arrangements *(legal, educational, financial, religious, special, etc.)* to ensure a smooth, rapid turnover of family member care responsibilities in case this plan is implemented.

E. I have arranged for necessary travel required to transfer my family members to a designated person. If my principal designee is not in the local area, I have arranged with a nonmilitary person in the local area to assume temporary guardianship of my family members until they are transferred to my principal care designee, or that designee arrives to assume responsibility for their care.

F. A copy of DA Form 5841-R *(Power of Attorney)* or **equivalent documents** and a copy of DA Form 5840-R *(Certificate of Acceptance as Guardian)* for each escort or guardian whether temporary or long-term is attached to this plan.

G. The following additional required documents are completed, included in this plan, and will be put into effect as part of my Family Care Plan.

1. DD Form 1172 *(Application for Uniformed Services Identification Card)* for each family member whether they have a currently valid ID card or not.

2. DD Form 2558 *(Authorization to Start, Stop or Change an Allotment for Active Duty or Retired Personnel)* or other proof of financial support for expenses incurred by guardian and family members.

3. Copies of Letters of Instruction *(which have been forwarded to designated escorts or guardians along with powers of attorney and other pertinent documents),* outlining all special instructions concerning the care of my family members have also been included in my Family Care Plan.

H. I have thoroughly briefed escorts and guardians on the full extent of their responsibilities and on procedures for gaining access to military/civilian facilities, services, entitlements and benefits on behalf of my family members.

I. I am confident that my Family Care Plan is workable, and to the best of my knowledge, the guardian *(s)* and escort *(s)* I have designated will be both willing and able to carry out the responsibilities of caring for my family members.

PART II - DESIGNATION OF GUARDIANS/ESCORTS

A. *I (We) have designated the following temporary guardian to care for my (our) family member (s) until responsibility is transferred to escort or principal (long-term) guardian.*

1. TYPED OR PRINTED NAME

2a. COMPLETE ADDRESS *(Including Street, Apartment Number, P.O. Box Number, Rural Route Number, City, State, and ZIP + 4 where applicable)*

3. TELEPHONE NUMBER *(Include Area Code)*

2b. E- MAIL ADDRESS

DA FORM 5305-R, APR 1999   DA FORM 5305-R, MAR 1992 IS OBSOLETE   USAPA V1.00

B. I (We) have designated the following individual(s) as principal long-term guardian(s) for my (our) family member (s). The designated guardian(s) reside in the continental United States or United States territories.

1. TYPED OR PRINTED NAME	2a. COMPLETE ADDRESS (Including Street, Apartment Number, P.O. Box Number, Rural Route Number, City, State, and ZIP + 4 where applicable)
3. TELEPHONE NUMBER (Include Area Code)	
	2b. E-MAIL ADDRESS

C. I (We) have designated the following individual(s) as escort for my (our) family member(s) if evacuation from OCONUS becomes necessary (applies only to persons assigned OCONUS):

1. TYPED OR PRINTED NAME	2a. COMPLETE ADDRESS (Including Street, Apartment Number, P.O. Box Number, Rural Route Number, City, State, and ZIP + 4 where applicable)
3. TELEPHONE NUMBER (Include Area Code)	
	2b. E-MAIL ADDRESS

PART III - DUAL MILITARY COUPLES ONLY
MILITARY SPOUSE AND COMMANDER CERTIFICATION

A. **Spouse:** We have made arrangements and will maintain arrangements for the care of our family member (s) in all circumstances required by our commitment to the military and our family.

1. SIGNATURE OF SPOUSE					2. DATE (YYYY/MM/DD)	
3. TYPED OR PRINTED NAME OF SPOUSE				4. SSN		

5. Recertification	a. INIT.	DATE	b. INIT.	DATE	c. INIT.	DATE	d. INIT.	DATE	e. INIT.	DATE

B. **Commander:** I have counseled the military spouse assigned to my unit, reviewed the Family Care Plan, and I am satisfied that the members have made adequate family care arrangements.

1. SIGNATURE OF COMMANDER	2. DATE	3. UNIT ADDRESS
4. TYPED OR PRINTED NAME OF COMMANDER		

5. Recertification	a. INIT.	DATE	b. INIT.	DATE	c. INIT.	DATE	d. INIT.	DATE	e. INIT.	DATE

PART IV - SOLDIER AND COMMANDER CERTIFICATION

A. **Soldier:** I (We) have made arrangements and will maintain arrangements for the care of my (our) family member(s) in all circumstances required by my (our) commitment to the military and my (our) family.

1. SIGNATURE OF SOLDIER					2. DATE (YYYY/MM/DD)	
3. TYPED OR PRINTED NAME OF SOLDIER				4. SSN		

5. Recertification	a. INIT.	DATE	b. INIT.	DATE	c. INIT.	DATE	d. INIT.	DATE	e. INIT.	DATE

B. **Commander:** I have reviewed the Family Care Plan, and I am satisfied that the members have made adequate family care arrangements that will allow for a full range of military duties and for worldwide availability as defined here.

1. SIGNATURE OF COMMANDER	2. DATE	3. UNIT ADDRESS
4. TYPED OR PRINTED NAME OF COMMANDER		

5. Recertification	a. INIT.	DATE	b. INIT.	DATE	c. INIT.	DATE	d. INIT.	DATE	e. INIT.	DATE

would be distributed according to the descent and distribution laws of your state of legal residence, or in the case of real property located in another state, the laws of that state.

If you are married, both you and your spouse should have wills, even if each will makes the same distribution of property and assets. It is particularly important to have a will if you have minor children so that their interests can be protected through a guardianship of your choice in the event both you and your spouse die.

Once you have made your will, review it periodically to keep it up-to-date. As circumstances change, you may want to update it to be sure that it still expresses your desires about the distribution of your property and assets.

Keep your will in a safe place. The safest place to keep it (and other important papers) is in a safe-deposit box at your bank. It is not a bad idea to send a copy of your will together with a statement as to the location of the original to the principal beneficiary or the person named in the will as the executor.

Life Insurance
It is beyond the scope of this book to discuss all the things to look for when you are shopping for life insurance. What kind of policy to get and how much insurance you may need depends strictly upon your individual or family situation. You are particularly insurable if you are still relatively young and you have school-age children who depend upon you. Shop around. There are numerous good individual and group insurance plans available; there are some pretty bad ones available as well—and plenty of unscrupulous insurance agents willing to take your money. Be vigilant when you buy insurance!

Servicemembers Group Life Insurance (SGLI)
Maximum coverage is $400,000, unless you decline coverage or request a reduced amount of coverage. DOD currently pays the premiums to service members who are deployed in a designated combat zone for $150,000 of SGLI coverage. When you leave the service, your SGLI is convertible to Veterans Group Life Insurance (VGLI).

Servicemembers Civil Relief Act (SCRA)
This piece of federal law provides protection of rights, privileges, immunities, and benefits to servicemembers while serving on active duty. These benefits include: protection against paying taxes in both the home state and the state in which service members are stationed, exemption from personal property taxes when stationed in a state that is not their domicile, the ability to have civil court cases delayed, and special treatment of certain financial obligations. Servicemembers may also qualify for lowering their interest rates to six percent for obligations incurred prior to entering active service. For more information go to *www.defenselink.mil/specials/relief_act/-index.html* or see a legal assistance attorney. All mobilized reserve component (RC) soldiers can receive finance support and information from the local servicing finance office or defense military pay office (DMPO).

Guide for Obtaining Information and Assistance

	YOUR CHAIN OF COMMAND	PERSONNEL NCO OR OFFICER	REENLISTMENT NCO	JUDGE ADVOCATE	INSPECTOR GENERAL	FINANCE OFFICER	CHAPLAIN	HOUSING OFFICER	TRANSPORTATION OFFICER	AMERICAN RED CROSS	ARMY COMMUNITY SERVICES	ARMY EMERGENCY RELIEF	EDUCATION OFFICER/ADVISOR
Appeals	1	2		2	2		2						
Assignment, reassignment, MOS, and proficiency pay	1	1			2								
Reenlistment	1		1										
Personnel matters: promotion, reduction, discharge, retirement	1	1	2	2									
Veterans' benefits													
Complaints (requests for assistance)	1	2	2	2	2	2	2	2	2	2	2	2	
Debts and civilian creditors	1	1		2		2	2				2		
Dependents' schools	1	1									2		
Family and religious affairs	1	2					1			2	2		
Travel of dependents, shipment of POV and household goods	1	2					2		1		2		
Medical service (individual and dependents)	1	1											
Pay, allowances, and incentive pay	1	2				1							
Leaves and passes	1	2											
Insurance, all types (SGLI and commercial)	1	1				2							
Legal assistance, including U.S. and foreign law, wills, and powers of attorney	1			1									
Military education	1	2	2										
Nonmilitary education	1	2											2
PX, commissary, QM sales store	1				2								
Government quarters, off-post housing	1	2						1					
Registration/operation of privately owned vehicle (POV), registration of firearms	1												
Entry into U.S., passport, visa, naturalization, immigration, birth certificate (children born in foreign country)	1	2		1							2		
Home conditions and emergency leave	1	2					2			2	2	2	
Emergency financial assistance	1	2				1				2	2	2	
Postal service	1												
Drug and alcohol rehabilitation program	1						2				1		

1. Primary source
2. Other sources as appropriate

One of the most significant provisions of the Servicemembers Civil Relief Act (SCRA) for RC soldiers is the right of reemployment. RC Soldiers who are mobilized are exempt from the Uniformed Services Employment and Reemployment Act (USERRA) five-year limit for retaining reemployment rights. In regard to questions about employment or reemployment rights servicemembers can check the Employer Support of the Guard and Reserve (ESGR) Web site at: *www.ESGR.org.*

HOUSING

Military families often must rent local housing while waiting for government quarters to become available. If you find yourself in that situation, you might want to consider renting an apartment on a month-by-month basis. Should you sign a lease for a specified period of time and then have to break it because a set of quarters unexpectedly becomes available, you have to forfeit your deposit (usually an amount equal to a month's rent).

Renting an apartment gives single soldiers a degree of independence and privacy not available in the barracks, and for this reason, many soldiers want to move off post.

Whether a single soldier can move off post depends on the following:

- Your post commander's policy. It is also up to the commanding officer of your unit. Some commanders are liberal in granting this privilege; it depends upon your unit's mission. Commanders of headquarters units can be more liberal than those of tactical or combat support units.
- The amount and quality of troop housing available. Some small, specialized units have trouble finding adequate troop housing, especially at overcrowded installations in metropolitan areas. Where sufficient troop housing is available, however, commanders normally fill the billets up first before allowing lower-ranking single personnel to move off post.
- Nonabuse of the privilege. Your commander will revoke permission to live off post as soon as you start coming to work late, running up debts, or causing disturbances among the local population.

Be sure that you can afford to live off post. Your military pay combined with your housing and subsistence allowances may be enough, depending on the geographical area, but just enough and no more. If supporting yourself in an apartment leaves you flat broke at the end of the month, you are better off living in the barracks.

Some soldiers find it a good idea to team up with two or three friends and rent a place by splitting all the costs. This is an excellent idea if your companions can be trusted to pay their share, take care of the communal areas, and respect your privacy and personal property.

PERSONAL PROPERTY

Joint ownership of property can have certain advantages in establishing an automatic and known passage of ownership upon the death of one owner and can also

have certain disadvantages. Inquire into federal and state laws regarding ownership of family property, and take actions that put your estate in the most favorable ownership positions.

In the event of your death, your immediate personal effects will be forwarded at government expense to the person entitled to their custody. This does not give the recipient legal title to them, but they should be retained for disposition under the law.

If you own real estate in your name and it is not paid for, show on your personal affairs record whether there is a mortgage or a deed of trust against it, along with the name of the person or organization to whom you are indebted. Also include information about property taxes and insurance.

Transfer of automobile ownership is sometimes complicated because of varying state laws. Remember that joint titling may make you or your spouse subject to personal property taxes; active-duty personnel are generally exempt from payment of personal property taxes, so adding your spouse's name to an automobile title can cost you a lot of money.

INCOME TAXES

Military pay in general is subject to income tax. You do not pay tax on subsistence, quarters, and uniform allowances. Dislocation allowance, special duty pays, and hardship pay, however, are taxable.

Any nonmilitary earnings, including the pay received while employed during off-duty hours and the income of any of your dependents, are taxable. Military pay is excluded from federal income tax for service in any area that the president of the United States designates by executive order to be a combat zone. This exclusion is unlimited for enlisted members. If you spend a single qualifying day in the combat zone, your pay for the entire month is excluded from taxable income. Bonuses and special pays are also excluded from taxable income if within the previously stated limitations and earned in the same month in which you served in a combat zone.

The Soldiers' and Sailors' Civil Relief Act assures that a state in which a soldier is stationed but which is not the servicemember's legal residence cannot tax service pay. Legal residence is established at enlistment or thereafter when a soldier executes DD Form 2058, *State of Legal Residence Certificate.*

The following states do not withhold income tax from the pay of military personnel: Alaska, Florida, Nevada, New Hampshire, South Dakota, Tennessee, Texas, Washington, and Wyoming. Soldiers claiming legal residence in foreign countries or U.S. territories are also exempt from paying state income taxes. Appendix K, "State Tax Withholding," to AR 37-104-3 contains specific information relative to each state for which withholding tax applies.

WHERE TO FIND HELP

In addition to what follows, you can refer to the Guide for Obtaining Information and Assistance table on page 246 for more information.

Army Community Services (ACS)

The ACS is an official Department of the Army organization established to provide information, aid, guidance, and referral services to military personnel and their families. ACS activities are monitored by the Army adjutant general. The ACS Web page is at *www.myarmylifetoo.com/*.

The ACS provides a wide variety of services, including the following:
- Referrals for handicapped dependents.
- Family counseling services.
- Financial planning services.
- Lending services to provide bedding, linens, and housewares to military families until they can get settled at a new post.
- Volunteer services providing transportation to dependents when required.
- Child abuse information and referral.
- An emergency food locker from which needy families may draw supplies.

Army Emergency Relief (AER)

The Army Emergency Relief (AER) operates as a part of the Army Community Services. AER provides badly needed financial assistance to soldiers and their dependents. A local AER officer can authorize interest-free cash loans. Large loans must be approved by Headquarters, AER. The AER Web site is at *www.aerhq.org/*.

AER loans may be approved for the following purposes:
- Defray living expenses because of nonreceipt of military pay.
- Provide money to help defray emergency travel expenses.
- Help pay rents, security deposits, and utilities.
- Help pay "essential POV [privately owned vehicle] expenses."
- Pay funeral expenses above and beyond those allowed by the government.
- Pay grants to the widows and orphans of deceased soldiers, in some cases.
- Provide cash to buy food when it is not available from the Army Community Services (ACS) food locker.
- Provide money to replace lost funds.

Soldiers must apply for AER loans through their unit commanders by filling out DA Form 1103, *Application for AER Financial Assistance.* The soldier must document his or her expenses or financial situation, and an allotment must be executed before the AER will disburse any money.

Each year, AER disburses millions of dollars to help soldiers and their families. The only source for these funds is cash donations by Army members solicited annually during Army-wide fund-raising drives.

Army Family Action Plan (AFAP)

Today, more than half the active Army force is married. The Army now pays considerable attention to soldiers' families.

A partnership exists between the Army and Army families. The Army's unique missions, concept of service, and lifestyle of its members all affect the nature of this

partnership. Toward the goal of building a strong partnership, the Army remains committed to assuring adequate support to families in order to promote wellness, to develop a sense of community, and to strengthen the mutually reinforcing bonds between the Army and its families.

The Army Family Action Plan includes four major themes: relocation; medical concerns; family support and role identity; and education and care of youth. The specific areas range from developing videos for overseas orientation programs, developing family member support groups at installations and units, and attempting to correct medical staff shortages—to providing English-as-a-second-language instruction for family members whose native language is other than English. As an NCO, regardless of whether you now have a family or plan to have one someday, your understanding and full support of the Army Family Action Plan is essential to its success.

Following are brief definitions of the critical elements of the plan's philosophy. Their applications are much more far-reaching than to just the Army Family Action Plan itself—they are essential ingredients to the cohesion that makes the Army work.

Partnership. Partnership has to exist between the Army as an institution and the individuals who are part of it: soldiers, civilians, and family members. Partnership is a cohesion of the Army and family members based on mutual understanding of the mission and commitment to one another. It is a reciprocal relationship, based on moral and ethical responsibilities and statutory and regulatory requirements. Partnership between its members makes the Army an institution, not just a job or a workplace.

Wellness. Wellness is the concern for developing those strengths, skills, aptitudes, and attitudes that contribute to the wholeness and health of body, mind, and spirit. Wellness is achieved by concentrating on what is working well, and by drawing on the characteristics of the Army's many healthy families and then transmitting those characteristics to the people who need assistance.

Sense of Community. This is the center of the partnership, with all members offered the challenge and opportunity to work together for the common good. It means that each member of the Army community has a special responsibility to make the institution a better place in which to live and work.

Partnership, wellness, sense of community—all are important to military community residents and officials. The following are a few of the many examples that illustrate the value of the Army Family Action Plan (AFAP):

- Quality child care is a top priority to the increasing number of spouses who work. AFAP initiatives bring about increased appropriated fund support for child care, fees for child care based on family income, better-trained and higher-paid caregivers and more of them, parent advisory boards, and an ongoing study of the demand for child care.
- Since relocation assistance and sponsorship are paramount, AFAP requests increased allowances for transportation of household goods, especially for junior enlisted soldiers. An automated relocation assistance system provides

housing and other relocation information about areas in the United States and abroad.
- Because of the AFAP, reservists may shop in commissaries during a specified number of days during the year.

Since the first AFAP conference was held in 1983, many laws have been passed or amended to resolve more than 100 quality-of-life issues affecting the Army family.

Legal Assistance

A legal assistance officer will advise you on such matters as a will, power of attorney, divorce and separation actions, estates, tax problems, and other civil matters. The legal assistance officer can also provide you with a very useful "legal checkup," which is designed to identify any potential legal problems that you may have.

This officer is not normally permitted to represent you in civil court or to give you advice in matters of a criminal nature. Neither may he or she advise you about court-martial investigations or charges (a military counsel appointed by the judge advocate will assist you in such cases). If your problem requires the services of a civilian lawyer, the legal assistance officer can refer you, through cooperating bar associations, to civilian legal advisors or legal aid bureaus.

The *Servicemember's Legal Guide*, 5th edition, published by Stackpole Books, provides comprehensive information on what soldiers and their families need to know about the law.

Chaplains

Chaplains are available to help soldiers, family members, and civilians with any type of concern they may have, be it spiritual, work related, or otherwise. Chaplains can help in areas ranging from marriage and family counseling to stress management and suicide prevention. Soldiers seeking counseling don't necessarily have to be churchgoers to use the chaplains to help them through the rough times. Lastly, Army chaplain regulations state that any communications to a chaplain acting as a spiritual advisor must be kept in confidence and cannot be told to anyone else without permission.

Disability Soldier Support System (DS3)

The Disability Soldier Support System (DS3) program provides each soldier seriously injured during combat operations in the global war on terrorism and his/her family with a personal DS3 advocate, called a soldier/family management specialist. When a soldier receives a disability rating of 30 percent or greater and a special category designation, the soldier is designated DS3. Soldiers will continue to receive DS3 support for five years after they leave active duty.

MEDICAL INSURANCE—TRICARE

Army health-care beneficiaries—you and your family—should take a long-term view toward medical and dental health. Eat foods that contribute to a longer life.

Exercise regularly for the same reason. Rest properly. Brush and floss after meals. Get periodic physical and dental examinations. Follow the advice of doctors, dentists, and other Army health- and medical-care providers. Stay healthy to limit the effects of illness or disease. Beware of unsafe acts and unsafe conditions to avoid injury. When a person is ill or injured, nothing matters more than recovery.

When an active-duty soldier becomes sick or gets hurt, the Army direct-care medical system provides care at no cost. In fact, AR 40-3, *Medical, Dental, and Veterinary Care*, prohibits active-duty soldiers, including active-duty reserve component soldiers, from seeking and obtaining medical and dental care from civilian sources without prior authorization from the local Army medical treatment facility commander. So, while soldiers are on active duty, they do not need medical and dental insurance. But Army family members do—and they have it provided by TRICARE and the Dependent Dental Plan, which is offered through TRICARE.

Eligibility for TRICARE is determined by the Defense Enrollment Eligibility Reporting System (DEERS), a database of uniformed services members (sponsors), family members, and others worldwide who are entitled under the law to TRICARE benefits. Active duty and retired servicemembers are automatically registered in DEERS, but it's the sponsor's responsibility to ensure that his or her eligible family members are registered correctly in DEERS. All sponsors should ensure that their family members' status (marriage, divorce, new child, etc.), residential address, telephone numbers, and e-mail address are current in DEERS so that TRICARE can send out information and have claims processed quickly and accurately.

TRICARE

TRICARE is a health-care program for members of the uniformed services and their families, and survivors and retired members and their families. TRICARE brings together the health-care resources of each of the military services and supplements them with networks of civilian health-care professionals to provide better access and high-quality service while maintaining the capability to support military operations. There are three TRICARE regions in the United States, each with an assigned lead agent who is responsible for the military health services system in that region.

Under TRICARE, family members have two basic choices for seeking medical care: (1) the Enrolled Choice (TRICARE Prime) and (2) the Nonenrolled Choice (TRICARE Extra/TRICARE Standard). Active-duty members must enroll in TRICARE Prime, and thus are not eligible for the Nonenrolled Choice.

Choice 1. Enrolled Choice (TRICARE Prime) provides the most comprehensive health-care benefits to the patient at the lowest cost. TRICARE Prime guarantees priority access to care at a military treatment facility or, where available, an off-post, civilian, contracted doctor's office.

All active-duty military members must enroll in this choice and must use military facilities. Family members must also enroll to use this option. Those who select the Enrolled Choice will be assigned to a primary care manager (PCM). This is a

health-care provider who you will see first for all of your medical needs. If necessary, your PCM will refer you to specialty medical care, when needed. There are no enrollment fees for active-duty families in TRICARE Prime.

Choice 2. The Nonenrolled Choice (TRICARE Extra/TRICARE Standard) allows family members to seek medical care from any physician of their choice in the civilian community. The Nonenrolled Choice is a more costly option than the Enrolled Choice. This choice incorporates two programs (TRICARE Extra and TRICARE Standard). Medical expenses are covered under these programs when family members are not enrolled in TRICARE Prime. A single deductible covers the use of either program.

Active enrollment and preauthorization are not required for your family to use the Nonenrolled Choice, but a nonavailability statement must be obtained for civilian inpatient care. See your local health benefits advisor for more information.

TRICARE Standard is the basic TRICARE health-care program, offering comprehensive health-care coverage, for people not enrolled in TRICARE Prime. (Active-duty service members are automatically enrolled in Prime, and many other beneficiaries choose to enroll.) Standard does not require enrollment.

Fee-for-service flexibility: Standard is a fee-for-service plan that gives beneficiaries the option to see any TRICARE-certified/authorized provider—doctor, nurse-practitioner, lab, clinic, etc. Standard offers the greatest flexibility in choosing a provider, but it will also involve greater out-of-pocket expenses for you, the patient. You also may be required to file your own claims.

Costs: Standard requires that you satisfy a yearly deductible before TRICARE cost sharing begins, and you will be required to pay co-payments or cost shares for outpatient care, medications, and inpatient care. A nonavailability statement for civilian inpatient care may be required for areas surrounding military treatment facilities.

TRICARE Extra is an option that allows Standard beneficiaries to save money by making appointments with civilian doctors, nurse practitioners, labs, clinics, etc., who are "participating" providers. Providers who participate in TRICARE agree to accept as payment in full for services they render, the TRICARE maximum allowable charge (TMAC).

Nonparticipating providers may, by law, charge up to 15 percent above the TMAC for their services, and the TRICARE Standard beneficiary is responsible for the amount above the TMAC.

Participating providers will file claims forms for the TRICARE beneficiary. (Certified providers may or may not file claims on behalf of the Standard patient; the doctor may choose to do so, or not, on a case by case basis.)

Using the Nonenrolled Choice allows family members the freedom to choose any civilian physician. Some physicians' services will be less costly than others. Your family members may continue to use military facilities on a space-available basis, but obtaining appointments will become very difficult.

TRICARE Pharmacy

Prescriptions may be filled (up to a ninety-day supply for most medications) at a military treatment facility (MTF) pharmacy free of charge, although not all medications are available at MTF pharmacies. The TRICARE Mail Order Pharmacy (TMOP) is available for prescriptions you take on a regular basis. You can receive up to a ninety-day supply (for most medications) of your prescription through the mail by using TMOP. Finally, prescription medications that your doctor requires you to start taking immediately can be obtained though a retail network pharmacy as part of the TRICARE Retail Pharmacy (TRRx) program.

What Will TRICARE Cost?

The charts below provide examples of cost shares for families using TRICARE. Health benefits advisors at the military treatment facilities or representatives at the TRICARE Service Centers can assist you and your family in obtaining the medical care and services you need.

Active-Duty Family Members

If you have questions about your military health-care benefits under TRICARE, there are many places to get answers. A member handbook may be obtained by visiting or calling your local TRICARE Service Center; by calling the health benefits advisor at your nearest military hospital or clinic; or by visiting the Web site at *www.tricare.osd.mil.* Each medical facility has a health benefits advisor, Managed Care Office, or TRICARE Service Center. This should be your first contact for information. Additionally, below are telephone numbers for each region, where you can call and get information about TRICARE and your health-care benefits.

ACTIVE-DUTY FAMILY MEMBERS

	TRICARE Prime E-1 through E-4	TRICARE Prime E-5 and above	TRICARE Extra/Standard Families of E4 and Above	TRICARE Extra/Standard Families of E5 and Below
Annual Deductible (Individual/Family)	None	None	$50/$100	$150/$300
Civilian Outpatient Visit	$0	$0	Extra: 15 percent; Standard: 20 percent	Extra: 15 percent; Standard: 20 percent;
Civilian Inpatient Admission	$0	$0	Greater of $25 or $13.90/day	Greater of $25 or $13.90/day
Civilian Inpatient Mental Health	$0	$0	$20 per day	$20 per day

TRICARE REGIONS

TRICARE   *www.triwest.com*
West   (888) TRIWEST; (888) 874-9378
Alaska, Arizona, California, Colorado, Hawaii, Idaho, Iowa
(except for the Rock Island Arsenal area), Kansas, Minnesota,
Missouri (except for the St. Louis area), Montana, Nebraska,
Nevada, New Mexico, North Dakota, Oregon, South Dakota, the
extreme western portion of Texas, Utah, Washington, and
Wyoming.

TRICARE   *www.healthnetfederalservices.com*
North   (877) TRICARE; (877) 874-2273
Connecticut, Delaware, the District of Columbia, Illinois, Indi-
ana, the Rock Island Arsenal area of Iowa, Kentucky, Maine,
Maryland, Massachusetts, Michigan, the St. Louis area of Mis-
souri, New Hampshire, New Jersey, New York, North Carolina,
Ohio, Pennsylvania, Rhode Island, Fort Campbell area of Ten-
nessee, Vermont, Virginia, West Virginia, and Wisconsin.

TRICARE   *www.humana-military.com*
South   (800) 444-5445
Alabama, Arkansas, Florida, Georgia, Louisiana, Mississippi,
Oklahoma, South Carolina, most of Tennessee, and the eastern
portion of Texas.

TRICARE
Overseas   1-888-777-8343
TRICARE Prime and TRICARE Standard for active duty and
their families. Only TRICARE Standard is for Military retirees;
their families who live overseas cannot enroll in TRICARE
Prime, but they can use TRICARE Standard.

TRICARE Reserve Select (TRS)

TRICARE Reserve Select (TRS) is a new premium-based TRICARE health plan
offered for purchase by certain members and former members of the reserve component (RC) and their families, if specific eligibility requirements are met. TRS
coverage is available to eligible RC members who were called or ordered to active
duty, under Title 10, in support of a contingency operation on or after September
11, 2001. Reserve component members and their RC unit will need to agree for the

member to stay in the Select Reserve for one or more whole years to qualify. TRS coverage must be purchased. TRS members pay a monthly premium for health-care coverage (for self only or for self and family). Adjusted effective January 1 each year, the premiums for calendar year 2005 are: $75 for TRS member-only coverage, $233 for TRS member and family coverage.

TRICARE for Life (TFL) is a Medicare wraparound coverage available to:
- Medicare-entitled uniformed service retirees, including retired guard members and reservists,
- Medicare-entitled family members and widows/widowers (dependent parents and parents-in-law are excluded),
- Medicare-entitled Medal of Honor recipients and their family members, and
- Certain Medicare-entitled unremarried former spouses.

TRICARE pays the balance on the Medicare claim—everything Medicare did not pay—for everything that is a TRICARE benefit.

TRICARE Supplements

TRICARE supplements are not part of the TRICARE program. The different commercial plans are designed to be secondary coverage to TRICARE. Dependent on the level of coverage, TRICARE supplements pay the cost share, deductible, and eligible excess charges under the TRICARE Standard and Extra options so that on a combined basis, eligible participants have 100 percent coverage in most cases. For more detailed information, check with any of the various associations representing the different members of the armed forces.

TRICARE DENTAL PROGRAM

Active-duty soldiers receive all dental care, at no cost, from military dental treatment facilities and are therefore ineligible for the TRICARE Dental Program (TDP). The TDP is a voluntary dental plan open to families of all active-duty, selected reserve, and individual ready reserve soldiers ordered to active duty for more than thirty consecutive days.

Sponsors must have at least twelve months remaining on their service commitments at the time of enrollment. After completing the initial twelve-month enrollment period, they may continue in the TDP on a month-by-month basis.

Soldiers failing to pay premiums or disenrolling before completing the twelve-month lock-in are responsible for payment of all remaining premiums. Unless disenrolling for a valid reason, soldiers are prohibited from reentering the program for twelve months.

Soldiers may disenroll from the TDP before completion of the mandatory twelve-month enrollment for the following reasons: when a sponsor or family member loses Defense Enrollment Eligibility Reporting System (DEERS) eligibility, when TDP enrolled members relocate outside the CONUS service area, or when an active-duty member transfers with enrolled family members to a duty station where space-available dental care for the enrolled members is readily available at the local uniformed services dental treatment facility.

TRICARE Management Activity (TMA)

United Concordia Companies, Inc, administers and underwrites the TRICARE Dental Program (TDP). For further information, call the TRICARE Dental Program, United Concordia Companies, Inc. (UCCI), at (800) 866-8499. For enrollment information, call (888) 622-2256. See also the UCCI Web site: *www.ucci.com/was/ucci-web/tdp/tdp.jsp*, or you can contact your nearest TRICARE Service Centers, a military dental treatment facility, or a uniformed services personnel office.

LONG-TERM CARE

TRICARE or Medicare do not cover long-term care. The Federal Long-Term Care Insurance Program is an important benefit for members of the Army family, including retiree members and qualified relatives. It is insurance that helps you pay for care to help you perform daily activities if you have an ongoing illness or disability. It also includes the kind of care you would need if you had a severe cognitive problem such as Alzheimer's disease. It is help with eating, bathing, dressing, transferring from a bed to a chair, toileting, continence, etc. This type of care isn't received in a hospital and isn't intended to cure you. It is not acute care. It is chronic care that you might need for the rest of your life. It can be received in your own home, at a nursing home, or at another long-term care facility.

If you are younger than forty and healthy when you retire, the Federal Long-Term Care Insurance Program may not be the best deal. You may obtain comparable coverage at a lower monthly premium from one of the large companies that handle long-term care. Check the premiums calculator offered by the Office of Personnel Management on the Internet at *www.ltcfeds.com/ltcWeb/do/assessing_your_needs/ratecalc* for more information. To qualify, you must answer more questions about your health and habits than regular military personnel. Retirees can also call (800) 582-3337, Monday through Friday, from 8 A.M. to 8 P.M. EST.

Appendix 1

Chain of Command

It is to your benefit to know your chain of command. Listed here are the personnel normally found in the formal chain of command. Check with your first sergeant to fill in the names. The number of personnel and the terminology for the positions within the chain vary in some Army units.

CHAIN OF COMMAND

Commander in Chief	President of the United States
Secretary of Defense	_____
Secretary of the Army	_____
Chairman of the Joint Chiefs of Staff	_____
Chief of Staff, Army	_____
MACOM Commander	_____
Corps Commander	_____
Post/Division/Command Commander	_____
Brigade/Group Commander	_____
Battalion Commander	_____
Company Commander	_____
Platoon Leader	_____
Squad/Section Leader	_____

The NCO support channel complements and parallels the chain of command and provides a structure for the day-to-day activities of the Army.

NCO SUPPORT CHANNEL

Sergeant Major of the Army   _____

MACOM Command Sergeant Major   _____

Corps Command Sergeant Major   _____

Post/Division/Command Command
Sergeant Major   _____

Brigade/Group Command Sergeant Major   _____

Battalion Command Sergeant Major   _____

First Sergeant   _____

Platoon Sergeant   _____

Squad Leader   _____

Appendix 2

Acronyms

ISG	first sergeant
AAFES	Army and Air Force Exchange Service
AAM	Army Achievement Medal
AAR	after-action review
ABCMR	Army Board for the Correction of Military Records
AC	active component
ACAP	Army Career and Alumni Program
ACE	American Council on Education
ACES	Army Continuing Education System
AC PLDC	Advanced Component Primary Leadership Development Course
ACS	Army Community Services
ACT	American College Testing Program Assessment
ACTPEP	American College Testing Proficiency Examination Program
ACU	Army combat uniform
ADA	air defense artillery
ADAPCP	Alcohol and Drug Abuse Prevention and Control Program
AEA	assignment eligibility and availability
AEC	Army Education Center
AEN	Army Employment Network
AEPS	Army electronic product support
AER	Army Emergency Relief
AFAP	Army Family Action Plan
AFQT	Armed Forces Qualification Test
AG	Adjutant General
AGR	Active Guard and Reserve
AI	assignment instruction
AIDS	acquired immunodeficiency syndrome
AIP	Assignment Incentive Pay
AIPD	Army Institute for Professional Development
AIT	advanced individual training
AKO	Army Knowledge Online
ALC	Army Learning Center
ALI	automatic list integration

AM	Air Medal
AMD	Army Medical Department
AMOS	additional military occupational specialty
AMTP	Army Mission Training Plan
ANC	Army Nurse Corps
ANCOC	Advanced Noncommissioned Officer Course
AOL	Army Online
AP/CPB	Annenberg Project and Center for Public Broadcasting
APFT	Army Physical Fitness Test
APOD	aerial port of debarkation
APOE	aerial port of embarkation
AR	Army Regulation
ARC	American Red Cross
ARCAM	Army Reserve Components Achievement Medal
ARCOM	Army Commendation Medal
ARNG	Army National Guard
ARTEP	Army Training and Evaluation Program
ASAP	Army Substance Abuse Program
ASK	assignment satisfaction key
ASEP	Advanced Skills Education Program
ASI	additional skill identifier
ASK	Assignment Satisfaction Key
ATACMS	Army Tactical Missile System
ATIMP	Army Training Information Management Program
ATRRS	Army Training Requirements and Resources System
ATSC	Army Training Support Center
AUSA	Association of the U.S. Army
AUTODIN	Automated Digital Network
AWOL	absent without leave
BAH	basic allowance for housing
BAQ	basic allowance for quarters
BAS	basic allowance for substinence
BASD	basic active service date
BCT	basic combat training; brigade combat team
BDE	brigade
BDFS	bachelor's degree for soldiers
BDU	battle dress uniform
BEQ	bachelor enlisted quarters
BESD	basic enlisted service date
BNCOC	Basic Noncommissioned Officer Course
BSEP	Basic Skills Education Program
BSM	Bronze Star Medal
BT	basic training
CAP III	Centralized Assignment Procedure III System

CE	Commander's Evaluation
CFC	Combined Federal Campaign
CFP	contingency force pool
CHAMPUS	Civilian Health and Medical Program of the Uniformed Services
CIB	Combat Infantryman Badge
CID(C)	Criminal Investigation Division (Command)
CLEP	College Level Examination Program
CMF	career management field
CMH	Center for Military History
COHORT	Cohesion, Operational Readiness, and Training
COLA	cost-of-living allowance
CONAP	Continental United States Area of Preference
CONUS	continental United States
COT	Consecutive Overseas Tour
CPL/SPC	Corporal/Specialist
CPMOS	career progression military occupational specialty
CQ	charge of quarters
CS	combat support
CSM	command sergeant major
CSS	combat service support
CTT	common task training
CVC	combat vehicle crewman
DA	Department of the Army
DANTES	Defense Activity for Nontraditional Education Support
DCPC	Direct Combat Probability Coding
DBDU	desert battle dress uniform
DDSM	Defense Distinguished Service Medal
DEERS	Defense Enrollment Eligibility Reporting System
DEROS	date of estimated return from overseas
DFAS	Defense Finance and Accounting Service
DFC	Distinguished Flying Cross
DIEMS	date initially entered military service
DMOS	duty military occupational specialty
DMPO	defense military pay office
DMSM	Defense Meritorious Service Medal
DOD	Department of Defense
DODDS	Department of Defense Dependents Schools
DOE	Department of Education
DOR	date of rank
DRF	Deployment Ready Force
DROS	date returned from overseas
DSC	Distinguished Service Cross
DSM	Distinguished Service Medal
DSN	Defense Switched Network

DSSM	Defense Superior Service Medal
DSST	Defense Subject Standardized Tests
DUI	distinctive unit insignia
DVA	Department of Veterans Affairs
EAD	entry on active duty
EANGUS	Enlisted Association of the National Guard of the United States
eArmyU	Electronic Army University
EDAS	Enlisted Distribution and Assignment System
EDSAV	Educational Savings Allotment
EEMP	Exceptional Family Member Program
EFT	Electronic Funds Transfer
EHWBDU	enhanced hot weather battle dress uniform
EMF	enlisted master file
EML	environmental and morale leave
E/MSS	Employee/Member Self Service
ENTNAC	Entrance National Agency Check
EO	equal opportunity
EOD	explosive ordnance disposal
EOM	end of month
EPMD	Enlisted Personnel Management Directorate
EPMS	Enlisted Personnel Management System
EPW	enemy prisoner of war
ESGR	Employer Support of the Guard and Reserve
ETS	expiration of term of service; enlisted training system
FAO	Finance and Accounting Office
FAST	Functional Academic Skills Training
FININ	payment to a financial institution for credit to a member's account
FIST	fire support team
FM	field manual
FORSCOM	U.S. Army Forces Command
FSA	family separation allowance
FSA-T	family separation allowance for temporary duty
FTX	field training exercise
GCM	general court-martial, Good Conduct Medal
GCMCA	General Court-Martial Convening Authority
GED	General Educational Development
GRE	Graduate Record Examination
GWOT	Global War on Terror
GWOTEM	Global War on Terrorism Expeditionary Medal
GWOTSM	Global War on Terrorism Service Medal
HAAP	Homebase and Advance Assignment Program
HALO	high-altitude, low-opening (parachute jumps)
HDP-L	hardship duty pay for location assignment

HDP-M	hardship duty pay for mission assignment
HBA	health benefits adviser
HIV	human immunodeficiency virus
HMMWV	high-mobility multipurposed wheeled vehicle
HOR	home of record
HQDA	Headquarters, Department of the Army
HRC	Human Resources Command
HSCP	High School Completion Program
HW	hot weather
IBCT	Interim Brigade Combat Team
IET	Initial Entry Training
IFV	infantry fighting vehicle
IG	Inspector General
IHA	interim housing allowance
ISR	Individual Soldier's Report
ITEP	Individual Training Program
ITT	intertheater transfer
IVRS	Interactive Voice Response Telephone System
JAC	job assistance center
JAG	Judge Advocate General
JFTR	Joint Federal Travel Regulations
JSAM	Joint Service Achievement Medal
JSCM	Joint Service Commendation Medal
JSEP	Job Skills Education Program
JTR	Joint Travel Regulations
JUMPS	Joint Uniform Military Pay Schedule
JUSMAG	Joint U.S. Military Advisory Group
KDSM	Korea Defense Service Medal
KFOR	Kosovo Force
LDRSHIP	loyalty, duty, respect, selfless service, honor, integrity, and personal courage
LES	Leave and Earnings Statement
LI	leader's identification
LOD	line of duty
LTC	lieutenant colonel
MAAG	Military Assistance Advisory Group
MAC	Military Airlift Command
MACOM	Major Army Command
MACP	Married Army Couples Program
MCM	Manual for Courts-Martial
MEDDAC	Medical Department Activity
METL	Mission Essential Task List
MFT	master fitness trainer
MGIB/ACF	Montgomery GI Bill/Army College Fund

MI	military intelligence
MILES	Multiple Integrated Laser Identification System
MILPER	military personnel
MILPO	military personnel office
MLRS	Multiple Launched Rocket System
MOH	Medal of Honor
MOOTW	military operations other than war
MOS	military occupational specialty
MOVSM	Military Outstanding Volunteer Service Medal
MP	military police
MPRJ	military personnel records jacket
MRBM	medium-range ballistic missiles
MSC	Medical Service Corps
MSM	Meritorious Service Medal
MTOE	modified table of organization and equipment
NAC	National Agency Check
NATO	North Atlantic Treaty Organization
NBC	nuclear, biological, and chemical
NCO	noncommissioned officer
NCOA	Noncommissioned Officer Academy; Noncommissioned Officers Association
NCOER	Noncommissioned Officer Evaluation Report
NCOES	Noncommissioned Officer Education System
NMS	New Manning System
OCAR	Office of the Chief, Army Reserve
OCONUS	outside continental United States
OCS	Officer Candidate School
ODCSPER	Office of the Deputy Chief of Staff for Personnel
OEF	Operation Enduring Freedom
OIF	Operation Iraqi Freedom
OJE	on-the-job experience
OJT	on-the-job training
OMPF	Official Military Personnel File
OP	operating procedures
OPM	Office of Personnel Management
OSR	overseas service ribbon
OSUT	one-station unit training
PAC	Personnel Administration Center
PCM	primary care manager
PCS	permanent change of station
PDS	permanent duty station
PERSCOM	Total Army Personnel Command
PH	Purple Heart
PLDC	Primary Leadership Development Course

PMCS	preventive maintenance checks and services
PMOS	primary military occupational specialty
POR	preparation of replacements for overseas movement
POV	privately owned vehicle
POWM	Prisoner of War Medal
PPG	Priority Placement Group
PSB	personnel support battalion, personnel service branch
PSB/MPD	personnel services battalion/military personnel division
PSC	Personnel Service Center
PSNCO	personnel staff noncommissioned officer
PT	physical training
PX	post exchange
QM	Quartermaster
QMP	Qualitative Management Program
RA	Regular Army
RC	reserve component
RC-PLC	Reserve Component Primary Leadership Course
RC-PLDC	Reserve Component Primary Leadership Development Course
RC-PNCOC	Reserve Component Primary Noncommissioned Officer Course
RE Code	Reenlistment Code
ROE	Rules of Engagement
ROTC	Reserve Officers' Training Corps; Reserve Officers' Training Course
R&R	rest and recuperation
SAM	soldier assignment module
SAT	Scholastic Assessment Test
SB	special branches
SCRA	Servicemembers Civil Relief Act
SD	special duty
SDNCO	staff duty noncommissioned officer
SF	Special Forces
SFC	sergeant first class
SFOR	Stabilization Force
SGLI	Servicemen's Group Life Insurance
SGM	sergeant major
SGT	sergeant
SIDPERS	Standard Installation/Division Personnel Reporting System
SKB	skills, knowledge, and behavior
SL	skill level
SM	Soldier's Medal
SMOS	secondary military occupational specialty
SMP	Simultaneous Membership Program
SOC	Servicemembers Opportunity Colleges
SOCAD	Servicemembers Opportunity Colleges Army Degree

SOFA	status of forces agreement
SOP	standard operating procedures
SPC	specialist
SPT-V	payment to a dependent
SQI	special qualification identifier
SRB	selective reenlistment bonus
SS	Silver Star
SSB	special separation bonus
SSG	staff sergeant
SSN	Social Security Number
STP	Soldier Training Publication
SWASM	Southwest Asia Service Medal
TA	tuition assistance
TAO	tuition assistance officer; transition assistance office
TAPDB	Total Army Personnel Database
TASS	Total Army Schools System
TBD	to be determined
TC	Transportation Corps; Training Circular
TCO	test control officer
TDA	Table of Distribution and Allowances
TDP	TRICARE Dental Program
TDY	temporary duty
TE	technical escort
TEC	training extension course
TFL	TRICARE for Life
TIG	time in grade
TIS	time in service
TLA	temporary lodging allowance
TLE	temporary lodging expense
TMA	TRICARE Management Activity
TOE	table of organization and equipment
TOS	Time on Station
TRADOC	U.S. Army Training and Doctrine Command
TRS	TRICARE Reserve Select
TSO	test scoring officer
TSP	Thrift Savings Plan; Training Support Package
UA	Unit of Action
UCMJ	Uniform Code of Military Justice
USAEREC	U.S. Army Enlisted Records and Evaluation Center
USAR	U.S. Army Reserve
USASMA	U.S. Army Sergeants Major Academy
USASMC	U.S. Army Sergeants Major Course
USASSC	U.S. Army Soldier Support Center
USATC	U.S. Army Training Center

USCENTCOM AOR	U.S. Central Command's Area of Responsibility
USERRA	Uniformed Services Employment and Reemployment Act
USMA	U.S. Military Academy
USMAPS	U.S. Military Academy Preparatory School
USMC	U.S. Marine Corps
VA	Veterans Administration
VEAP	Veterans Educational Assistance Program
VGLI	Veterans Group Life Insurance
VHA	variable housing allowance
VSI	Voluntary Separation Incentive
VTC	Video Teleconferencing
YTD	year to date

Index

DECORATIONS, AWARDS, AND SERVICE MEDALS

U.S. ARMY AND DEPARTMENT OF DEFENSE MILITARY DECORATIONS

**Medal of Honor
(Army)**

**Distinguished Service
Cross (Army)**

**Defense
Distinguished Service
Medal**

**Distinguished Service
Medal (Army)**

Silver Star

**Defense
Superior Service
Medal**

Legion of Merit

Distinguished Flying Cross

Soldier's Medal (Army)

Bronze Star Medal

Purple Heart

Defense Meritorious Service Medal

Meritorious Service Medal

Air Medal

**Joint Service
Commendation
Medal**

**Army
Commendation
Medal**

**Joint Service
Achievement
Medal**

**Army
Achievement
Medal**

**Prisoner of War
Medal**

**Good Conduct Medal
(Army)**

**Army Reserve
Components
Achievement Medal**

**National Defense Service
Medal**

**Antarctica Service
Medal**

**Armed Forces
Expeditionary Medal**

**Vietnam Service
Medal**

Southwest Asia Service Medal

Kosovo Campaign Medal

Afghanistan Campaign Medal

Iraq Campaign Medal

Global War on Terrorism Expeditionary Medal

Global War on Terrorism Service Medal

Korean Defense Service Medal

Armed Forces Service Medal

Humanitarian Service Medal

Military Outstanding Volunteer Service Medal

Armed Forces Reserve Medal

U.S. ARMY SERVICE AND TRAINING RIBBONS

NCO
Professional Development
Ribbon

Army Service
Ribbon

Overseas Service
Ribbon (Army)

Army Reserve
Components Overseas
Training Ribbon

NON-U.S. SERVICE MEDALS

United Nations
Medal

NATO Medal

Multinational
Force and Observers
Medal

**Republic of Vietnam
Campaign Medal**

**Kuwait Liberation Medal
(Kingdom of *Saudi
Arabia*)**

**Kuwait Liberation Medal
(Government of
Kuwait)**

U.S. ARMY AND DEPARTMENT OF DEFENSE
UNIT AWARDS

**Presidential Unit
Citation (Army)**

**Joint Meritorious
Unit Award**

**Valorous Unit
Award**

**Meritorious Unit
Commendation (Army)**

**Army Superior Unit
Award**

U.S. ARMY BADGES AND TABS

Combat and Special Skill Badges

**Combat Infantryman Badge
1st Award**

**Combat Medical Badge
1st Award**

**Combat Infantryman Badge
2nd Award**

**Combat Medical Badge
2nd Award**

**Combat Infantryman Badge
3rd Award**

**Combat Medical Badge
3rd Award**

Expert Infantryman Badge

Expert Field Medical Badge

Combat Action Badge

**Master Astronaut
Badge**

**Basic Astronaut
Badge**

**Senior Astronaut
Badge**

**Master Aviator
Badge**

**Basic Aviator
Badge**

**Senior Aviator
Badge**

**Master
Flight Surgeon
Badge**

**Basic
Flight Surgeon
Badge**

**Senior
Flight Surgeon
Badge**

**Master
Aircraft Crewman
Badge**

**Basic
Aircraft Crewman
Badge**

**Senior
Aircraft Crewman
Badge**

**Master Parachutist
Badge**

**Basic Parachutist
Badge**

**Senior Parachutist
Badge**

**Combat Parachutist
Badge (1 Jump)**

**Combat Parachutist
Badge (2 Jumps)**

**Combat Parachutist
Badge (3 Jumps)**

**Combat Parachutist
Badge (4 Jumps)**

**Combat Parachutist
Badge (5 Jumps)**

Air Assault Badge

Glider Badge

**Special Forces Tab
(Metal Replica)**

**Ranger Tab
(Metal Replica)**

Sapper Tab

**Pathfinder
Badge**

**Salvage Diver
Badge**

**Second Class Diver
Badge**

**Master Diver
Badge**

**First Class Diver
Badge**

**Scuba Diver
Badge**

**Master Explosive
Ordnance Disposal
Badge**

**Basic Explosive
Ordnance Disposal
Badge**

**Senior Explosive
Ordnance Disposal
Badge**

**Nuclear Reactor
Operator Badge
(Basic)**

**Nuclear Reactor
Operator Badge
(Second Class)**

**Nuclear Reactor
Operator Badge
(First Class)**

**Nuclear Reactor
Operator Badge
(Shift Supervisor)**

**Parachute Rigger
Badge**

**Driver and Mechanic
Badge**

Marksmanship Badges

Marksman

Sharpshooter

Expert

Identification Badges

Presidential Service

Vice-Presidential Service

Secretary of Defense

Joint Chiefs of Staff

Army Staff

Guard,
Tomb of the Unknown Soldier

Drill Sergeant

U.S. Army Recruiter
(Active Army)

U.S. Army Recruiter
(Army National Guard)

U.S. Army Recruiter
(U.S. Army Reserve)